Introduction to Psychology

GUIDED NOTEBOOK

HAWKES LEARNING

Project Managers:
Laura Brown,
Cory Eno

Editors:
Caitlin Clark,
Katherine Cleveland,
Caitlin Edahl,
Cory Eno

Creative Director:
Tee Jay Zajac

Designers:
Trudy Gove,
Patrick Thompson,
Tee Jay Zajac

Cover Design:
Patrick Thompson

VP Research & Development: Marcel Prevuznak

Director of Content: Kara Roché

Program Manager, Humanities & Social Sciences: Katherine Cleveland

HAWKES LEARNING

A division of Quant Systems, Inc.

546 Long Point Road
Mount Pleasant, SC 29464

Printed in the United States of America

10 9 8 7 6 5 4 3 2

ISBN: 978-1-64277-080-3

Table of Contents

Chapter 10

Personality

Chapter 11

Social Psychology

Chapter 12

Industrial-Organizational Psychology

Chapter 13

Stress, Lifestyle, and Health

Chapter 14

Psychological Disorders

Chapter 15

Therapy and Treatment

Chapter 1
Psychological Science

Lesson 1.1
What Is Psychology?

OBJECTIVES

- ★ Appreciate Freud's influence on psychology.
- ★ Appreciate the important role that behaviorism played in psychology's history.
- ★ Associate various theorists with the appropriate psychological perspective.
- ★ Define empirical method, psyche, ology, and psychology.
- ★ Define psychology.
- ★ Explain the difference between competing schools of psychological thought.
- ★ Recognize the contributions made to early psychology by those who overcame significant racial and gender barriers.
- ★ Understand basic tenets of humanism.
- ★ Understand how the cognitive revolution shifted psychology's focus back to the mind.
- ★ Understand the importance of Wundt and James in the development of psychology.
- ★ Understand the merits of an education in psychology.

BIG IDEA

Psychology is a relatively new discipline that seeks to answer questions about the mind and behavior.

This lesson will discuss the following:

- Psychological Science
- Merits of an Education in Psychology
- History of Psychology

On Your Own

What images instantly come to mind when you think of psychology? Why do you think those are the first connections you make?

Psychology refers to the ________________ study of the ______________ and __________________.

Psychological Science

Fill in missing information about the steps in the scientific method.

1. A researcher with a question about how or why something happens will propose a tentative explanation, called a ________________.
2. A __________________ fits into the context of a scientific ______________, which is a broad __________________ for some aspect of the natural world.
3. The researcher makes _____________________ or carries out an __________________ to test the _________________ of the hypothesis.
4. That test and its results are ___________________ so that others can check the results or build on them.

Scientific explanations must be perceivable and ____________________, which makes our scientific understanding of the mind limited. An __________________ method, like the scientific method, is based on observation and __________________________.

On Your Own

Write a quick hypothesis about something involving the mind and behavior. How would you test it?

Merits of an Education in Psychology

List a job you're interested in and something you enjoy doing in your free time that would be enhanced by a better understanding of the mind and behavior. Explain how that knowledge would help.

Job	Activity
Example:	Example:

Explanation:	Explanation:

Wundt and Structuralism

Wilhelm Wundt is widely considered the first ________________. He used a process called ____________________, which required a person to observe their own conscious experience as __________________ as possible.

In 1879, Wundt established a psychology ________________ in Germany, where he developed an approach called ____________________. This approach was an attempt to understand the structure or _____________________ of the mind.

On Your Own

Imagine you're studying reactions and reaction time to receiving a text notification.

What would you want to know?	
How would you design the experiment?	
How would relying on self-reporting from subjects complicate your findings?	

James and Functionalism

William James, the first American psychologist, was focused on the adaptive ________________ of behavior as a result Darwin's theory of natural ______________. This led James to develop a perspective called ______________________. This approach looked at how mental activities helped an organism fit into its ____________________. It also paid attention to the operation of the whole mind rather than its ________________ parts, as ______________________ did.

Pioneering Women

List the accomplishments of the following pioneering psychologists.

Mary Whiton Calkins	
Margaret Floy Washburn	

On Your Own

Read "Feminist Psychology." What are some ways cultural biases create barriers for women in certain career paths today?

Freud and Psychoanalytic Theory

Psychoanalytic theory focuses on the role of:

1.

2.

On Your Own

Do you think your unconscious feelings play a role in how you behave? Give an example to support your opinion.

Wertheimer, Koffka, Köhler, and Gestalt Psychology

The word *Gestalt* roughly translates to "_____________"; a major emphasis of Gestalt psychology deals with the fact that although a sensory experience can be broken down into ________________ parts, how those parts relate to each other as a whole is often what the individual responds to in ________________.

Pavlov, Watson, Skinner, and Behaviorism

Behaviorists believed that ________________ analysis of the mind is impossible. A major study of behaviorists was _______________ behavior and its ___________________ with the inborn qualities of an organism.

On Your Own

Based on what you know about operant conditioning, discuss a way your behavior has been shaped by rewards or punishments. How effective was this method?

Maslow, Rogers, and Humanism

Humanism is a perspective within psychology that emphasizes the potential for ___________ that is innate to all humans. Two famous humanist psychologists were _________ Rogers and ________________ Maslow.

On Your Own

Now that you've been introduced to Maslow's hierarchy of needs, what are some reasons a person might not be reaching their full potential? Talk about a time when you performed poorly on something important due to these same reasons.

Rogers believed that a therapist needed to display three features to maximize the effectiveness of client-centered therapy: ____________________ positive regard, ________________, and empathy.

____________________ positive regard refers to the fact that the therapist accepts their clients for who they are, no matter what they might say.

The Cognitive Revolution

Cognitive psychologists and scientists in related disciplines, like linguistics, were dissatisfied with the focus on ______________ that was led by psychologists like Watson and Skinner. Cognitive psychology sought to return some of the focus to the ____________.

Multicultural Psychology

Just as with biases about gender, cultural and racial biases had long affected psychology and those who sought to practice it.

On Your Own

What is a cultural or racial issue today that could be addressed by psychology? Choose one and explain how psychology could contribute.

Psychology and You

Schools of Psychology

Which of the schools or approaches to psychology seems the most interesting to you? Why?

Lesson Wrap-up

Say It in a Sentence

In one sentence, explain why there have been so many approaches to psychology in the last 150 years.

Test Yourself

Choose the correct answer for each of the following questions. Check your work using the Answer Key in the back of the book.

____ 1. Based on your reading, which theorist would have been most likely to agree with the following statement?

"Perceptual phenomena are best understood as a combination of their components."

A. William James
B. Max Wertheimer
C. Carl Rogers
D. Noam Chomsky

____ 2. The operant conditioning chamber (aka ______ box) is a device used to study the principles of operant conditioning.

A. Skinner
B. Watson
C. James
D. Koffka

Next to each statement, write **T** for True or **F** for False. Check your work using the Answer Key in the back of the book.

3. ______ Sigmund Freud was an influential humanistic psychologist.

4. ______ Mary Whiton Calkins was the first female president of the American Psychological Association (APA).

5. ______ Humanists and cognitive psychologists believed that behaviorists put too much focus on behavior and that the inner workings of the mind were important.

Key Terms

Match each key term with its definition.

A. Behaviorism
B. Functionalism
C. Humanism
D. Introspection
E. Psychoanalytic Theory
F. Structuralism

_____ Focus on the role of the unconscious in affecting conscious behavior
_____ Focus on observing and controlling behavior
_____ Process by which someone examines their own conscious experience in an attempt to break it into its component parts
_____ Understanding the conscious experience through introspection
_____ Perspective within psychology that emphasizes the potential for good that is innate to all humans
_____ Focused on how mental activities helped an organism adapt to its environment

Lesson 1.2

Contemporary Psychology

OBJECTIVES

- ★ Appreciate the diversity of interests and foci within psychology.
- ★ Demonstrate familiarity with some of the major concepts or important figures in each of the described areas of psychology.
- ★ Understand basic interests and applications in each of the described areas of psychology.
- ★ Understand educational requirements for careers in academic settings.
- ★ Understand the educational requirements for careers in psychology.

BIG IDEA

Contemporary psychology is a diverse field that impacts a wide range of careers.

In the lesson we will discuss the following:

- Biopsychology and Evolutionary Psychology
- Sensation and Perception
- Cognitive Psychology
- Developmental Psychology
- Social Psychology
- Industrial-Organizational Psychology
- Health Psychology
- Sport and Exercise Psychology
- Clinical Psychology
- Forensic Psychology
- Careers in Psychology

American Psychological Association (APA)	Association for Psychological Science (APS)
• Professional organization representing diverse psychologists in the United States • Largest organization of psychologists in the world • Advances and disseminates psychological knowledge to improve understanding of the mind and behavior • 56 divisions • Members span from students to doctoral-level psychologists and can be found in educational settings, criminal justice systems, hospitals, the armed forces, and industry	• Advance the scientific orientation of psychology • Result of disagreements between members of the scientific and clinical branches of psychology within the APA • Publishes 5 research journals and engages in education and advocacy with funding agencies • Significant proportion of its members are international although the majority is located in the United States

Biopsychology and Evolutionary Psychology

List some of the topics within the scope of biopsychology.

-

-
-
-
-
-
-

On Your Own

Are you particularly moody or more even-keeled? Are there certain traits you find attractive in others? Do you think these things come naturally to you?

Evolutionary psychology seeks to study the ultimate ________________ causes of behavior.

Sensation and Perception

Our sensations are the sensory __________________ we're taking in from our environment, and our

___________________ is a complex process affected by our experiences, attention, and even our cultural backgrounds.

On Your Own

What are three questions that can be answered by the study of sensation and perception?

1.

2.

3.

Cognitive Psychology

Cognitive psychology is the area of psychology that focuses on studying cognitions, or _______________, and their relationship to our __________________ and actions. It is also ____________________, meaning that it is broad in scope and relates to a diverse range of fields of study.

Developmental Psychology

Developmental psychology is the scientific study of development across a ______________.

On Your Own

Do you think the way we develop has an impact on our mental health? Why?

Personality Psychology

Personality psychology focuses on patterns of thoughts and behaviors that make each individual ______________. To do this, research is focused on identifying and measuring personality traits and determining how those traits interact in a particular context to influence a person's behavior. Personality traits are relatively ____________________ patterns of thought and ________________, and many have proposed that five trait dimensions are sufficient to capture the ___________________ in personality across individuals.

On Your Own

After looking at the Five-Factor model, identify the trait you feel you'd score highest on and the one you'd score lowest on. Explain your answers.

Highest Score	Lowest Score
Trait:	Trait:
Why?	Why?

Social Psychology

Social psychology focuses on how we _____________ with and relate to ____________.

On Your Own

While this lesson highlights the Milgram study on obedience, what is another social question that you would like answered by social psychology?

Industrial-Organizational Psychology

Industrial-Organizational psychology (________ psychology) is a subfield of psychology that applies psychological theories, principles, and research findings in industrial and organizational settings. I-O psychologists are often involved in issues related to ______________ management, ___________________ structure, and _______________ environment.

On Your Own

List three problems you've had at work that could be addressed by I-O psychology.

1.
2.
3.

Health Psychology

Health psychology focuses on how health is affected by the interaction of _______________, psychological, and ___________________ factors. This particular approach is known as the ____________________ model.

Sport and Exercise Psychology

Researchers in sport and exercise psychology study the psychological aspects of sport _______________, including _______________ and performance _____________, and the effects of sport on mental and _________________ wellbeing.

On Your Own

Discuss a time when you found that sports or exercise had important mental aspects.

Clinical Psychology

Clinical psychology is the area of psychology that focuses on the ____________________ and ________________ of psychological disorders and other problematic patterns of _________________.

__________________ psychology is a similar discipline that focuses on emotional, social, vocational, and health-related outcomes in individuals who are considered psychologically _______________.

On Your Own

Although the field has changed a great deal, and therapeutic methods have become more positive, there is still a stigma around getting mental health treatment. What are some reasons a person might not seek help when they need it?

Forensic Psychology

Forensic psychology is a branch of psychology that deals with questions of psychology as they arise in the context of the ______________ system.

On Your Own

How might the portrayal of the justice system in television and movies create myths about forensic science?

Psychology and You

Fields of Study

Which contemporary psychology field could you learn the most about your own life from? Explain your answer.

Lesson Wrap-up

Say It in a Sentence

In one sentence, explain why the scope of contemporary psychology is so broad.

Test Yourself

Choose the correct answer for each of the following questions. Check your work using the Answer Key in the back of the book.

____ 1. In Milgram's controversial study on obedience, nearly ______ of the participants were willing to administer what appeared to be lethal electrical shocks to another person because they were told to do so by an authority figure.

A. 1/3
B. 2/3
C. 3/4
D. 4/5

____ 2. A researcher interested in how changes in the cells of the hippocampus (a structure in the brain related to learning and memory) are related to memory formation would most likely identify as a(n) ______ psychologist.

A. biological
B. health
C. clinical
D. social

Next to each statement, write **T** for True or **F** for False. Check your work using the Answer Key in the back of the book.

3. ______ Carl Rogers' ideas about client-centered therapy contributed greatly to the way clinicians operate.

4. ______ The "Big Five" or Five Factor model of personality includes dimensions of conscientiousness, agreeableness, introversion, openness, and extroversion.

5. ______ Cognitive psychologists often work in isolation because their field does not overlap with many other disciplines.

Key Terms

Match each key term with its definition.

A. American Psychological Association
B. Biopsychology
C. Biopsychosocial Model
D. Clinical Psychology
E. Cognitive Psychology
F. Counseling Psychology
G. Developmental Psychology
H. Forensic Psychology
I. Personality Psychology
J. Personality Trait
K. Sport and Exercise Psychology

_____ Area of psychology that focuses on improving emotional, social, vocational, and other aspects of the lives of psychologically healthy individuals

_____ Consistent pattern of thought and behavior

_____ Study of how biology influences behavior

_____ Scientific study of development across a lifespan

_____ Area of psychology that focuses on the diagnosis and treatment of psychological disorders and other problematic patterns of behavior

_____ Professional organization representing psychologists in the United States

_____ Area of psychology that applies the science and practice of psychology to issues within and related to the justice system

_____ Area of psychology that focuses on the interactions between mental and emotional factors and physical performance in sports, exercise, and other activities

_____ Study of cognitions, or thoughts, and their relationship to experiences and actions

_____ Perspective that asserts that biology, psychology, and social factors interact to determine an individual's health

_____ Study of patterns of thoughts and behaviors that make each individual unique

Lesson 1.3

Why Is Research Important?

OBJECTIVES

- ★ Explain how scientific research addresses questions about behavior.
- ★ Discuss how scientific research guides public policy.
- ★ Appreciate how scientific research can be important in making personal decisions.

BIG IDEA

Research is important because it allows individuals to gain accurate information about phenomena in the world rather than relying on common sense or opinions.

In this lesson, you will learn about the following:

- Use of Research Information
- The Process of Scientific Research

It is through ______________________________ scientific research that we divest ourselves of our preconceived notions and superstitions and gain an ___________________________ understanding of ourselves and our world.

The hallmark of scientific research is that there is ___________________________ to support a claim. Scientific knowledge is ___________________________; it is grounded in _______________, tangible evidence that can be observed time and time again.

Use of Research Information

Individuals should strive to think critically about information by exercising a degree of healthy

________________________.

On Your Own

Individuals are bombarded with information that is not necessarily supported scientifically. Can you provide an example of a piece of "news" that you saw that was not actually true? Why does this happen?

Imagine you're scrolling through social media and see the following headline shared by a few of your friends: "Large cat causes concern for residents of lake of the Ozarks." The headline is accompanied by a story tagline and a picture of a tiger. What questions might you ask before you share this piece of news?

What questions can you ask when faced with a claim (even if it sounds plausible)?

-
-
-
-

On Your Own

Imagine you are a governor who has to decide whether or not to support funding D.A.R.E. What would you decide, and why?

Research is what makes the difference between facts and opinions. ________________ are observable realities, whereas ____________________________ are personal judgements, conclusions, or attitudes that may or may not be accurate.

The Process of Scientific Research

The ________________ __________________ involves testing ideas against the real world and using those observations to generate more testable ideas. This process involves both ____________________________ reasoning (testing ideas against the empirical world), and inductive reasoning (empirical observations leading to new ideas).

Complete the following graphic.

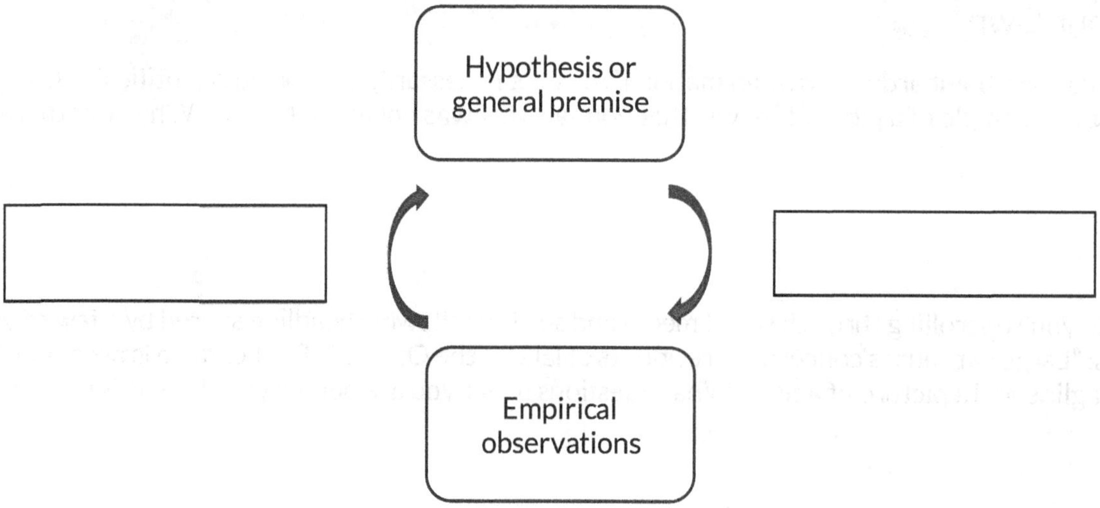

________________________ reasoning begins with a generalization that is used to reach logical conclusions about the real world. On the other hand, ________________________ reasoning uses empirical observations to construct broad generalizations.

On Your Own

Provide an example of a time when you used inductive reasoning.

A ________________ is a well-developed set of ideas that proposes an explanation for observed phenomena. Theories are often too ________________________ to be wholly tested, so ________________________, or testable predictions about how the world will behave if an idea is correct, are generated to test portions of the larger theory.

Complete the following graphic.

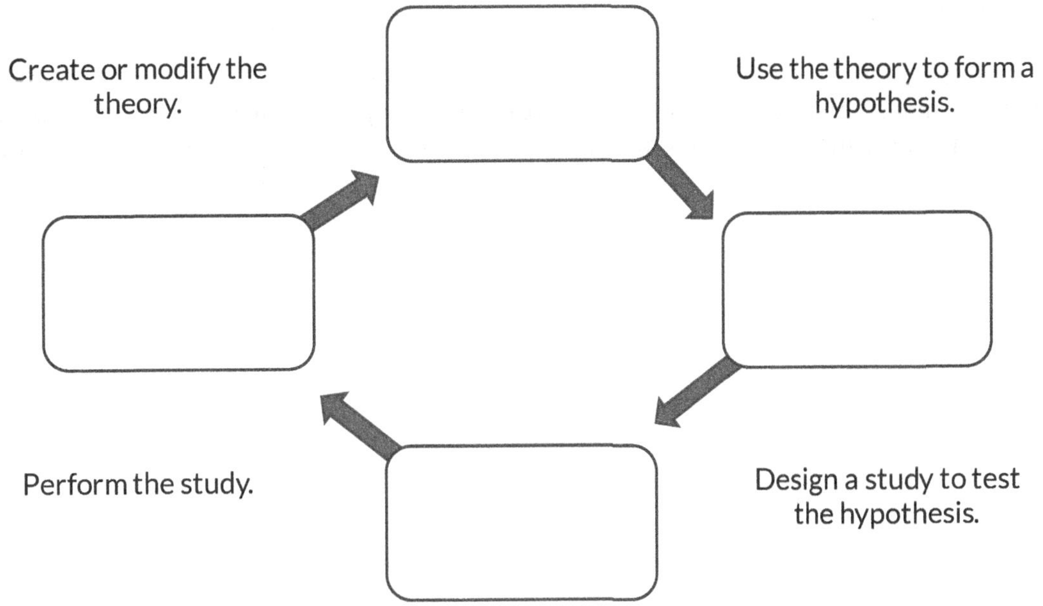
Create or modify the theory.
Use the theory to form a hypothesis.
Perform the study.
Design a study to test the hypothesis.

A scientific hypothesis is ________________________, or capable of being shown to be incorrect.

On Your Own

Provide an example of an idea or theory that is not falsifiable.

On Your Own

Identify the aspects of the scientific method that are illustrated in each of the following scenarios. Then, check the box next to the correct answer.

Dylan predicts that an expensive laundry detergent will be more effective than an inexpensive detergent.

- ☐ Theory
- ☐ Hypothesis
- ☐ Research
- ☐ Observation

Tracy designs an experiment in which she tests the benefits of exercise on cognitive performance.

- ☐ Theory
- ☐ Hypothesis
- ☐ Research
- ☐ Observation

Psychology and You

Recall a Time

Recall a situation in your life where scientific research and evidence were more beneficial than relying on opinion. For example, when you go to the doctor's office and say you have strep throat, the doctor performs tests to confirm the diagnosis rather than simply taking you at your word. Now, think of your own example.

Lesson Wrap-up

Say It in a Sentence

In one sentence, explain the importance of the scientific method.

Test Yourself

Next to each statement, write **T** for True or **F** for False. Check your work using the Answer Key in the back of the book.

1. _____ Within the process of the scientific method, ideas in the form of theories and hypotheses are tested against the real world in the form of empirical observations.
2. _____ In deductive reasoning, empirical observations lead to new ideas.
3. _____ In inductive reasoning, ideas are tested against the empirical world.
4. _____ A hypothesis is a testable prediction about how the world will behave if the idea is correct, and it is often worded as an if-then statement.

Key Terms

Match each key term with its definition.

A. Deductive Reasoning
B. Empirical
C. Fact
D. Falsifiable
E. Hypothesis
F. Inductive Reasoning
G. Opinion
H. Theory

_____ Objective and verifiable observation, established using evidence collected through empirical research

_____ Grounded in objective, tangible evidence that can be observed time and time again, regardless of who is observing

_____ Conclusions are drawn from observations

_____ Well-developed set of ideas that propose an explanation for observed phenomena

_____ Personal judgements, conclusions, or attitudes that may or may not be accurate

_____ Results are predicted based on a general premise

_____ Able to be disproven by experimental results

_____ Tentative and testable statement about the relationship between two or more variables

Lesson 1.4

Approaches to Research

OBJECTIVES

- ★ Describe the different research methods used by psychologists.
- ★ Discuss the strengths and weaknesses of case studies, naturalistic observation, surveys, and archival research.
- ★ Compare longitudinal and cross-sectional approaches to research.

BIG IDEA

Researchers use a variety of different research methods, all of which have particular strengths and weaknesses.

In this lesson, you will learn about the following:

- Clinical or Case Studies
- Naturalistic Observation
- Surveys
- Archival Research
- Longitudinal and Cross-Sectional Research

Clinical or Case Studies

In a ______________________________ or ______________ study, researchers focus on one person or just a few individuals.

On Your Own

Provide examples of three individuals or small groups of individuals that might be studied in a case study. Why would these individuals be of interest?

1.

2.

3.

____ is the ability to apply the findings of a particular research study to a larger population as a whole.

List a benefit and a drawback of case studies.

Benefit	Drawback

Naturalistic Observation

Naturalistic observation involves studying behavior in its ____________________ setting.

On Your Own

Imagine you want to study naturally occurring aggression in children. Specifically, you want to know how often it happens and the triggers that cause it. Describe how you might study this phenomenon using naturalistic observation. Be sure to address what you will do to prevent participants from knowing they are being observed.

Naturalistic observational studies are often conducted with animals. In fact, Jane Goodall spent nearly 50 years studying ____________________ in Africa.

On Your Own

There are a multitude of concerns when conducting an observational study. One concern is that the observer may become biased and incorrectly label or categorize behavior. For example, Jane Goodall was criticized for naming the chimpanzees she was observing rather than referring to them with their numbers. Do you feel this would significantly change her objectivity and affect the study? Explain.

List two benefits and two drawbacks of naturalistic observation.

Benefits	**Drawbacks**

______________ __________ refers to situations in which the observer may unconsciously skew observations to fit research goals or expectations. To protect against this type of bias, researchers should have ____________________ criteria for the types of behaviors that will be recorded. In addition, multiple raters should have a high degree of ________________ ________________, or agreement between researchers, regarding the variable of interest.

On Your Own

Earlier, you were asked to describe a study of aggressive behavior in children. For the same study, how would you protect against observer bias?

Surveys

________________ are lists of questions to be answered by research participants.

List two benefits and two drawbacks of surveys.

Benefits	Drawbacks

On Your Own

Individuals are not always honest on surveys, especially when the topic might be a difficult one. Give two examples of research areas that may be difficult to measure via survey because participants are more likely to lie.

Archival Research

Some researchers gain access to large amounts of ________________ without interacting with a single research participant. Instead, they use existing ________________ to answer various research questions. This ________________ research relies on looking at past records or data sets to search for interesting patterns or relationships.

List two benefits and two drawbacks of archival research.

Benefits	Drawbacks

Longitudinal and Cross-Sectional Research

______________________________ studies involve testing the same group of individuals repeatedly over an extended period of time. In contrast, ______________________________ research involves testing different segments of the population at the same time.

Label the following scenarios as *longitudinal* or *cross-sectional*.

Scenario	Research Type
Dr. Smith tests 2-, 4-, and 6-year-olds on the object permanence task during October 2018.	
Dr. Smith tests the children on object permanence when they are 2, 4, and 6 years of age.	

List two benefits and two drawbacks of longitudinal research.

Benefits	Drawbacks

On Your Own

If you were a researcher interested in conducting longitudinal research, how would you combat possible attrition?

On Your Own

Identify the type of research approach illustrated in each of the following scenarios. Then, check the box next to the correct answer.

Katy was conducting an experiment to determine if individuals on a college campus were willing to help someone pick up dropped books. She dropped all her books around varying areas of campus and had an observer watch the interactions to note if the bystanders helped or continued walking past.

- ☐ Archival Research
- ☐ Survey
- ☐ Naturalistic Observation

Dr. Dylan must review past research to determine the difference in attention span in the 2000s versus the 1960s. Dr. Dylan decides to review the use of microfiche.

- ☐ Archival Research
- ☐ Survey
- ☐ Naturalistic Observation

Dawn hands out a written questionnaire to her classes to gather information for research.

- ☐ Longitudinal study
- ☐ Survey
- ☐ Archival Research

Psychology and You

Study Design

Choose a topic you would want to study if you were a researcher. Briefly discuss several ways to study your topic, using different research methods. How could you study the topic using naturalistic observation? A survey? What about archival data?

Lesson Wrap-up

Say It in a Sentence

In one sentence, explain the importance of generalizability.

Test Yourself

Next to each statement, write **T** for True or **F** for False. Check your work using the Answer Key in the back of the book.

1. ______ Longitudinal research is a research design in which data-gathering is administered repeatedly over an extended period of time.

2. ______ Archival research involves studying existing data sets to answer research questions.
3. ______ Naturalistic observation often lacks validity.
4. ______ Observer bias is an issue with survey-based research.

Key Terms

For the following key terms, make groupings out of the related terms. Be sure to explain how they are related.

Key Terms: archival research, attrition, clinical or case study, generalize, inter-rater reliability, longitudinal research, naturalistic observation, observer bias, population, sample, survey

Lesson 1.5

Analyzing Findings

OBJECTIVES

★ Explain what a correlation coefficient tells us about the relationship between variables.
★ Recognize that correlation does not indicate a cause-and-effect relationship between variables.
★ Discuss our tendency to look for relationships between variables that do not really exist.
★ Explain random sampling and assignment of participants into experimental and control groups.
★ Discuss how experimenter or participant bias could affect the results of an experiment.
★ Identify independent and dependent variables.

BIG IDEA

When conducting research, it is important to understand how to interpret results to ensure that researchers do not reach faulty conclusions.

In this lesson, you will learn about the following:

- Correlational Research
- Causality: Conducting Experiments and Using the Data
- Reliability and Validity

Correlational Research

______________________________ means that there is a relationship between two or more variables such that, as one variable changes, the other variable changes as well. The correlation between two items is denoted by the __________________ ____________________(*r*), a number between -1 and _____.

Indicate the stronger correlations in the following table.

Correlation A	Use > or < to indicate which correlation is stronger	Correlation B
-.28		-.57
.98		.37
.57		-.87
-.88		.25

Are the correlations in the following statements positive or negative?

Correlation	Type
The longer you sleep at night, the better your grades.	

The more you party the night before an exam, the lower your grade on the exam.	
The more alcohol you drink, the slower reaction time you have when driving.	
The taller you are, the more you weigh.	
The younger you are, the fewer wrinkles you have.	

Correlation Does Not Indicate Causation

Correlation is limited because establishing the existence of a relationship tells researchers little about_______________ __________ ______________. There is a common saying that "correlation does not equal causation." In fact, there are times when relationships between variables are actually caused by ____, which affects the variable of interest.

On Your Own

Consider this headline: "Does being left-handed make you an angry person?" Given what you have learned in this lesson, react to the legitimacy of this study.

Illusory Correlations

Individuals often make illusory, or ______________, correlations between different variables. For example, many people swear that individuals "act crazy" during a full moon. However, over _________ different studies have demonstrated no such relationship between the moon and human behavior.

Causality: Conducting Experiments and Using the Data

________________________________ are the only way to truly determine cause and effect.

The Experimental Hypothesis

The first step in an experiment is to develop an experimental ______________________________ that can be tested within a research design. Hypotheses may come from ___________

______________________ of the real world or careful review of the existing research literature.

Designing an Experiment

The most basic experimental design consists of two groups: the experimental group and the control group. The ____________________________ group receives the experimental manipulation, whereas the ____________________ group does not. Researchers must also ______________________________ define variables of interest.

It is best practice to avoid __________________________________ bias, or the possibility that a researcher's beliefs will skew the results of the study. Using _________________________-blind (participants are unaware of their group assignment) or __________________________-blind (both participants and researchers are unaware of participant group assignment) procedures can help reduce this bias.

Independent and Dependent Variables

The independent variable is the variable that the researcher ______________________________ or controls. On the other hand, the dependent variable is what the researcher _________________________ to determine if the independent variable had an effect.

For each study design, indicate the independent and dependent variables in the following table.

Study Design	Independent Variable	Dependent Variable
Children are shown differing levels of violence on television. Afterward, their behavior is observed to determine their levels of aggression.		
Rats are tested on maze memory after consuming either alcohol or saline solution.		
One group of students is taught the "read, recite, review" system of studying, whereas another is taught rote memorization. Exam scores are compared.		

Selecting and Assigning Experimental Participants

Researchers must often select a ___________________________ (or a subset of the population of interest) to study. These participants are often selected randomly to ensure that experimental groups differ in only the independent variable. Having a _____________________________________ group is important to ensure generalizability.

On Your Own

What are your thoughts regarding the idea that a great deal of psychological literature is based on the results of work with undergraduate students? Do you feel this work is generalizable?

If you had a jar of 1,000 jellybeans that was 45% blue jellybeans, 30% red, and 25% yellow, which would be a better sample: 10 jellybeans or 100 jellybeans? Be sure to explain your answer.

Interpreting Experimental Findings

Statistical analysis determines how likely any difference found in the experiment is due to ________________________. In psychology, group differences are considered significant if the odds of these findings occurring by chance is __________ __________________or less.

Reporting Research

Unlike popular magazines or even *Psychology Today*, research projects are published in ______________-____________________ scholarly journal articles. These articles have been reviewed in-depth by field experts to ensure they contain good science and are well presented. Peer review provides some degree of ________________ control for psychological research.

On Your Own

Recently, long-standing psychological "truths" have been challenged due to failure of replication. As the lesson points out, if a medical breakthrough found in one study is not found in subsequent studies, one would begin to doubt the reality of the medical breakthrough. Does the same logic apply to psychology? That is, can the human experience change with time such that a universal "truth" can no longer apply in a later generation? Explain your answer.

Your aunt claims, "Andrew Wakefield found a correlation between vaccines and autism! I will *not* vaccinate my child." What do you say?

Reliability and Validity

______________________________ refers to the ability to consistently produce a given result, whereas

______________________________ refers to the extent to which a given instrument or tool accurately

measures what it is supposed to measure.

On Your Own

Check the box next to the correct answer.

For a correlation coefficient, the number (rather than the sign) indicates the ________ of the relationship.

- ☐ strength
- ☐ direction
- ☐ meaningfulness

For a correlation coefficient, the sign (rather than the number) indicates the ________ of the relationship.

- ☐ strength
- ☐ direction
- ☐ meaningfulness

Psychology and You

Peer-Reviewed Scholarly Articles

Use the library resources at your school to locate a peer-reviewed scholarly article about a topic in psychology that interests you. Summarize the abstract here (2 to 3 sentences).

Lesson Wrap-up

Say It in a Sentence

In one sentence, explain the difference between an independent and dependent variable.

Test Yourself

Answer the following questions. Check your work using the Answer Key in the back of the book.

1. A correlation coefficient of 0 means what?

2. What type of correlation is represented in the image?

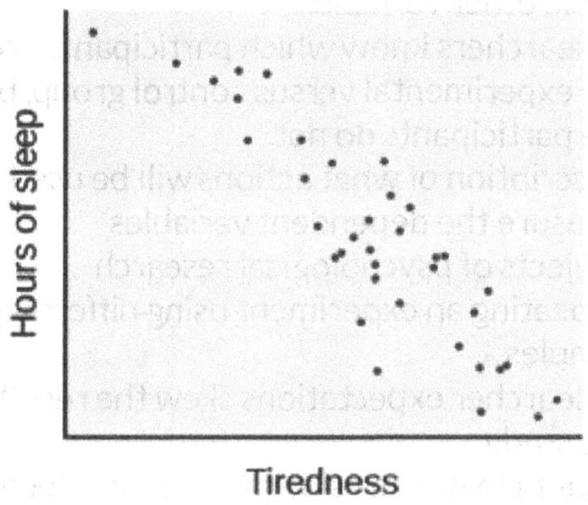

3. What is the major limitation of correlational studies?

Key Terms

Match each key term with its definition.

A. Cause-and-Effect Relationship
B. Confirmation Bias
C. Confounding Variable
D. Control Group
E. Correlation
F. Correlation Coefficient
G. Dependent Variable
H. Double-Blind Study
I. Experimental Group
J. Experimenter Bias

_____ Group designed to answer the research question

_____ Experiment in which both the researchers and the participants are unaware of group assignments

_____ Subset of a larger population in which every member of a population has an equal chance of being selected

_____ Accuracy of a given result in measuring what is it designed to measure

K. Illusory Correlation
L. Independent Variable
M. Negative Correlation
N. Operational Definition
O. Participants
P. Peer-Reviewed Journal Article
Q. Placebo Effect
R. Positive Correlation
S. Random Assignment
T. Random Sample
U. Reliability
V. Replicate
W. Single-Blind Study
X. Statistical Analysis
Y. Validity

_____ Relationship between two or more variables
_____ Determines how likely any difference between experimental groups is due to chance
_____ Two variables change in the same direction
_____ Variable that is influenced or controlled by the experimenter
_____ Seeing relationships between two things when in reality no such relationship exists
_____ Tendency to ignore evidence that disproves beliefs or ideas
_____ Serves as a basis for comparison and controls for chance factors that might influence the results of a study
_____ Number between -1 and +1
_____ Expectations or beliefs can determine experience in a given situation
_____ Consistency and reproducibility of a given result
_____ Changes in one variable cause the changes in the other variable
_____ Researchers know which participants are in the experimental versus control group, but the participants do not
_____ Description of what actions will be used to measure the dependent variables
_____ Subjects of psychological research
_____ Repeating an experiment using different samples
_____ Researcher expectations skew the results of the study
_____ Unanticipated outside factor that affects both variables of interest in a correlation
_____ Variable that the researcher measures
_____ Two variables change in different directions
_____ Article read by several other scientists with expertise in the subject
_____ Method of group assignment in which all participants have an equal chance of being assigned to either group

Lesson 1.6

Ethics

OBJECTIVES

- ★ Discuss how research involving human subjects is regulated.
- ★ Summarize the processes of informed consent and debriefing.
- ★ Explain how research involving animal subjects is regulated.

BIG IDEA

Today, researchers are expected to follow certain ethical guidelines to ensure that both human participants and animals do not undergo unduly aversive conditions in the name of science.

In this lesson, you will learn about the following:

- Research Involving Human Participants
- Research Involving Animal Subjects

Research Involving Human Participants

Experiments that involve human participants are subject to extensive and strict guidelines to ensure that participants do not face ________________. Research proposals must be reviewed by the

____ (IRB), which ensures that the research is safe for participants in a variety of ways.

What are the elements of informed consent?

-
-
-
-

On Your Own

Think of an experiment in which deception would be necessary for the goals of the study.

What are the elements of debriefing?

-
-
-
-

On Your Own

What is your reaction to the Tuskegee syphilis study? What ethical practices were violated?

Research Involving Animal Subjects

On Your Own

How do you feel about research on animals? Are there certain animals that you favor for research purposes over others? Why?

On Your Own

Check the box next to the correct answer.

Animal experimental proposals are reviewed by this group.

- ☐ Institutional Review Board (IRB)
- ☐ Institutional Animal Care and Use Committee (IACUC)
- ☐ Debriefing

This form provides a written description of what participants can expect during the experiment, including potential risks and implications of the research.

- ☐ IRB
- ☐ Debriefing
- ☐ Informed consent

This is a committee of individuals, often made up of members of the institution's administration, scientists, and community members.

- ☐ Institutional Review Board (IRB)
- ☐ Institutional Animal Care and Use Committee (IACUC)
- ☐ Debriefing

Psychology and You

Reasoned Argument

Your friend tells you, "Psychologists do whatever they want. They can play mind games and do a lot of harm in their research studies. Look at the Tuskegee study! They can't be trusted." Provide a counterargument.

Lesson Wrap-up

Say It in a Sentence

In one sentence, explain informed consent.

Test Yourself

Next to each statement, write **T** for True or **F** for False. Check your work using the Answer Key in the back of the book.

1. _____ Debriefing is always necessary in research.
2. _____ Most of the animals used in research are cats and dogs.
3. _____ Sixty percent of the animals used in research are birds and rodents.
4. _____ The IRB reviews protocols for both human and non-human subjects.

Key Terms

Write a paraphrased definition for each key term.

Debriefing:

Deception:

Informed Consent:

Institutional Animal Care and Use Committee:

Institutional Review Board:

Chapter 2

Biopsychology

Lesson 2.1

Human Genetics

OBJECTIVES

- ★ Explain the basic principles of the theory of evolution by natural selection.
- ★ Describe the differences between genotype and phenotype.
- ★ Discuss how gene-environment interactions are critical for expression of physical and psychological characteristics.

BIG IDEA

The study of human genetics is important to psychological theorists in order for them to better understand biological factors that contribute to human behavior.

In this lesson, you will learn about the following:

- Genetic Variation
- Gene-Environment Interactions

Psychological researchers study ______________________________ to better understand the biological basis that contributes to certain behaviors.

_______________________-_______________ __________________ is a genetic condition in which red blood cells take on a __________________________ shape, and these changes cause these cells to form ____________________________ due to their abnormal shape. In some cases, individuals with sickle-cell anemia die early; however, some individuals are protected from ____________________________ because they carry the gene for sickle-cell anemia. In this way, the environment and ______________________ can interact.

___________________ ___________________ theorized that organisms that are better suited for their environments will survive and reproduce, whereas those that are poorly suited for their environments will die off.

On Your Own

What are the differences between evolutionary psychology and behavior genetics?

1.

2.

Genetic Variation

Genetic variation, the genetic ______________________________ between individuals, is what contributes to a species' adaptation to its environment. At the start of human conception, an egg and sperm combine, bringing together two different sets of _______ chromosomes that will make up gene pairings for the individual.

An individual's underlying genetic makeup comprises his/her ______________________________, whereas the individual's physical appearance is the person's ______________________________.

Phenotypes and Genotypes (B = cleft chin; b = no cleft chin)			
Mom's genetic contribution	**Dad's genetic contribution**	**Child genotype**	**Child phenotype**
B	B		
B	b		
b	B		
b	b		

Many traits are determined by pairs of genes; however, there are cases in which a human characteristic is controlled by a ____________________ gene. Most traits are ______________________________.

Harmful genes can come from genetic ______________________________, which are sudden, permanent changes in a gene.

On Your Own

Provide an example of a beneficial mutation (i.e., one that resulted in the animal/human being better suited to its environment).

Gene-Environment Interactions

On Your Own

Compare range of reaction and genetic environmental correlation.

The lesson discussed a situation in which a child, raised by an NBA player, was exposed to basketball at an early age, leading to different fulfillment of genetic potential than the same child born to a different non-NBA playing parent. What is an example of a match between genetics and environment from your own life?

______________________________ studies how the same genotype can be expressed in different ways. For example, even ______________________________ twins can show a great deal of variability over the course of their lives.

Say It in a Sentence

The lesson provided information about the prevalence of schizophrenia depending on the individual's genetics and environmental upbringing. Summarize this information in one sentence.

On Your Own

Check the box next to the correct answer.

These are long strips of genetic material known as deoxyribonucleic acid (DNA).

- ☐ Genotype
- ☐ Phenotype
- ☐ Chromosomes
- ☐ Genes

This is a specific version of a gene.

- ☐ Allele
- ☐ Homozygous
- ☐ Heterozygous

When someone has two copies of the same allele, they are said to be:

- ☐ Heterozygous
- ☐ Homozygous
- ☐ Phenotype
- ☐ Genotype

Psychology and You

Describe a Scenario

Describe two scenarios; one scenario will illustrate what seems to be behavior associated with a person's genotype, and the other will illustrate a behavior associated with a phenotype. For example, consider identical twins raised in two separate homes, in which one of the twins is academically motivated and the other is not.

1.

2.

Lesson Wrap-up

Say It in a Sentence

In one sentence, explain the importance of studying human genetics for the purpose of psychological research.

Test Yourself

Next to each statement, write **T** for True or **F** for False. Check your work using the Answer Key in the back of the book.

1. ______ The following is an example of a range of reaction: if an individual's genetic makeup predisposes her to high levels of intellectual potential, and she is reared in a rich, stimulating environment, she will be more likely to achieve her full potential than if she was raised under conditions of significant deprivation.
2. ______ Genetic environmental correlation is the theory that our genes influence our environment and our environment influences the expression of our genes.
3. ______ Genes do not affect more than our physical characteristics.

4. ______ Different versions of a gene are called alleles.

Key Terms

Match each key term with its definition.

A. Allele
B. Chromosome
C. Deoxyribonucleic Acid
D. Dominant Allele
E. Epigenetics
F. Fraternal Twins
G. Gene
H. Genetic Environmental Correlation
I. Genotype
J. Heterozygous
K. Homozygous
L. Identical Twins
M. Mutation
N. Phenotype
O. Polygenic
P. Range of Reaction
Q. Recessive Allele
R. Theory of Evolution by Natural Selection

______ Helix-shaped molecule made of nucleotide base pairs
______ Specific version of a gene
______ Asserts our genes set the boundaries within which we can operate, and our environment interacts with the genes to determine where in that range we will fall
______ Sudden, permanent change in a gene
______ Consisting of two different alleles
______ Long strand of genetic information
______ Allele whose phenotype will be expressed in an individual that possesses that allele
______ Study of gene-environment interactions, such as how the same genotype leads to different phenotypes
______ States that organisms that are better suited for their environments will survive and reproduce compared to those that are poorly suited for their environments
______ Individual's inheritable physical characteristics
______ Twins who develop from two different eggs fertilized by different sperm, so their genetic material varies the same as in non-twin siblings
______ Multiple genes affecting a given trait
______ Genetic makeup of an individual
______ Sequence of DNA that controls or partially controls physical characteristics
______ Consisting of two identical alleles
______ View of gene-environment interaction that asserts our genes affect our environment and our environment influences the expression of our genes
______ Twins that develop from the same sperm and egg
______ Allele whose phenotype will be expressed only if an individual is homozygous for that allele

Lesson 2.2

Cells of the Nervous System

OBJECTIVES

- ★ Identify the basic parts of a neuron.
- ★ Describe how neurons communicate with each other.
- ★ Explain how drugs act as agonists or antagonists for a given neurotransmitter system.

BIG IDEA

Understanding how cells and organs, such as the brain, function can help psychologists understand the biological basis underlying human behavior.

In this lesson, you will learn about the following:

- Neuron Structure
- Neuronal Communication
- Neurotransmitters and Drugs

On Your Own

What are the functions of glial cells?

1.

2.

3.

4.

5.

Neuron Structure

____________________ are the central building blocks of the nervous system.

Label the following figure.

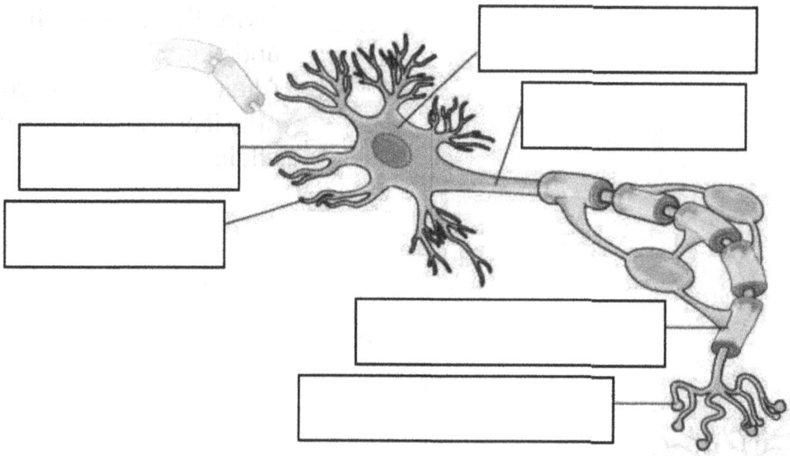

On Your Own

What is the pathway that a neuronal signal takes?

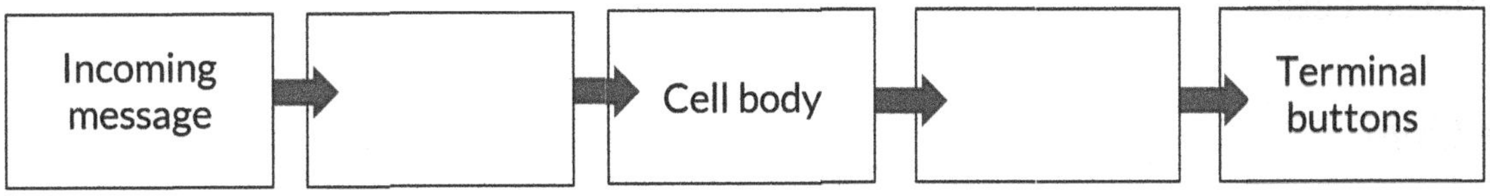

The myelin sheath is a fatty substance made of ________________ cells that coats the axon and acts as an ____________________. At the end of the axon, terminal buttons contain __________________of neurotransmitters that can cross the _______________________, or space, between cells. Once the neurotransmitters have been released, they bind to receptors via a ___________-________-__________ mechanism—only certain neurotransmitters will bind to certain receptors.

Neuronal Communication

When neurons are at rest, they have a _______________________ potential that is created by the movement of ions across the cell membrane. In this resting state, _______________________ ions are in higher concentrations outside of the cell, whereas __________________________ ions are in higher concentration within the cell. When a strong enough signal is received by the cell, gates open up, allowing ____________________ to come into the cell. This influx causes the inside of the cell to become _____________________ charged, causing potassium ions to leave. This rapid change is an ____________________ potential.

On Your Own

Why would cells have a period of hyperpolarization?

What does it mean that an action potential is "all or none"?

When the action potential arrives at the terminal button, the synaptic ______________________ release neurotransmitters into the synapse. These neurotransmitters bind to available __________________, activating the next cell.

On Your Own

What happens to excess neurotransmitters?

1.

2.

3.

Why is neuronal communication considered an "electrochemical" event?

Neurotransmitters and Drugs

Psychotropic medications are drugs that treat psychiatric symptoms by restoring ____________________________________ balance.

Complete the following table.

Neurotransmitter	Involved in	Potential Behavioral Effect
	muscle action, memory	
Beta-endorphin		
	mood, sleep, learning	
	brain function, sleep	
Glutamate		
	heart, intestines, alertness	
Serotonin		

Psychoactive drugs can be either __________________________(promoting neurotransmitter action) or

______________________________(decreasing neurotransmitter action).

Determine if an agonist or an antagonist should be prescribed in the following instances.

Disorder	Neurotransmitter Levels	Agonist or Antagonist?
Depression	Decreased serotonin	
Parkinson's	Decreased dopamine	
Schizophrenia	Increased dopamine	

On Your Own

Check the box next to the correct answer.

What receives the neural impulse?

- ☐ Soma
- ☐ Axon
- ☐ Myelin sheath
- ☐ Dendrites

What sends the neural impulse?

- ☐ Soma
- ☐ Axon
- ☐ Myelin sheath
- ☐ Dendrites

If someone was suffering from a disorder resulting from too much of a neurotransmitter, what would you prescribe?

- ☐ Agonist
- ☐ Antagonist

Psychology and You

Understanding the Biological Function of the Brain

Discuss why it's important for psychologists to understand the biological function of the brain.

Lesson Wrap-up

Say It in a Sentence

In one sentence, describe the path that a neuronal impulse takes once it reaches the neuron.

Test Yourself

Next to each statement, write **T** for True or **F** for False. Check your work using the Answer Key in the back of the book.

1. ______ The neuronal membrane is impermeable.
2. ______ Glutamate is responsible for alertness.
3. ______ There are 10 billion neurons at birth.

Key Terms

For the following key terms, make groupings out of related terms. Be sure to explain how they are related.

Key Terms: action potential, agonist, all-or-none, antagonist, axon, biological perspective, dendrite, glial cell, membrane potential, myelin sheath, neuron, neurotransmitter, psychotropic medication, receptor, resting potential, reuptake, semipermeable membrane, soma, synapse, synaptic vesicle, terminal button, threshold of excitation

Lesson 2.3

Parts of the Nervous System

OBJECTIVES

★ Describe the difference between the central and peripheral nervous systems.

★ Explain the difference between the somatic and autonomic nervous systems.

★ Differentiate between the sympathetic and parasympathetic divisions of the autonomic nervous system.

BIG IDEA

The peripheral nervous system is made up of the somatic and autonomic nervous systems and is largely responsible for day-to-day operations of the body.

In this lesson, you will learn about the following:

- Central Nervous System
- Peripheral Nervous System

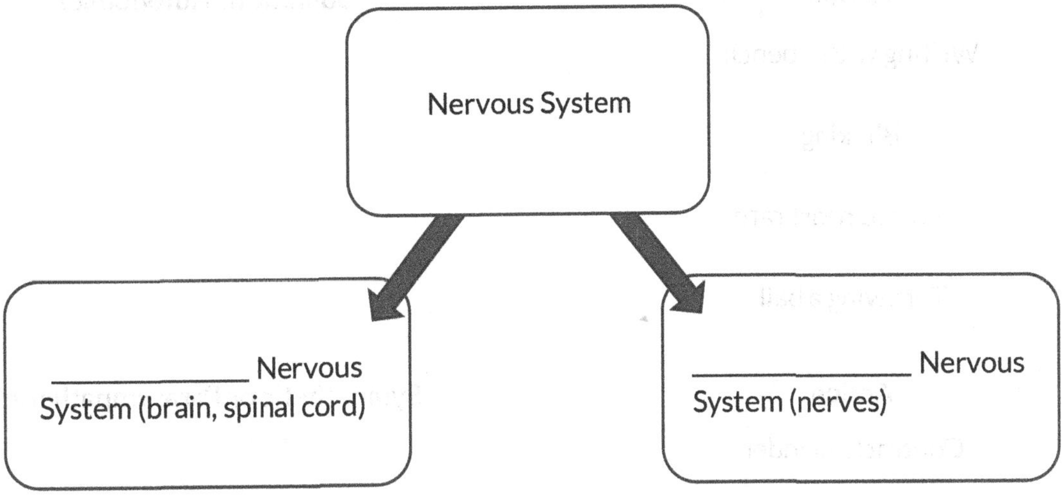

Peripheral Nervous System

The peripheral nervous system is made up of thick bundles of _______________, called nerves, that carry messages back and forth between the central nervous system and the _____________________, organs, and senses in the periphery of the body.

Complete the following graphic with details of the peripheral nervous system.

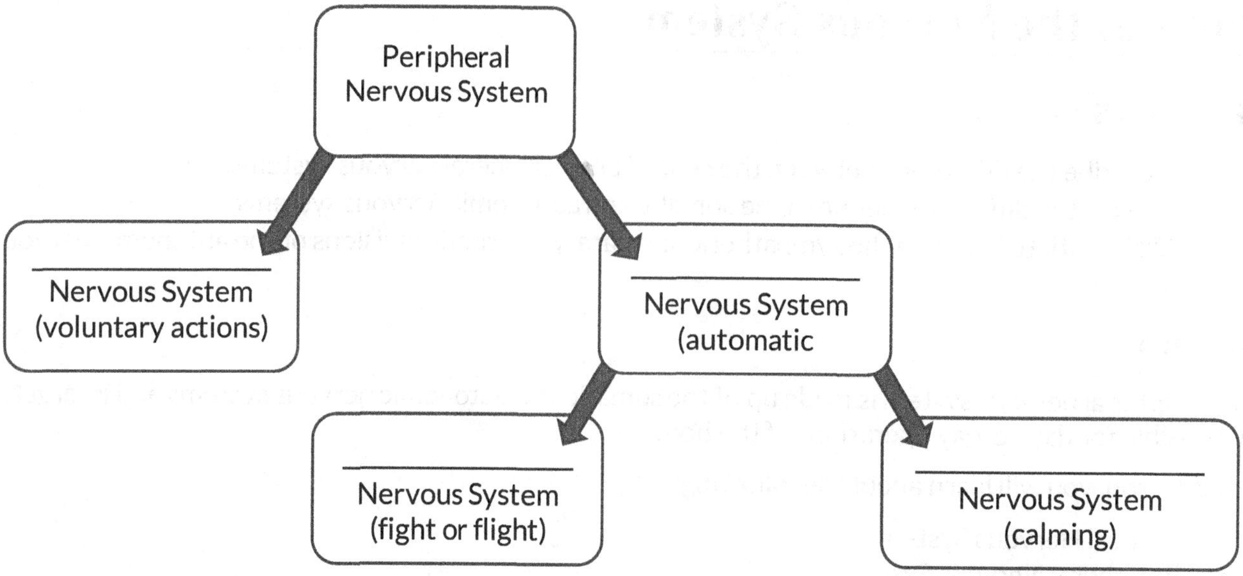

Action	Somatic or Autonomic?
Writing with a pencil	
Blinking	
Elevated heart rate	
Throwing a ball	

Action	Sympathetic or Parasympathetic?
Contracts bladder	
Slows heart rate	
Inhibits salivation	
Dilates pupils	

On Your Own

What tends to trigger your fight-or flight-response?

Provide an example of a situation in which someone would experience activation of the sympathetic nervous system.

Provide an example of a situation in which someone would experience activation of the parasympathetic nervous system.

Psychology and You

Fight-or-Flight Reaction

Describe a time when you had a fight-or-flight reaction. What were the physiological experiences that accompanied the situation?

Lesson Wrap-up

Say It in a Sentence

In one sentence, describe the role of the peripheral nervous system.

Test Yourself

Choose the correct answer for each of the following questions. Check your work using the Answer Key in the back of the book.

____ 1. When you are terrified as someone jumps out at you in a haunted house, your ____________ nervous system is at work.

A. somatic
B. parasympathetic
C. sympathetic

____ 2. When you calm down after exiting the haunted house, your nervous ____________ system is at work.

A. somatic
B. parasympathetic
C. sympathetic

____ 3. Dancing to your favorite song is controlled by the ____________ nervous system.

A. somatic
B. parasympathetic
C. sympathetic

Key Terms

Write a paraphrased definition for each key term.

Autonomic Nervous System:

Central Nervous System:

Fight or Flight Response:

Homeostasis:

Parasympathetic Nervous System:

Peripheral Nervous System:

Somatic Nervous System:

Sympathetic Nervous System:

Lesson 2.4

The Brain and Spinal Cord

OBJECTIVES

- ★ Explain the functions of the spinal cord.
- ★ Identify the hemispheres and lobes of the brain.
- ★ Describe the types of techniques available to clinicians and researchers to image or scan the brain.

BIG IDEA

The brain has a multitude of components that each uniquely contribute to human abilities, from memory to vision to language.

In this lesson, you will learn about the following:

- The Spinal Cord
- The Two Hemispheres
- Forebrain Structures
- Midbrain and Hindbrain Structures
- Brain Imaging

The Spinal Cord

On Your Own

What are some facts about the spinal cord?

1.

2.

3.

4.

5.

The Two Hemispheres

The surface of the brain is known as the ______________________________, and it is covered in bumps (__________) and grooves (____________). In addition, it is broken up into two __________________________.

On Your Own

What are your thoughts about individuals with split brains as a result of surgery to reduce epileptic symptoms?

Forebrain Structures

Complete the following table.

Work with Patients with Split Brains			
Show object in which visual field?	**Information goes to which hemisphere of the brain?**	**Does this side of the brain contain language capability?**	**Can patient verbally identify object?**
Left visual field			
Right visual field			

Lobes of the Brain

Label the following graphic organizer.

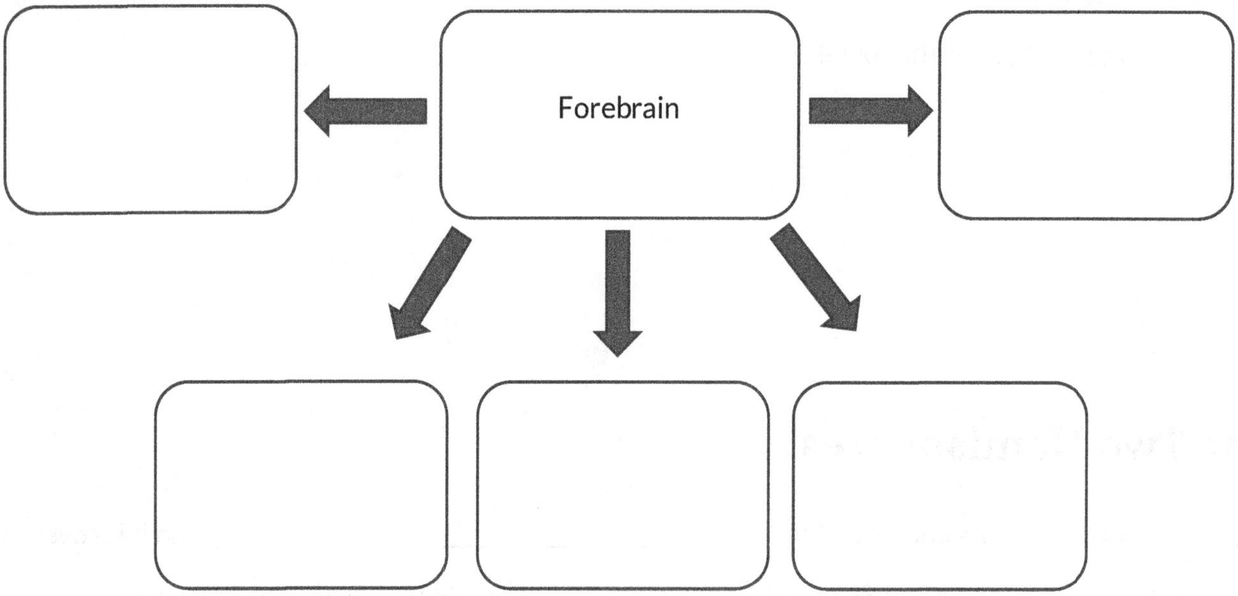

Lobes of the Brain

Label the following diagram.

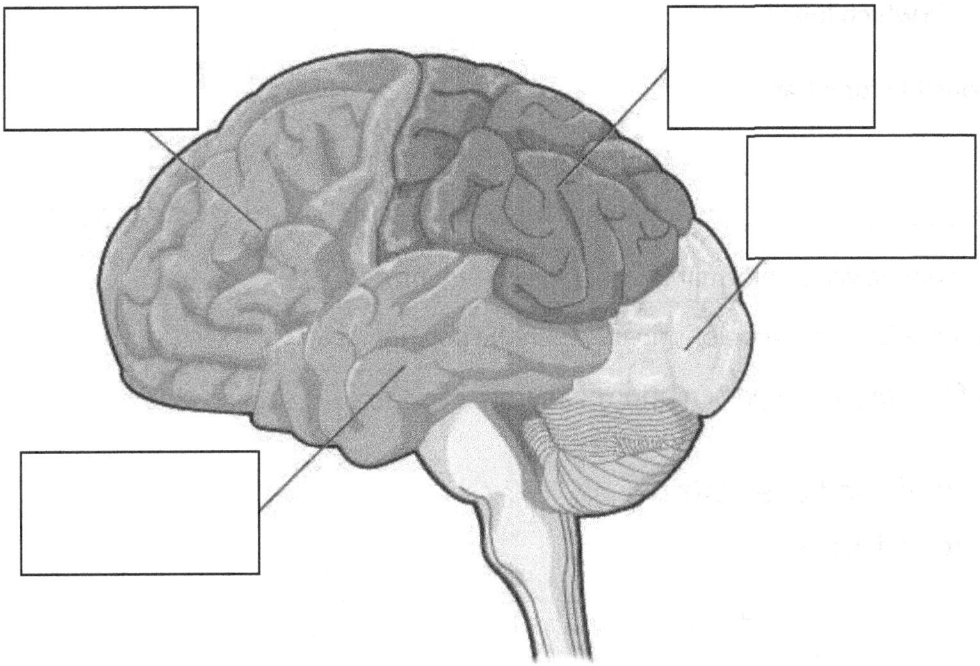

On Your Own

What are the functions of the frontal lobe?

1.

2.

3.

4.

What is your reaction to the story about Phineas Gage?

The brain's ______________________ lobe is involved in processing information from the body's senses, and it contains the somatosensory cortex.

On Your Own

What are the functions of the temporal lobe?

1.

2.

3.

4.

Broca's and Wernicke's Areas		
	Broca's Area	**Wernicke's Area**
Found in which lobe?		
Responsible for what?		

The ______________________ lobe contains the primary visual cortex, which is responsible for interpreting incoming visual information. This area is organized ______________________, which means there is a close relationship between the position of an object in a person's visual field and the position of that object's representation on the ______________________.

Other Areas of the Forebrain

Complete the following graphic organizer.

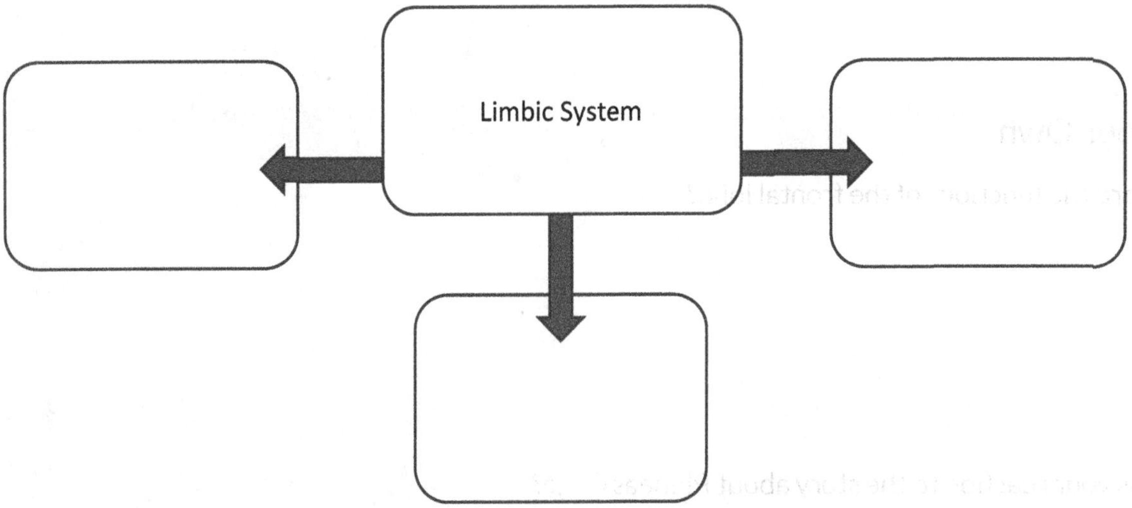

The Case of Henry Molaison (H. M.)

On Your Own

What is your reaction to the story of Henry Molaison? Would you have agreed to the surgical fix for epilepsy?

Midbrain and Hindbrain Structures

The ____________________ is comprised of structures located deep within the brain. For example, the substantia ________________ and ventral __________________________ area are in the midbrain. The hindbrain is located at the back of the head and contains the medulla, ________________, and cerebellum.

The medulla controls _________________________ processes. The pons connects the brain to the spinal cord and helps regulate ________________. The cerebellum is responsible for balance, coordination, movement, and _________________ skills.

On Your Own

What is your reaction to the Terri Schiavo case? Would you want to be kept alive if you were brain dead?

Brain Imaging

Techniques Involving Radiation

A __________________________ tomography (CT) scan involves taking a number of x-rays of a particular section of the body or brain. A _____________________ ________________________ tomography (PET) scan involves imaging of a radioactive tracer in the bloodstream that can show where the brain is more active.

Techniques Involving Magnetic Fields

______________________________ ______________________________ imaging involves the displacement of hydrogen atoms in the person's cells. These atoms give off an electromagnetic signal that can be read by the machine.

Techniques Involving Electrical Activity

Electroencephalography (EEG) involves measuring the brain's ________________________ activity.

Psychology and You

Provide an Example

Provide an example of a time when your amygdala "remembered" an experience from years past. For example, certain smells may trigger memories.

Lesson Wrap-up

Say It in a Sentence

In one sentence, explain the function of the lobes.

Test Yourself

Next to each statement, write **T** for True or **F** for False. Check your work using the Answer Key in the back of the book.

1. _____ The reticular formation is centered in the midbrain, but it actually extends up into the forebrain and down into the hindbrain.
2. _____ The two hemispheres are connected by a thick band of neural fibers known as the cerebral cortex.
3. _____ The occipital lobe is located in the forebrain.
4. _____ The two hemispheres of the cerebral cortex are part of the forebrain, which is the largest part of the brain.

Choose the correct part of the brain for each of the following descriptions. Check your work using the Answer Key in the back of the book.

____ 5. This part of the brain regulates a number of homeostatic processes, including the regulation of body temperature, appetite, and blood pressure.

A. Hippocampus
B. Amygdala
C. Hypothalamus
D. Cerebellum

____ 6. This is a sensory relay for the brain. All our senses, with the exception of smell, are routed through this area before being directed to other areas of the brain for processing.

- **A.** Amygdala
- **B.** Thalamus
- **C.** Hypothalamus
- **D.** Hippocampus

____ 7. This area of the brain is involved in our experience of emotion and in tying emotional meaning to our memories.

- **A.** Amygdala
- **B.** Thalamus
- **C.** Hypothalamus
- **D.** Hippocampus

Key Terms

Match each key term with its definition. Some terms will not be used.

A. Amygdala
B. Auditory Cortex
C. Broca's Area
D. Cerebellum
E. Cerebral Cortex
F. Corpus Callosum
G. Forebrain
H. Frontal Lobe
I. Hemisphere
J. Hindbrain
K. Hippocampus
L. Hypothalamus
M. Limbic System
N. Longitudinal Fissure
O. Medulla
P. Midbrain
Q. Motor Cortex
R. Occipital Lobe
S. Parietal Lobe
T. Pons

_____ Thick band of neural fibers connecting the hemispheres
_____ Strip of cortex in the temporal lobe that is responsible for processing auditory information
_____ Region in the left hemisphere that is essential for language production
_____ Structure in the temporal lobe associated with learning and memory
_____ Part of the cerebral cortex associated with visual processing
_____ Strip of cortex involved in planning and coordinating movement
_____ Structure in the limbic system involved in emotion and tying emotional meaning to our memories
_____ Hindbrain structure that controls balance, coordination, movement, and motor skills
_____ Surface of the brain that is associated with our highest mental capabilities
_____ Hindbrain structure that controls automated processes like breathing, blood pressure, and heart rate
_____ Part of the cerebral cortex involved in reasoning, motor control, emotion, and language
_____ Division of the brain containing the medulla, pons, and cerebellum
_____ Largest part of the brain; contains the cortex, thalamus, and limbic system
_____ Collection of structures involved in processing emotion and memory
_____ Division of the brain located between the forebrain and the hindbrain

Lesson 2.5

The Endocrine System

OBJECTIVES

- ★ Identify the major glands of the endocrine system.
- ★ Identify the hormones secreted by each gland.
- ★ Describe each hormone's role in regulating bodily functions.

BIG IDEA

The endocrine system and its related hormones often influence human behavior in long-lasting and widespread ways.

In this lesson, you will learn about the following:

- Major Glands

Finish labeling the following diagram.

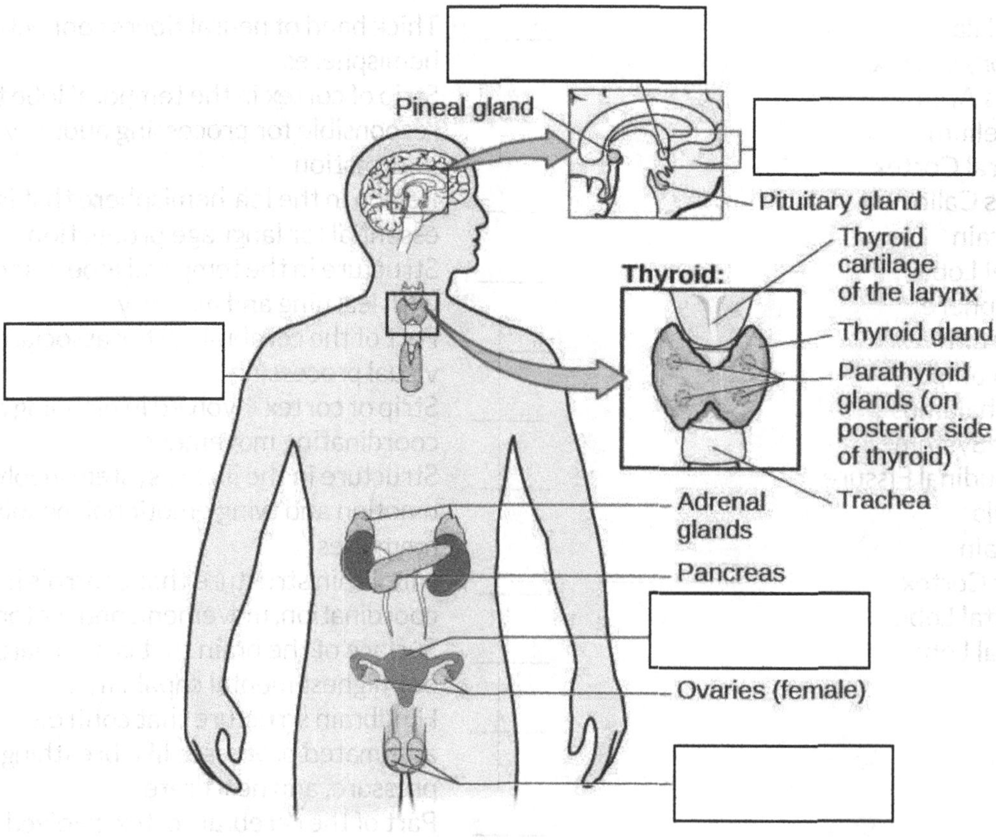

Complete the following table that illustrates the differences between hormones and neurotransmitters.

	Hormones	Neurotransmitters
Range of effect		
Speed of action		
How long in effect?		

Major Glands

The ________________ ________________, also known as the "master gland," descends from the hypothalamus and uses its messenger hormones to control all other glands in the endocrine system.

On Your Own

What are the functions of the pituitary gland?

1.

2.

3.

4.

The ____________________ gland releases hormones that regulate growth, metabolism, and appetite. In ____________________________, the thyroid makes too much thyroxine, whereas reduction in this hormone results in ______________________________. The ____________________ glands secrete hormones involved in the stress response, such as epinephrine and norepinephrine. The ____________________ secretes hormones to help regulate blood sugar levels. The ____________ secrete sex hormones and mediate both sexual motivation and behavior.

On Your Own

What are negative consequences of steroid use?

1.

2.

3.

4.

Do you think athletes should be able to use performance enhancing substances? Explain.

Psychology and You

Hypothyroidism vs. Hyperthyroidism

Explain hypothyroidism and hyperthyroidism. Why is it important to understand both in the field of psychology?

Lesson Wrap-up

Say It in a Sentence

In one sentence, explain why understanding the endocrine system is important to the field of psychology.

Test Yourself

Choose the correct answer for the following questions. Check your work using the Answer Key in the back of the book.

____ 1. This "master gland" controls all other glands in the endocrine system.

- **A.** Thyroid
- **B.** Gonads
- **C.** Pituitary

____ 2. These glands sit atop our kidneys and secrete hormones involved in the stress response.

- **A.** Adrenal
- **B.** Gonads
- **C.** Hypothalamus

____ 3. This gland releases hormones that regulate growth, metabolism, and appetite.

- **A.** Thyroid
- **B.** Adrenal
- **C.** Pituitary

Next to each statement, write **T** for True or **F** for False. Check your work using the Answer Key in the back of the book.

4. ______ The pancreas secretes hormones that regulate blood sugar levels.
5. ______ The thyroid serves as the master gland, controlling secretion of all other glands.
6. ______ The gonads (ovaries for females, testes for males) mediate sexual motivation and behavior.

7. _____ Hormones are involved in regulating bodily functions and are ultimately controlled through interactions between the hypothalamus and pituitary gland.

Key Terms

Match each key term with its definition.

A. Adrenal Gland
B. Diabetes
C. Endocrine System
D. Gonad
E. Hormone
F. Pancreas
G. Pituitary Gland
H. Thyroid

_____ Secretes hormones that regulate blood sugar
_____ Disease related to insufficient insulin production
_____ Secretes hormones involved in the stress response
_____ Secretes hormones that regulate growth, metabolism, and appetite
_____ Series of glands that produce chemical substances known as hormones
_____ Chemical messenger released by endocrine glands
_____ Secretes a number of hormones that regulate fluid levels in the body and help control other glands in the endocrine system
_____ Secretes sex hormones that mediate both sexual motivation and behavior

Chapter 3
States of Consciousness

Lesson 3.1
What Is Consciousness?

OBJECTIVES

- ★ Understand what is meant by consciousness.
- ★ Explain how circadian rhythms are involved in regulating the sleep-wake cycle and how circadian cycles can be disrupted.
- ★ Discuss the concept of sleep debt.

BIG IDEA

States of consciousness vary across the day and are influenced by a variety of internal and external factors.

In this lesson, you will learn about the following:

- Biological Rhythms
- Problems with Circadian Rhythms

Consciousness describes our ____________________ of internal and external stimuli. We experience different states of ________________________ and different levels of awareness on a regular basis.

On Your Own

If consciousness was placed on a continuum, what would the labels be?

[ ] ←——→ [ ]

What are different states of consciousness?

1.
2.
3.
4.
5.
6.
7.

Biological Rhythms

Biological rhythms are ______________________ rhythms of biological activity. These rhythms can last different lengths of time, from moments to months.

On Your Own

Provide examples of biological rhythms.

1.
2.
3.
4.
5.
6.

Finish labeling the following figure.

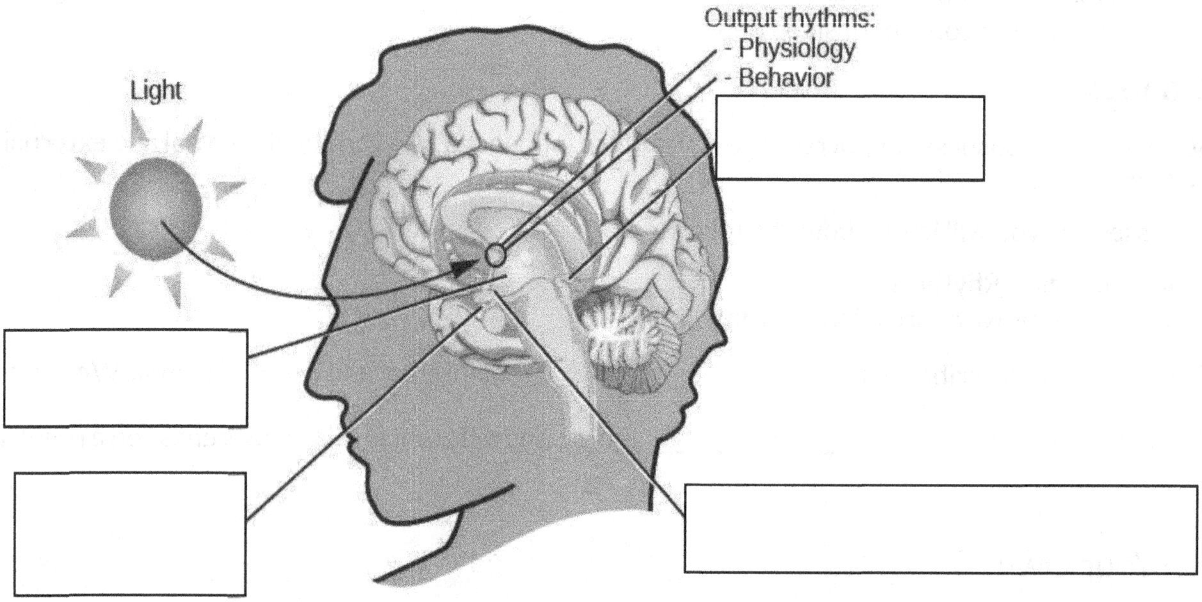

Problems with Circadian Rhythms

One important regulator of sleep is the hormone melatonin, which is released from the pineal gland in response to darkness and light in the environment.

Disruptions of Normal Sleep

On Your Own

Have you ever experienced jet lag? Describe the symptoms.

Insufficient Sleep

On Your Own

Examine the figure related to recommended sleep amounts per age. About how much sleep should someone in your age range get? Do you usually fall within this range? Why or why not?

Fill in the missing negative consequences of sleep deprivation.

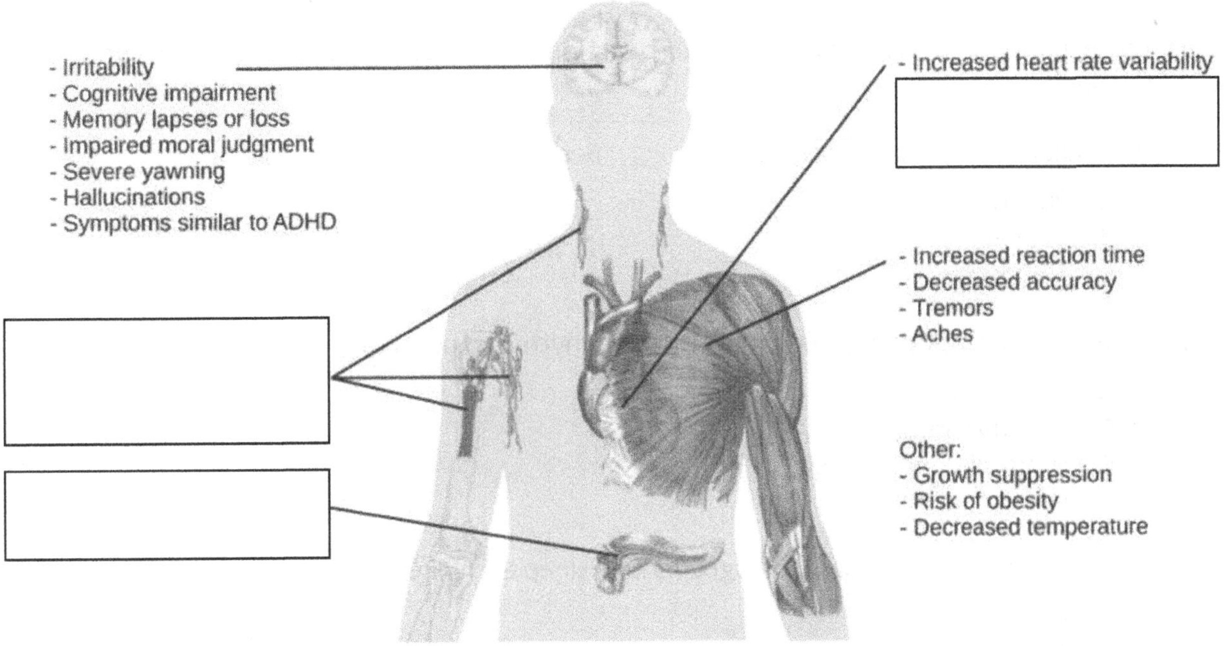

Why do you think humans need less sleep as they age?

Psychology and You

Provide an Example

Recall a time when you personally experienced a lack of sleep. What health problems led to or resulted from it?

Lesson Wrap-up

Say It in a Sentence

In one sentence, explain why getting the proper amount of sleep is important.

Test Yourself

Choose the correct answer for each of the following questions. Check your work using the Answer Key in the back of the book.

____ 1. Circadian rhythms occur across a ________ period.

- **A.** 28-day
- **B.** 24-hour
- **C.** 12-hour

____ 2. The internal clock that governs the circadian rhythm is the:

- **A.** Pituitary gland
- **B.** Hypothalamus
- **C.** Suprachiasmatic nucleus
- **D.** Inferotemporal cortex

____ 3. If individuals continuously do not get enough sleep each night, they accrue:

- **A.** A sleep debt
- **B.** A sleep rebound

Next to each statement, write **T** for True or **F** for False. Check your work using the Answer Key in the back of the book.

4. _____ A lunar rhythm lasts 30 days.
5. _____ Only sleep and full wakefulness are states of consciousness.
6. _____ Body temperature increases over the course of the day.
7. _____ Sleep is necessary for normal functioning.

Key Terms

Match each key term with its definition.

A. Biological Rhythm
B. Circadian Rhythm
C. Consciousness
D. Homeostasis
E. Insomnia
F. Jet Lag
G. Melatonin
H. Meta-analysis

_____ State marked by relatively low levels of physical activity and reduced sensory awareness that is distinct from periods of rest that occur during wakefulness

_____ Work schedule that changes from early to late on a daily/weekly basis

_____ Collection of symptoms that result from traveling across time zones

I. Pineal Gland
J. Rotating Shift Work
K. Sleep
L. Sleep Debt
M. Sleep Regulation
N. Suprachiasmatic Nucleus
O. Wakefulness

_____ Biological rhythm over approximately 24 hours
_____ Awareness of internal and external stimuli
_____ Endocrine structure that releases melatonin
_____ High levels of sensory awareness, thought, and behavior
_____ Internal cycle of biological activity
_____ Tendency to maintain a balance
_____ Hormone that serves important role in sleep-wake cycle
_____ Brain's control of switching between sleep and wakefulness
_____ Consistent difficulty falling or remaining asleep
_____ Brain's biological clock
_____ Result of insufficient sleep on a chronic basis
_____ Study that combines results of several related studies

Lesson 3.2

Sleep and Why We Sleep

OBJECTIVES

★ Describe areas of the brain involved in sleep.
★ Understand hormone secretions associated with sleep.
★ Describe several theories aimed at explaining the function of sleep.

BIG IDEA

Humans sleep a great deal of the time, but the true purpose of sleep is still debated.

In this lesson, you will learn about the following:

- What Is Sleep?
- Why Do We Sleep?

On Your Own

Why do you think humans spend so much time sleeping?

What is Sleep?

Sleep is a homeostatically regulated phenomenon. We need sleep, as evidenced by ______________

____________________: when individuals who have been deprived of sleep tend to fall asleep faster when given a chance to sleep.

What brain areas contribute to sleep? Complete the following graphic.

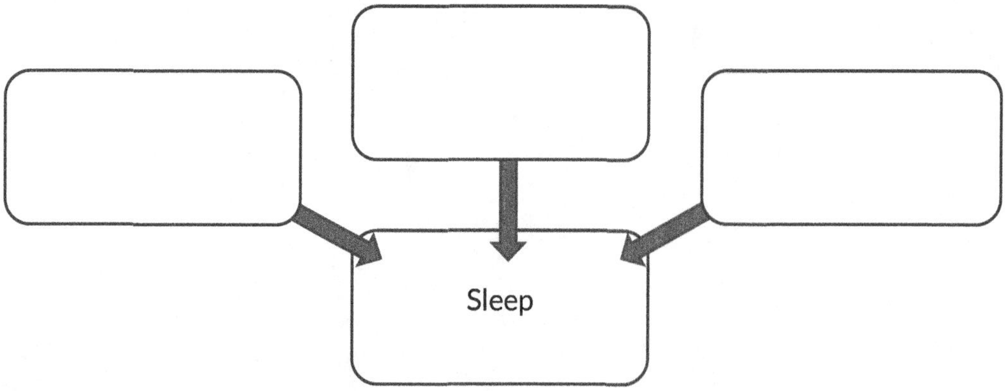

What hormones are secreted during sleep? Complete the following graphic.

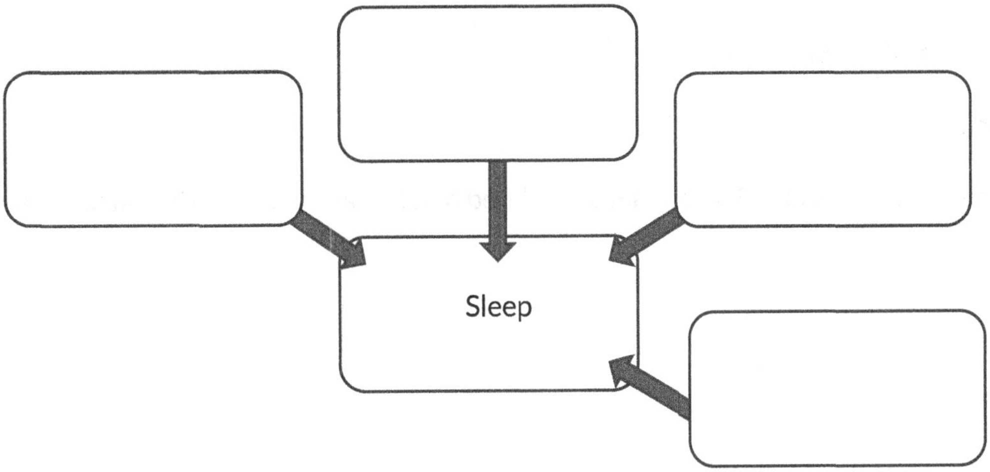

Complete the following chart.

Hormone	Endocrine Gland	Effects
	Pineal gland	Regulation of biological rhythms
	Pituitary gland	Regulation of reproductive system
	Pituitary gland	Regulation of reproductive system
	Pituitary gland	Physical growth and maturation

Label the following figure.

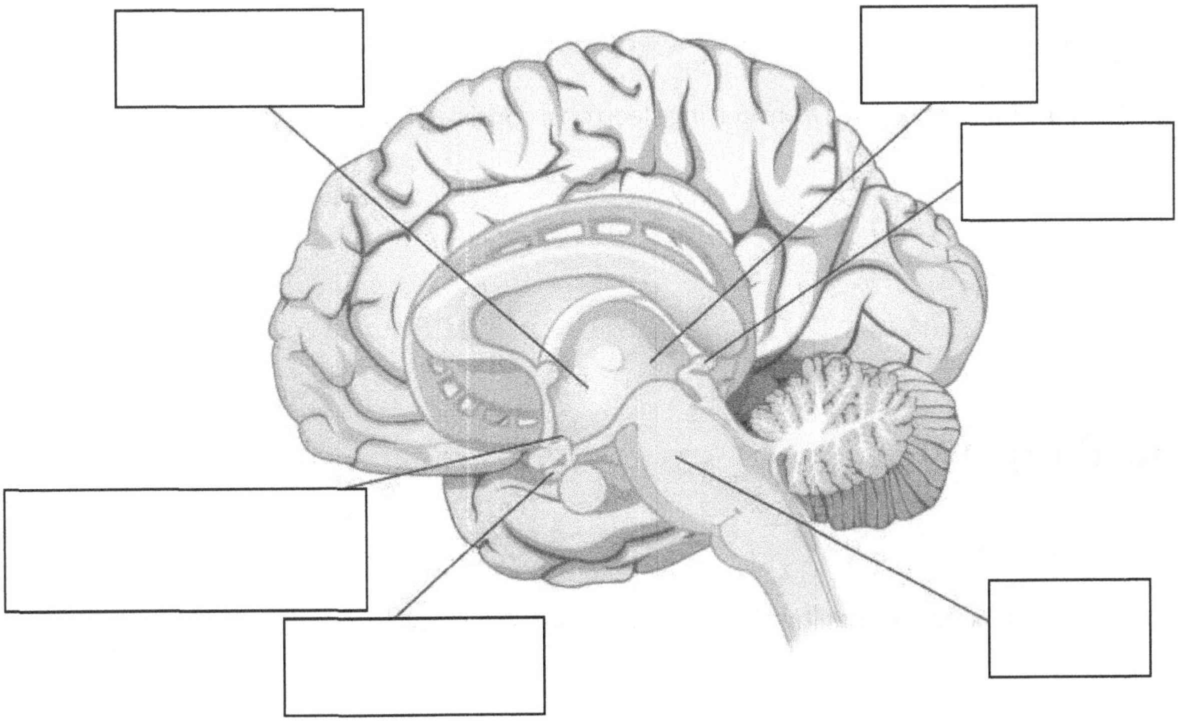

What Is Sleep?

Adaptive Function of Sleep

On Your Own

Compare the two theories about sleep that are related to adaptation. Which do you feel is more likely?

What are the benefits of good sleep?

1.
2.
3.
4.
5.

Cognitive Function of Sleep

Sleep appears to be important for ____________________ function and memory formation. Sleep deprivation results in disruptions in cognition and memory ________________. These deficits increase as sleep ____________________ becomes more severe.

Psychology and You

Sleep Benefits

Explain the benefits humans receive from getting sleep on a consistent basis.

Lesson Wrap-up

Say It in a Sentence

In one sentence, summarize the cognitive benefits of a healthy sleep cycle.

Test Yourself

Choose the correct answer for each of the following questions. Check your work using the Answer Key in the back of the book.

____ 1. This phenomenon occurs when a sleep-deprived individual takes a shorter-than-average time to fall asleep during opportunities for sleep.

- **A.** Natural selection
- **B.** Evolutionary psychology
- **C.** Sleep debt
- **D.** Sleep rebound

____ 2. This discipline studies how universal patterns of behavior and cognitive processes have evolved over time as a result of natural selection.

- **A.** Evolutionary psychology
- **B.** Natural selection
- **C.** Sleep rebound

Next to each statement, write **T** for True or **F** for False. Check your work using the Answer Key in the back of the book.

3. _____ Several hormones important for physical growth and maturation are secreted during sleep.
4. _____ Sleep is not important for memory.
5. _____ Sleep is not important for learning.
6. _____ Sleep is associated with secretion of melatonin, FSH, LH, and growth hormones.

Key Terms

Write a paraphrased definition for each key term.

Evolutionary Psychology:

Sleep Rebound:

Lesson 3.3

Stages of Sleep

OBJECTIVES

★ Differentiate between REM and non-REM sleep.
★ Describe the differences between the four stages of non-REM sleep.
★ Understand the role that REM and non-REM sleep play in learning and memory.

BIG IDEA

Sleep occurs in stages with different attributes, including one stage during which dreams occur.

In this lesson, you will learn about the following:

- NREM Stages of Sleep
- REM Sleep

Sleep is comprised of several stages that can be differentiated from one another by the patterns of

________________ ______________________, measured using EEG. They can be broken up into either

__________________ (rapid eye movement) sleep or non-REM sleep.

NREM Stages of Sleep

Complete the following chart.

Sleep Stages	Waves Present	Characteristics
	Alpha, theta	Transitional phase, light sleep phase
Stage 2		
	Delta	Deep sleep, hard to awake
	Delta	Deep sleep, hard to awake

REM Sleep

On Your Own

What are the notable properties of REM sleep?

1.
2.
3.
4.
5.

What does it mean that REM sleep is paradoxical?

There is evidence to suggest that ____________ sleep deprivation, or sleep deprivation in general, may affect and improve symptoms of ________________________. In fact, sleep deprivation may change ______________________ processing so that various stimuli are more likely to be perceived as positive rather than negative.

On Your Own

Explain the following hypnogram:

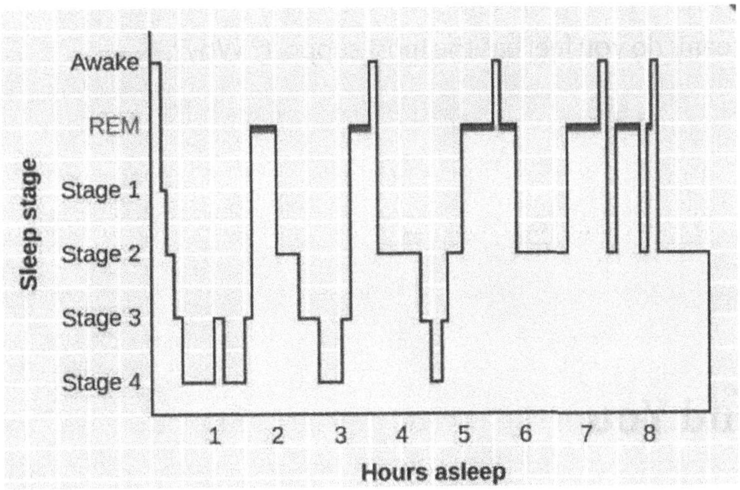

Dreams

Sigmund Freud felt that dreams were a way to interpret ________________________ desires by investigating the __________________ (hidden meaning) content of the dream instead of the ______________________ (actual) content.

On Your Own

What do you think of Freud's idea of dream analysis?

Carl Jung believed that dreams were a way to tap into the collective ______________________________.

Rosalind Cartwright believes that dreams reflect __________ ____________________ that are important to the dreamer.

Neuroscientists theorize that dreams may be a way of creating a ____________________ reality that dreamers can use in wakeful reality.

On Your Own

Which theory about dreams do you feel has the most support? Why?

Psychology and You

Dream Analysis

Describe a dream you had recently. How might Sigmund Freud analyze this dream?

Lesson Wrap-up

Say It in a Sentence

In one sentence, summarize the difference between REM and NREM sleep.

Test Yourself

Choose the correct answer for each of the following questions. Check your work using the Answer Key in the back of the book.

____ 1. This is often referred to as deep sleep or slow wave sleep because it is characterized by low-frequency, high-amplitude delta waves.

A. Stage 2 sleep
B. Stage 3 sleep
C. REM sleep

____ 2. Thomas became aware during a dream that he was having a dream. This characterization would best fit:

A. NREM sleep
B. REM sleep
C. Lucid dreams

____ 3. In which stage of sleep do K-complexes occur?

A. Stage 1
B. Stage 2
C. Stage 3

____ 4. In which stage of sleep do sleep spindles occur?

A. Stage 1
B. Stage 2
C. Stage 3
D. Stage 4

Next to each statement, write **T** for True or **F** for False. Check your work using the Answer Key in the back of the book.

5. ______ A K-complex is a high amplitude pattern of brain activity that may in some cases occur in response to environmental stimuli.

6. ______ Stage 1 sleep is a stage of deep relaxation.

7. ______ A sleep spindle is a rapid burst of higher frequency brain waves that may be important for learning and memory.

8. ______ Humans sleep about a 10th of their lives away.

Key Terms

For the following key terms, make groupings out of the related terms. Be sure to explain how they are related.

Key Terms: alpha wave, delta wave, collective unconscious, K-complex, latent content, lucid dream, manifest content, non-REM, rapid eye movement sleep, sleep spindle, stage 1 sleep, stage 2 sleep, stage 3 sleep, stage 4 sleep, theta waves

Lesson 3.4

Sleep Problems and Disorders

OBJECTIVES

- ★ Describe the symptoms and treatments of insomnia.
- ★ Recognize the symptoms of several parasomnias.
- ★ Describe the symptoms and treatments for sleep apnea.
- ★ Recognize risk factors associated with sudden infant death syndrome (SIDS) and steps to prevent it.
- ★ Describe the symptoms and treatments for narcolepsy.

BIG IDEA

There are several kinds of sleep disturbances. Sleep issues can affect not only the person experiencing them but others too.

In this lesson, you will learn about the following:

- Insomnia
- Parasomnias
- Sleep Apnea
- Narcolepsy

On Your Own

What are the different types of sleep disturbances?

	Consistent difficulty in falling or staying asleep
Parasomnia	
Others	

Insomnia

Insomnia is experienced by most people on occasion. Symptoms include difficulty falling asleep, waking during the night, and fatigue during the day. To be diagnosed, the symptoms must occur at least

_______________ nights a week for at least _____________ month's time.

On Your Own

What other psychological condition is insomnia associated with?

- ☐ Bipolar disorder
- ☐ Social phobia
- ☐ Depression

Identify three safe treatments for insomnia.

1.

2.

3.

Parasomnias

Define **parasomnias.**

Some parasomnias include sleepwalking, RBD (REM Sleep Behavioral Disorder), restless leg syndrome, and night terrors.

Sleepwalking

What is the medical term for sleepwalking?

Sleepwalking

- People may drive, eat, use bathroom while sleeping
- Not dangerous to wake sleepwalker
- Not a sign of a psychological problem
- More common in children
- More common when sleep-deprived

On Your Own

Read "A Sleepwalking Defense?". If you were a juror on this case, what information would you use to make a decision? Do you think sleepwalking can be a valid defense? Please explain.

Complete the following table.

Sleep Disturbance	Scenario
	Ryan experiences no muscle paralysis during REM sleep. She may kick, hit, punch, or engage in other active behavior.
	Olivia suffers from dreams that are different from nightmares in that she acts awake and panics. She does not remember them upon awakening.
	Charlie tells his physician he has trouble falling asleep because he has a "pins and needles" sensation in his legs. Kicking or moving his legs seems to be the only remedy.

Sleep Apnea

Sleep apnea consists of episodes in which a person stops breathing while sleeping.

Two types of apnea include:

1. Obstructive sleep apnea: due to blocked airway
2. Central sleep apnea: due to disruption in brain signals that regulate breathing

On Your Own

Describe how the CPAP device is used to treat sleep apnea.

Sudden Infant Death Syndrome (SIDS)

- Babies may stop breathing and die in their sleep
- Smoking is a risk factor
- Dressing baby too warmly is a risk factor
- Place babies on their backs to sleep
- Do not use blankets or pillows, which may suffocate

Narcolepsy

Narcolepsy is a neurological disorder. Symptoms include:

- Falling asleep during the day unexpectedly
- Falling immediately into REM sleep
- Sudden loss of muscle tone (cataplexy)
- Falling asleep when emotional or aroused

What is a treatment for narcolepsy?

On Your Own

Fill in the table by writing the correct name of the sleep disturbance described in each column.

Tyler falls asleep suddenly during the day. This happens even when he is actively doing something, like having a good time with friends.	Nick is violently active during his sleep. Nick also has Parkinson's disease.	For the past month, Rohit has been tired during the day, several days a week. He can fall asleep at night, but he awakens several times and has trouble getting back to sleep.	Joyce is exhausted during the day but doesn't know why. Her husband reports that she snores loudly and seems to awaken several times throughout the night.

Psychology and You

Offer Some Advice

A friend mentions to you that she is thinking about using over-the-counter medicine to help her sleep at night. Discuss the potential risks. What alternative advice can you offer?

Lesson Wrap-up

Say It in a Sentence

In one sentence, summarize the types of sleep disturbances that can occur.

Test Yourself

Next to each statement, write **T** for True or **F** for False. Check your work using the Answer Key in the back of the book.

1. ______ Sleep apnea increases the risk of heart disease.
2. ______ Smoking is associated with sudden infant death syndrome.
3. ______ Night terrors are an indication of a serious psychological disorder.
4. ______ People have driven while sleeping.
5. ______ Muscle paralysis is a normal part of REM sleep.
6. ______ People who have sleep apnea are always aware that they have it.
7. ______ Caffeine can cause insomnia.

Key Terms

Match each key term with its definition.

A. Central Sleep Apnea
B. Parasomnia
C. Somnambulism
D. Night Terror
E. Restless Leg Syndrome
F. Obstructive Sleep Apnea
G. CPAP
H. Cataplexy
I. RBD

______ Sleepwalking

______ Disorder of interrupted breathing due to blockage of airway

______ Disorder in which the muscle paralysis of REM does not occur

______ Sleep disruption due to sensations in legs

______ Disorder of interrupted breathing due to disruption in brain signals that regulate breathing

______ A group of sleep disorders marked by disruptive movements or unwanted experiences

______ Continuous positive airway pressure mask used to keep airway open while sleeping

______ Panic, yelling, screaming while sleeping

Lesson 3.5

Substance Use and Abuse

OBJECTIVES

★ Describe the diagnostic criteria for substance use disorders.
★ Identify the neurotransmitter systems impacted by various categories of drugs.
★ Describe how different categories of drugs affect behavior and experience.

BIG IDEA

Using drugs can create an altered state of consciousness. Drugs are categorized by their effects on the body and mind. Many drugs can lead to physical or psychological addiction.

In this lesson, you will learn about:

- Substance Use Disorders
- Drug Categories

Substance Use Disorders

How do psychologists diagnose substance use disorders?

Drug use disorders are addictive disorders. People diagnosed with an addictive disorder:

- Often use more of the drug than they intend
- Use the drug despite negative consequences
- Experience physical tolerance
- Give up activities for the drug
- Experience unpleasant withdrawal symptoms

On Your Own

How would you differentiate substance use from a substance disorder?

Drug Categories

Alcohol and Other Depressants

Depressants are also called ____________________. They slow down brain and behavioral activity. Two sedatives that have been widely abused are ____________________ (used to reduce seizures) and benzodiazepines (used for anxiety and depression). All depressants ____________________ central nervous system activity by activating the neurotransmitter ______________, which has a quieting effect on the brain.

In the following table, list at least four short-term and two long-term effects of using alcohol.

Short-Term Effects	Long-Term Effects

Drinking while pregnant may cause _______________ alcohol syndrome, a permanent, brain-damaging condition.

Write the name of the correct drug category for the following list.

____
I slow down the central nervous system.
Barbiturates, Benzodiazepines, Alcohol
People become physically dependent on me. Withdrawal is very uncomfortable and causes both physical and emotional problems.

On Your Own

Your friend thinks he might have a substance abuse problem with alcohol. What could you do to help him?

Stimulants

Stimulants ________________ brain activity by activating the neurotransmitter ________________, which is associated with reward and craving.

Examples of stimulant drugs include ________________, amphetamines, MDMA, nicotine, and the most common, ____________________.

________________ cocaine is less expensive than powder cocaine. Therefore, it tends to be more accessible.

On Your Own

Read the article "5 Myths About That Demon Crack." What is your analysis of the use of harsh sentences to deter drug use? What alternative approaches can you offer to address crack cocaine use?

Opioids

You have probably heard about the opioid epidemic in the United States and across the world. Each day, more than 100 people in the U.S. die after overdosing on opioids.

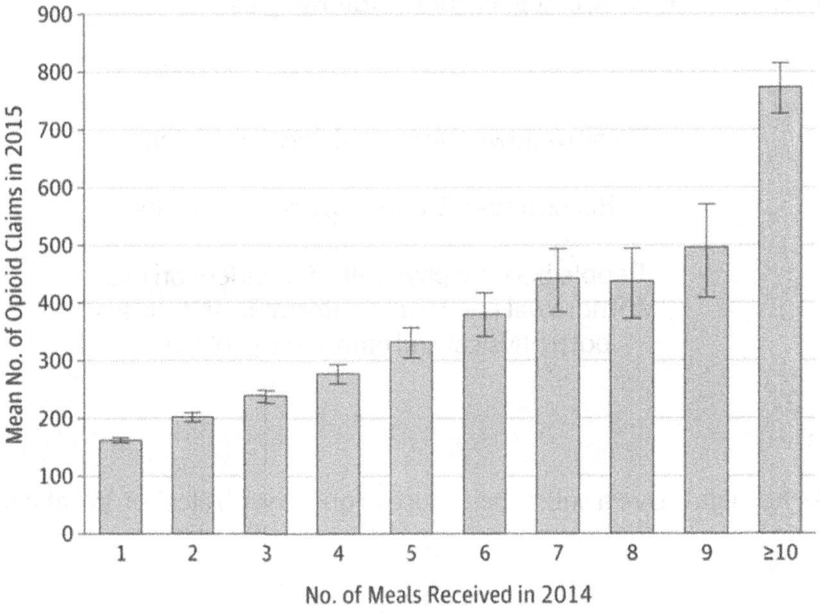

The bar graph shows the relationship between the number of opioid prescriptions written and the number of free meals received by physicians from opioid companies. Does this suggest that buying meals causes doctors to write more opioid prescriptions? Explain your answer.

On Your Own

Write the name of the correct drug category above the list.

____
I have a high potential for abuse. (Human body makes these natural pain killers)
I am made from the poppy plant. (Methadone, codeine)
I am an analgesic. (Morphine, heroin)

Hallucinogens

________________________ are a group of drugs that cause changes in mood and sensory perception. For people who use them, time may seem to slow down. Users may report feeling out of control or disconnected from their body.

Drugs in this category include mescaline and LSD. _______________________ interfere with the neurotransmitter __________________, which is the most abundant neurotransmitter in the body.

Mescaline and LSD are agonists for the neurotransmitter __________________.

On Your Own

What is your opinion on legalizing marijuana for medical or recreational use?

On Your Own

Write the name of the correct drug category above the list.

____
I have a lower potential for abuse than other drugs.
Some of my kind are serotonin agonists.
Some of my kind are glutamate antagonists.
I create distortions in sensory perceptions and perceptions of time.

Psychology and You

Effects of Stimulants

Your friends use caffeine, nicotine, and other drugs to stay up late studying or working. What do they need to know about the short-term and long-term effects of these drugs?

Sally went to her physician because she couldn't sleep, and she felt worried all the time. The physician diagnosed her with an anxiety disorder. As part of her treatment, the physician advised Sally to reduce caffeine, nicotine, and other stimulants. Why do you think the physician offered that advice?

Lesson Wrap-up

Say It in a Sentence

In one sentence, describe how drugs affect human consciousness.

Test Yourself

Choose the correct answer for each of the following questions. Check your work using the Answer Key in the back of the book.

____ 1. This highly addictive stimulant is legal and associated with heart disease, stroke, and a variety of cancers.

- **A.** Caffeine
- **B.** Diet pills
- **C.** Nicotine

____ 2. This drug is considered safe, but too much can result in twitching, nausea, irregular heartbeat, and insomnia.

- **A.** Cocaine
- **B.** "Crystal Meth"
- **C.** Caffeine

____ 3. Using these types of drugs leads to depletion of dopamine, norepinephrine, and serotonin, making people want to use the drugs more to replenish the neurotransmitters.

- **A.** Depressants
- **B.** Stimulants
- **C.** Hallucinogens

Next to each statement, write **T** for True or **F** for False. Check your work using the Answer Key in the back of the book.

4. ______ GABA is a neurotransmitter that increases arousal in the brain.
5. ______ Alcohol is experienced as a stimulant but is actually a depressant.
6. ______ Quitting alcohol or barbiturates can be life-threatening.
7. ______ Depressants are GABA agonists.
8. ______ Depressants have a low potential of becoming addictive.

Key Terms

Match each key term with its definition.

A. Psychological Dependence
B. Tolerance
C. Withdrawal
D. Methadone
E. Stimulant
F. Hallucinogen
G. Depressant
H. GABA

_____ Needing more of a drug in order to feel its effects
_____ Drug that increases heart rate, activity of central nervous system (upper)
_____ Negative symptoms are experienced when a drug isn't taken
_____ Is used to treat opioid withdrawal
_____ An emotional need for a drug
_____ A drug that reduces brain activity (downer)
_____ A drug that causes hallucinations, distortions in time perception
_____ Neurotransmitter activated by depressants

Lesson 3.6

Other States of Consciousness

OBJECTIVES

- ★ Define hypnosis and meditation.
- ★ Understand the similarities and differences of hypnosis and meditation.

BIG IDEA

Hypnosis and meditation are unique forms of consciousness used for relaxation, pain management, and managing stress. Meditation can be practiced alone, while hypnosis requires a helper.

In this lesson, you will learn about the following:

- Hypnosis
- Meditation

Hypnosis

____________________ is a state of extreme self-focus and attention in which minimal attention is given to external stimuli.

Brain imaging studies have demonstrated that hypnotic states are associated with

________________ ______________________ in brain functioning.

On Your Own

List some movies, television shows, books, and other media that have discussed hypnosis. How was it portrayed?

What are the four steps a patient must go through to be open to hypnosis?

1.

2.

3.

4.

People vary in terms of their ability to be hypnotized, but research suggests that most people are at least

__________________________ hypnotizable.

On Your Own

What are some conditions that hypnosis is said to be somewhat effective in treating?

For each myth in the following table, write the corresponding truth. The first one is done for you.

Myth	Truth
People can be made to do embarrassing things while under hypnosis because they aren't aware of what they are doing.	People are aware of what they do under hypnosis and can only be hypnotized if they are open to it.
The hypnotist controls the patient's mind.	
The patient does not remember what happens while under hypnosis.	

What are the two theories for how hypnosis works?

1.

2.

Meditation

Meditation is the act of focusing on a single target to increase __________________________ of the

moment.

Meditation is not an altered state of consciousness; however, patterns of brain waves exhibited by

expert meditators may represent a ___________________ state of consciousness.

The central feature of all mediation is clearing the mind in order to achieve a state of

_______________________ ______________________________ and focus.

What are some positive effects of mediation?

-
-
-
-
-
-

On Your Own

Think about where and when you can meditate. How do you think it might benefit you?

What similarities and differences do you see between meditation and hypnosis?

Psychology and You

Two-Minute Mindfulness Meditation

Think you're too busy to meditate? You can experience the benefits of meditation in only 2 minutes per day. Follow these steps to do a two-minute meditation.

1. Sit comfortably, relax, close your eyes.
2. Focus on your breathing, and take slow, deep breaths.
3. Hear the sounds around you. What do you hear?
4. Do a body scan from head to toe. How does your head feel? Your back? Slowly notice every part of your body to the soles of your feet.
5. Keep breathing slowly. If your mind wanders, just smile and bring it back to your breathing. Everyone's mind wanders.
6. Develop an attitude of self-acceptance. Whatever you're feeling is perfectly okay. Stay with that feeling. Allow it to happen. Continue breathing.
7. You can do this anywhere, at any time of day.

Lesson Wrap-up

Say It in a Sentence

In one sentence, explain how hypnosis and meditation help people.

Test Yourself

Next to each statement, write **T** for True or **F** for False. Check your work using the Answer Key in the back of the book.

1. ______ Very few people in the world can truly be hypnotized.
2. ______ There are competing theories about why hypnosis works.
3. ______ Hypnosis is effective for treating depression.
4. ______ Hypnosis and meditation are the same thing.
5. ______ Meditation can be performed alone.

Choose the correct answer for each of the following questions. Check your work using the Answer Key in the back of the book.

____ 6. Meditation originates from:

- **A.** Western philosophy
- **B.** Buddhist religion
- **C.** Eastern medicine

____ 7. Research is being conducted to evaluate the effectiveness of hypnosis in:

- **A.** Educational settings
- **B.** Marriage therapy
- **C.** Child therapy

____ 8. Hypnosis is associated with changes in:

- **A.** Heart functioning
- **B.** Lung functioning
- **C.** Brain functioning

Key Terms

Write the definition for each of the following terms.

Hypnosis:

Meditation:

Chapter 4

Sensation and Perception

Lesson 4.1

Sensation versus Perception

OBJECTIVES

- ★ Distinguish between sensation and perception.
- ★ Describe the concepts of absolute threshold and difference threshold.
- ★ Discuss the roles attention, motivation, and sensory adaptation play in perception.

BIG IDEA

The way we experience the world is not just a function of our five senses; our personality, motivations, and attention all play a role too.

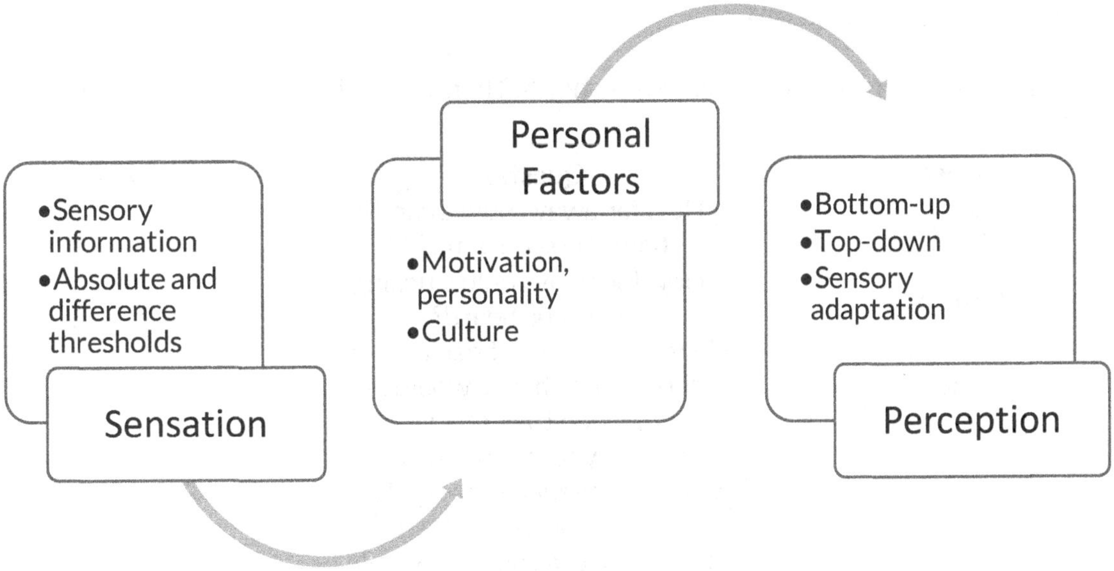

In this lesson, you will learn about the following:

- Sensation
- Perception

Sensation

What is the faintest sound a person can hear? How far away can a candle flame be seen on a clear night? How different do two things need to be in order for a person to notice? Psychologists study human sensation and perception to answer these and similar questions.

Absolute thresholds are the __________________ amount of energy we can detect ________% of the time.

Example:

Put a ticking clock on a table and walk away from it until you can't hear it. Then, gradually move toward it. Do this several times and record the different distances from which you can hear the clock. Where you detect it 50% of the time is your absolute threshold for hearing the clock.

The __________________ threshold is the smallest degree of difference required to discriminate one ________________ from another 50% of the time.

Example:

How different must two colors be for you to notice? If you visit the paint section of a hardware store, notice the dozens of shades of every single color! Similarly, how much salt is needed to notice a difference in taste?

Difference thresholds __________________ as a stimulus becomes stronger. At low levels of stimulation, we can notice a small change. At high levels of stimulation, we do not notice small changes. This is called _______________ Law.

Take a guess about the following absolute thresholds. Then, do a quick internet search to see how accurate you were.

Sense	Question	Answer
Vision	How far away could a candle flame be seen at night?	
Hearing	How far away could a ticking clock be heard?	
Smell	How many drops of perfume in a three-room house would be needed to detect it?	
Taste	How many teaspoons of sugar would be needed in two gallons of water for it to be tasted?	
Touch	How far from your face would the wing of a fly need to fall for you to feel it?	

Perception

Perception is how we interpret sensory information.

Perception is a top-____________ and bottom-_________ process.

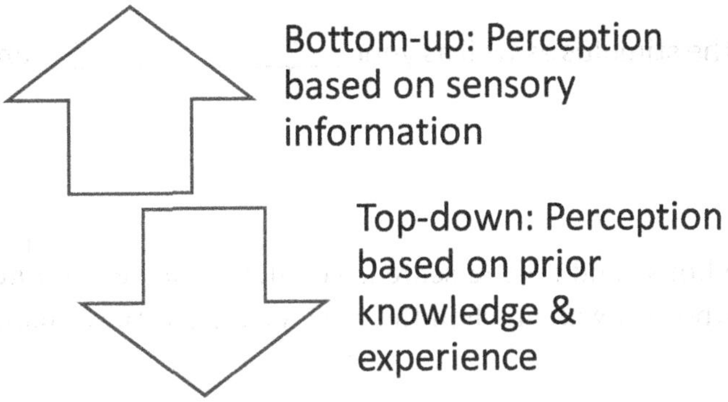

On Your Own

What type of processing is being used in the following scenario?

A six-year-old child is learning to read. She first recognizes each letter, slowly sounding out individual words.

What type of processing is being using in the following scenario?

"It deosn't mttaer in waht oredr the ltteers in a wrod are, the olny iprmoetnt tihng is taht the frist and lsat ltteer be at the rghit pclae. The rset can be a toatl mses and you can sitll raed it wouthit porbelms. Tihs is bcuseae the huamn mnid deos not raed ervey lteter by istlef but the wrod as a wlohe."

Do we perceive all sensations? No. When a stimulus is constant, we may not perceive it. This is called

_____________ ____________________.

Write at least one example of your experience with the following:

Top-down processing	
Bottom-up processing	
Sensory adaptation	

What we perceive depends on what we pay ________________ to. We might, for example, focus on how someone looks and completely miss what the person is saying to us. This failure to notice something because our attention is elsewhere is called ____________________ blindness.

Signal Detection Theory states that detecting a stimulus from its ___________________ is a product of the _________________ of the stimulus as well as your _________________ and _______________ state.

Example:

When you're alone in the house and a little scared, you detect noises you never noticed before. Similarly, mothers of newborns awaken when the baby cries, but they sleep through other sounds.

Psychology and You

Experience Reflection

Two people can experience the same event (e.g. a football game, movie, or business meeting) and perceive widely different things. Discuss a time when this has happened in your life.

Lesson Wrap-up

Say It in a Sentence

In one sentence, summarize how perception occurs.

Test Yourself

Choose the correct answer for each of the following questions. Check your work using the Answer Key in the back of the book.

____ 1. When you first start wearing a ring, you notice how it feels, but after a while you forget it's there. Why?

- **A.** The just-noticeable difference has been reached.
- **B.** Transduction has occurred.
- **C.** Sensory adaptation has occurred.

____ 2. Your phone receives a text message, but you don't hear it, see it, or detect the vibration. Which of the following explanations is most logical?

- **A.** The absolute threshold was not reached.
- **B.** Sensory adaptation did not occur.
- **C.** There was too little transduction.

____ 3. Research finds that people may perceive pictures and visual illusions differently based on what type of differences?

- **A.** Gender differences
- **B.** Educational differences
- **C.** Cultural differences

Next to each statement, write **T** for True or **F** for False. Check your work using the Answer Key in the back of the book.

1. _____ The detection of sensory information is called perception.
2. _____ Motivation has no significant impact on perception.
3. _____ Because culture impacts perception, Westerners are more likely to perceive the Müller-Lyer illusion.

Key Terms

Match each key term with its definition.

A. Absolute Threshold	_____	Amount of change needed to detect a difference in a stimulus
B. Bottom-Up Processing	_____	Experiencing a stimulus for the first time, no expectations
C. Inattentional Blindness	_____	The senses detect something (sight, sound, etc.)
D. Just Noticeable Difference	_____	Experiencing a stimulus using previous knowledge and experience
E. Perception	_____	Missing something because our attention is focused elsewhere
F. Sensation	_____	Failure to perceive a stimulus because you've become accustomed to it
G. Sensory Adaptation	_____	The process of interpreting sensory information
H. Signal Detection Theory	_____	The minimum amount of a stimulus needed to detect it
I. Top-Down Processing	_____	Detecting a stimulus among a distracting background
J. Transduction	_____	Conversion from sensory stimulus energy to action potential

Lesson 4.2

Waves and Wavelengths

OBJECTIVES

- ★ Describe important physical features of wave forms.
- ★ Show how physical properties of light waves are associated with perceptual experience.
- ★ Show how physical properties of sound waves are associated with perceptual experience.

BIG IDEA

Light waves and sound waves make it possible for us to see and hear. There are spectrums of light and sound, and humans can detect only part of them.

In this lesson, you will learn about the following:

- Amplitude and Wavelength
- Light Waves
- Sound Waves

Amplitude and Wavelength

Both light and sound travel in waves. The height of a wave is its ________________. The space between two peaks is called a ________________.

Wavelengths are described in terms of their ________________, which is measured in cycles per second, or hertz (Hz).

On Your Own

Refer to the figure in the lesson that illustrates the wavelengths of different colors.

Which wavelength has the lowest frequency?

Which has the highest frequency?

Light Waves

The colors we perceive are a function of the ________________ (peaks and troughs) of the wavelength.

Match each color with the size of its wavelength.

Long	Blues and violets
Medium	Red
Short	Green

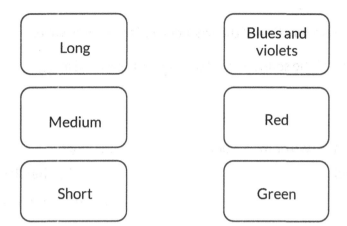

The amplitude of light waves also affects the brightness of color.

Large amplitude = High peaks and low troughs = Bright, intense colors

Small amplitude = Moderate peaks and troughs = Duller, less intense colors

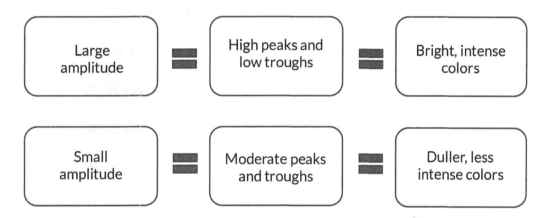

The ____________________ ____________________ is comprised of all the light waves, yet we humans are only able to see those in the ____________________ ____________________. The light waves we can see are measured in nanometers (nm), ranging from about 400 to 700 nm.

On Your Own

What acronym can you use to remember the order of the colors?

Why are the colors of the rainbow in this order?

Sound Waves

The __________ we perceive is a function of the frequency of the sound wave. ________________ is associated with the amplitude of the sound wave. Loudness is measured in ________________.

On Your Own

Fill in the table with examples of two or more sounds at each decibel range.

Sound	Decibel Range
	140 dB or more (Harmful)
	120-125 dB (Pain threshold)
	110 dB (Risk of hearing loss)
	80-100 dB
	60-70 dB
	40-50 dB
	20-30 dB

Psychology and You

Everyday Threats to Hearing

What are some common habits/experiences that can have a negative effect on hearing?

Hearing and Occupations

List five occupations for which good hearing is necessary.

List five occupations that put hearing at risk.

Lesson Wrap-up

Say It in a Sentence

In one sentence, summarize the relationship between hearing, vision, and wavelengths.

Test Yourself

Next to each statement, write **T** for True or **F** for False. Check your work using the Answer Key in the back of the book.

1. _____ Frequency is the same thing as amplitude.
2. _____ There are light waves that are invisible to humans.
3. _____ Animals can hear sound waves that humans cannot.

Choose the correct answer for each of the following questions. Check your work using the Answer Key in the back of the book.

_____ 4. Which of the following best characterizes the relationship between wavelengths and vision perception?

A. Wavelength is associated with color perception.
B. Wavelength is associated with depth perception.
C. Wavelength is associated with perceiving movement.
D. Wavelength is associated with size perception.

_____ 5. The visible spectrum consists of:

A. All the wavelengths in the electromagnetic spectrum
B. The wavelengths that humans can see
C. The colors of the rainbow
D. Both B and C
E. All of these are correct

_____ 6. Which of the following best characterizes the relationship between wavelengths and sound perception?

A. High-frequency sounds are more pleasant than low-frequency sounds.
B. Low-frequency sounds are more pleasant than high-frequency sounds.
C. There is no relationship between wavelengths and sound perception.
D. Perceived pitch is derived from the frequency of the wavelength.

Key Terms

Match the key term with its definition.

A. Amplitude	______	How we perceive a sound's frequency
B. Decibel	______	How the loudness of sound is measured
C. Electromagnetic Spectrum	______	All of the light waves
D. Frequency	______	The height of a wave
E. Pitch	______	Portion of the electromagnetic spectrum we can see
F. Visible Spectrum	______	The number of waves per second

Lesson 4.3

Vision

OBJECTIVES

- ★ Describe the basic anatomy of the visual system.
- ★ Discuss how rods and cones contribute to different aspects of vision.
- ★ Describe how monocular and binocular cues are used in the perception of depth.

BIG IDEA

There's more to the visual system than meets the eye. Our eyes and brain work together to sense and perceive the visual world around us.

In this lesson, you will learn about the following:

- Anatomy of the Visual System
- Color and Depth Perception

Anatomy of the Visual System

Fill in the following diagram with the correct parts of the eye.

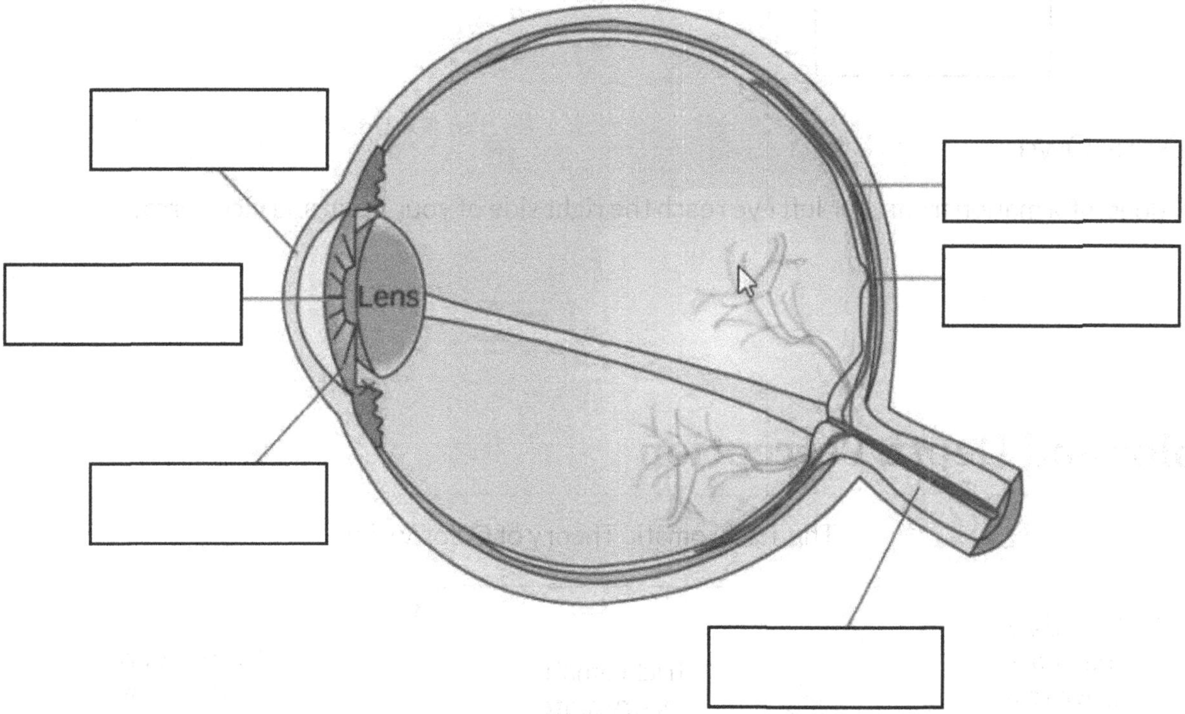

The ____________ ______________ runs from the back of the eye to the brain.

The ____________ ____________ is where the optic nerve leaves the eye; there are no photoreceptors there.

The ____________ contains the photoreceptors (sensory registers) for color and movement.

The _______________ require light and enable us to see color and detail.

The other photoreceptors are _______________, which work well in low light and help us see movement.

Fill in the following diagram.

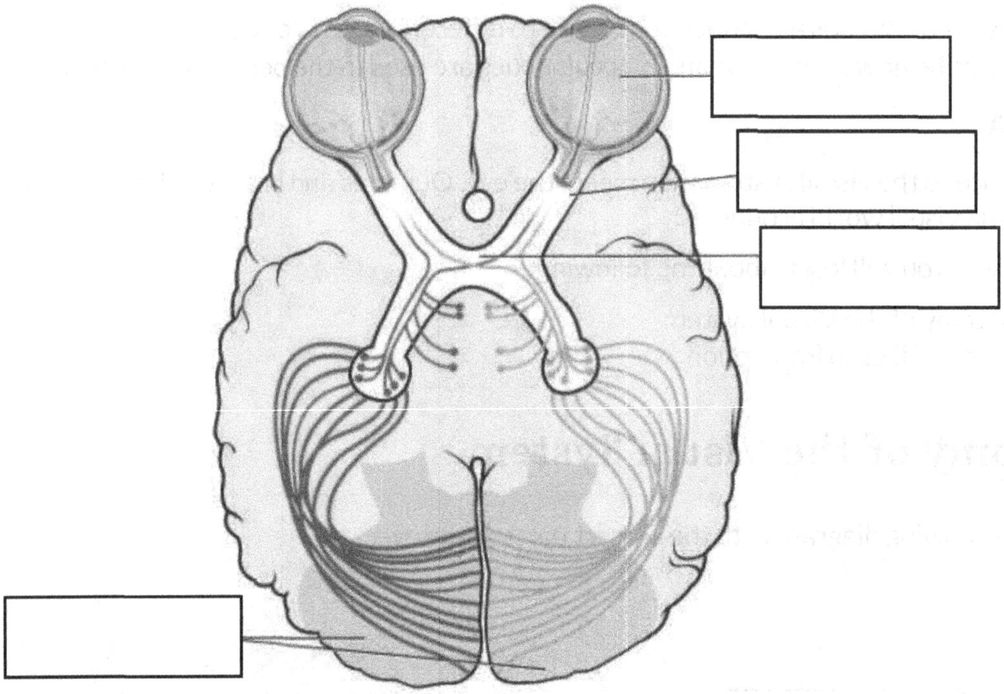

On Your Own

How does information from your left eye reach the right side of your brain and vice versa?

Color and Depth Perception

The Trichromatic Theory of Color Vision

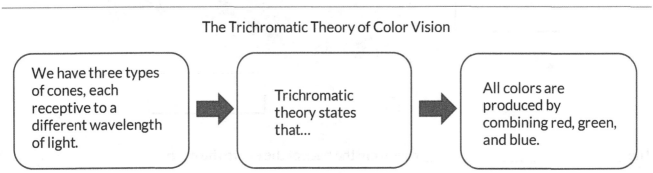

We have three types of cones, each receptive to a different wavelength of light. → Trichromatic theory states that… → All colors are produced by combining red, green, and blue.

The Opponent-Process Theory of Color Vision

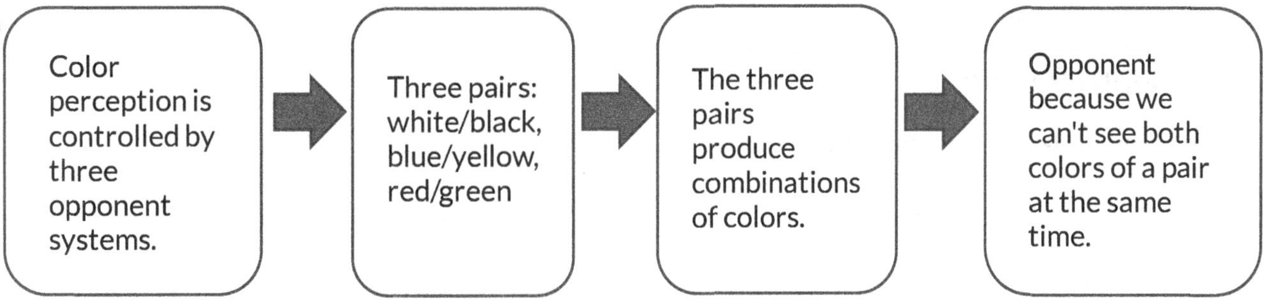

Color perception is controlled by three opponent systems.
Three pairs: white/black, blue/yellow, red/green
The three pairs produce combinations of colors.
Opponent because we can't see both colors of a pair at the same time.

On Your Own

The Trichromatic Theory of color vision came first. What does the opponent-process theory add to our understanding of color vision?

We use both binocular and monocular cues to perceive depth.

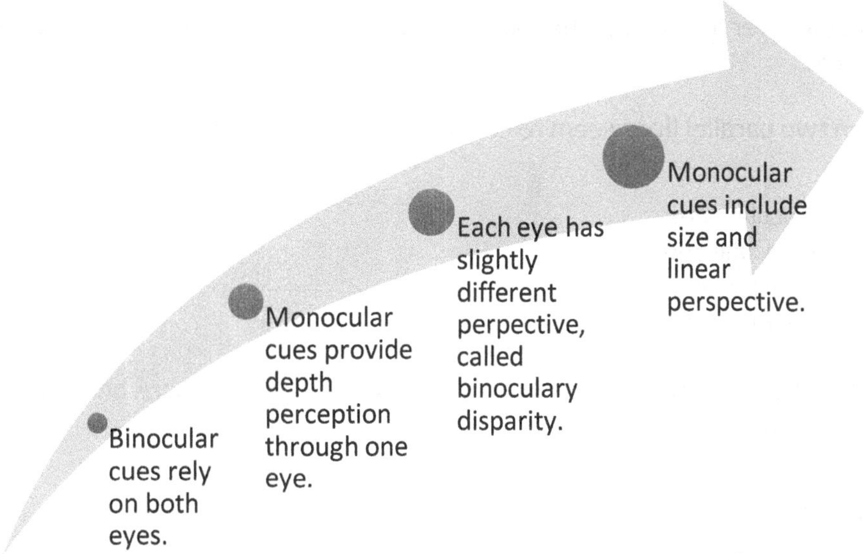

Binocular cues rely on both eyes.
Monocular cues provide depth perception through one eye.
Each eye has slightly different perpective, called binoculary disparity.
Monocular cues include size and linear perspective.

On Your Own

If a person could not see out of one eye, would he or she still have depth perception? Explain.

Psychology and You

Test Your Depth Perception

What are some everyday situations that test our depth perception?

Lesson Wrap-up

Say It in a Sentence

In one sentence, summarize how vision and depth perception work.

Test Yourself

Choose the correct answer for each of the following questions. Check your work using the Answer Key in the back of the book.

____ 1. When two parallel lines seem to converge, creating an illusion of depth on a flat service, it is called:

A. Binocular cues
B. Monocular cues
C. Depth perception
D. Linear perspective

____ 2. What is it called when we can see colors that aren't really there because our cones have been saturated?

A. Color illusion
B. Afterimage
C. Blind spot image
D. Monocular cue

____ 3. Which of the following pairs is not part of the opponent-process theory of color vision?

A. Blue-grey
B. Blue-yellow
C. Green-red
D. White-black

____ 4. Axons from the ganglion cells of the retina form the:

A. Occipital lobe
B. Optic chiasm
C. Optic nerve
D. Optic fovea

Key Terms

Match each key term with its definition.

A. Binocular Disparity	______	Area of eye where there are no photoreceptors
B. Cones	______	Center of the eye where light enters
C. Cornea	______	Theory of color vision: red, green, blue
D. Depth Perception	______	Photoreceptors sensitive to color
E. Lens	______	Layer at back of eye sensitive to light
F. Opponent-Process	______	Transparent layer over the eye
G. Pupil	______	Ability to perceive spatial relationships in 3-D
H. Retina	______	Theory of color vision: color is coded in pairs
I. Rods	______	Photoreceptors sensitive to movement and dim light
J. Tri-chromatic	______	Light enters through pupil, then passes through this; can change shape to focus

Lesson 4.4

Hearing

OBJECTIVES

- ★ Describe the basic anatomy and function of the auditory system.
- ★ Explain how we encode and perceive pitch.
- ★ Discuss how we localize sound.

BIG IDEA

Hearing is a complex mechanical process that involves the outer, inner, and middle ear as well as neural components to ensure comprehension of pitch and localization of sound.

In this lesson, you will learn about the following:

- Anatomy of the Auditory System
- Pitch Perception
- Sound Localization
- Hearing Loss

Anatomy of the Auditory System

What are the parts of the ear?

Outer Ear

Middle Ear

Inner Ear

Label the following figure.

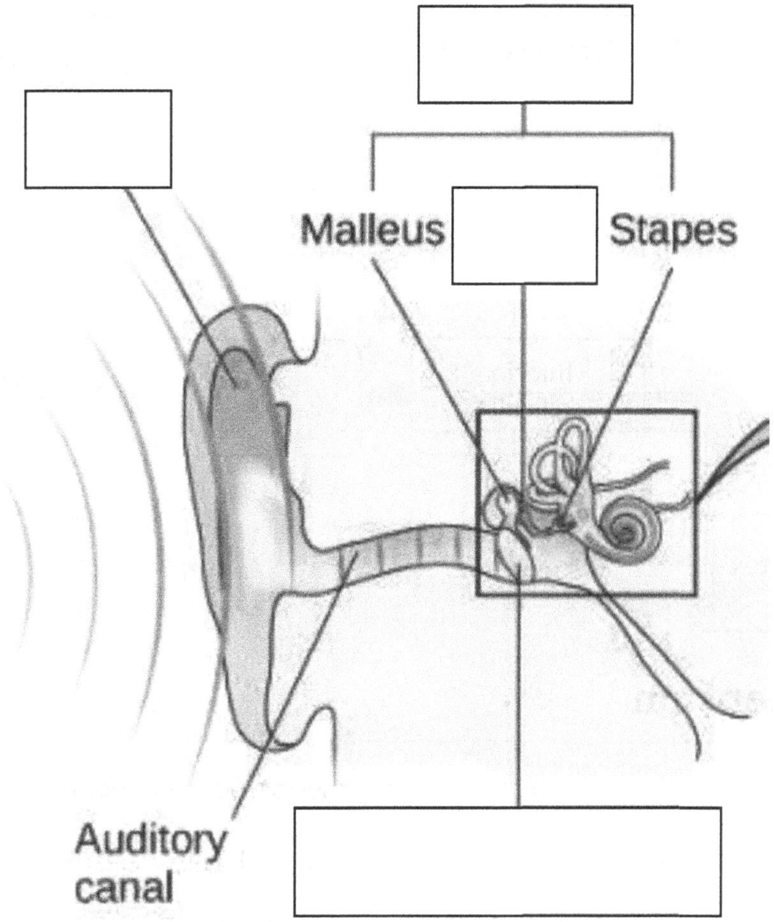

Label the following figure.

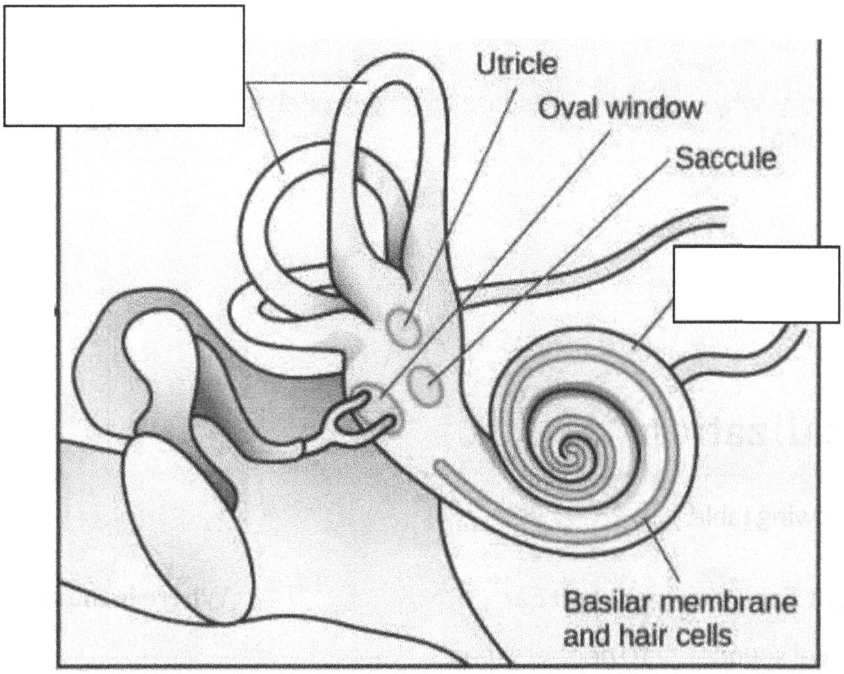

Complete the pathway for sound.

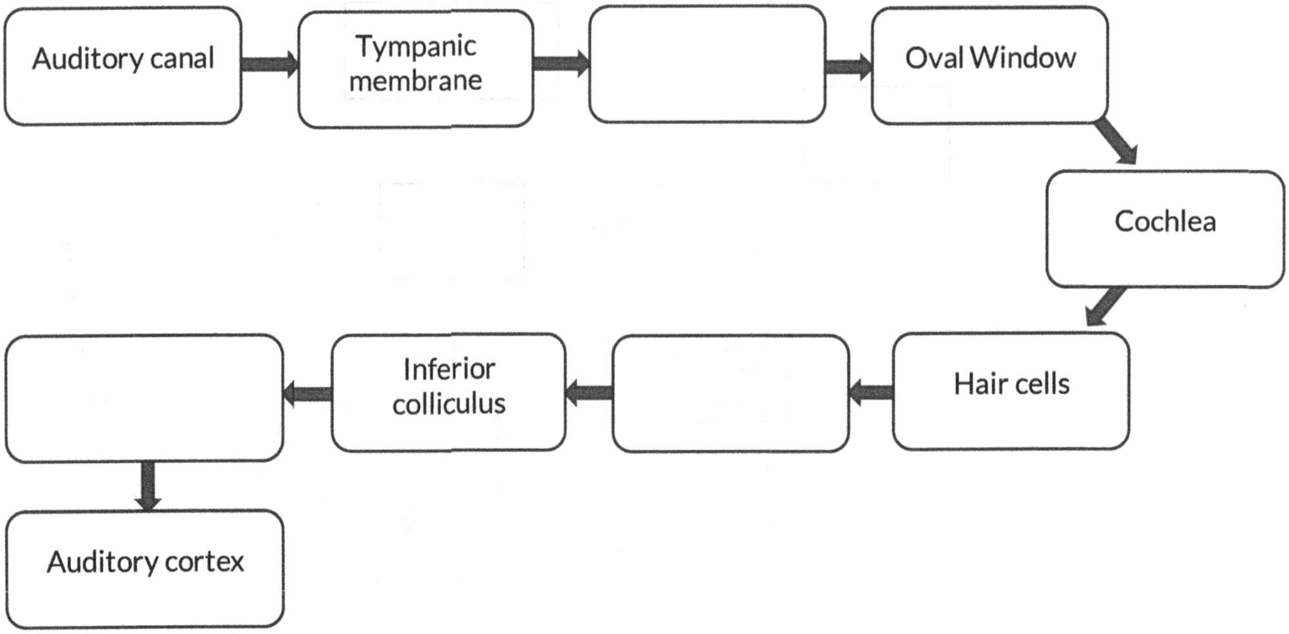

Pitch Perception

The ________________ theory of pitch perception asserts that frequency is coded by the ______________ level of the sensory neuron. This would mean that a given hair cell would fire action potentials related to the frequency of the sound wave. The _______________ theory of pitch perception suggests that different portions of the _________________ membrane are sensitive to sounds of different frequencies.

On Your Own

Based on place theory, why would it make sense that high-pitched sounds are located closer to the oval window of the cochlea?

Sound Localization

Complete the following table.

Right Ear	Left Ear	Where is the sound?
10 decibel sound	10 decibel sound	

10 decibel sound	15 decibel sound	
15 decibel sound	10 decibel sound	

The auditory system uses both ________________ (one ear) and ______________(two ear) cues to localize sound.

Hearing Loss

On Your Own

Imagine you suddenly become deaf. What aspects of your life would be challenging?

Do you feel it would be more difficult to have congenital deafness or total conductive hearing loss later in life? Explain your answer.

Psychology and You

Reflection

If your child was born deaf, would you choose to have your child verbalize, read lips and be part of the deaf culture, or some combination? Explain your answer.

Lesson Wrap-up

Say It in a Sentence

In one sentence, compare place theory and temporal theory of pitch perception.

Test Yourself

Choose the correct answer for each of the following questions. Check your work using the Answer Key in the back of the book.

____ 1. Auditory information passes through the ________ colliculus.

- **A.** superior
- **B.** inferior
- **C.** dorsolateral

____ 2. If pitch information is dependent upon nerves firing differing numbers of action potentials, this evidence would support which theory of pitch perception?

- **A.** Place theory
- **B.** Temporal theory

____ 3. If pitch information is dependent upon certain areas of the basilar membrane responding, this evidence would support which theory of pitch perception?

- **A.** Place theory
- **B.** Temporal theory

Next to each statement, write **T** for True or **F** for False. Check your work using the Answer Key in the back of the book.

4. ______ The hair cells are located in the semi-circular canals.

5. ______ The medial geniculate nucleus is found in the amygdala.

6. ______ Research suggests that the temporal theory of pitch perception is correct, and the place theory is incorrect.

7. ______ Failure to transmit neural signals from the cochlea to the brain is called sensorineural hearing loss.

Key Terms

Match each key term with its definition.

A. Basilar Membrane
B. Binaural Cue
C. Cochlea
D. Cochlear Implant
E. Conductive Hearing Loss
F. Congenital Deafness
G. Deafness

______ Spinning sensation
______ One-eared cue to localize sound
______ Failure in the vibration of the eardrum and/or movement of the ossicles
______ Middle ear ossicle known as the hammer
______ Middle ear ossicle known as the stirrup
______ Middle ear ossicle known as the anvil

H. Hair Cell
I. Incus
J. Interaural Level Difference
K. Interaural Timing Difference
L. Malleus
M. Ménière's Disease
N. Monaural Cue
O. Pinna
P. Place Theory of Pitch Perception
Q. Sensorineural Hearing Loss
R. Stapes
S. Temporal Theory of Pitch Perception
T. Tympanic Membrane
U. Vertigo

_____ Thin strip of tissue within the cochlea that contains the hair cells
_____ Two-eared cue to localize sound
_____ Visible part of the ear
_____ Different portions of the basilar membrane are sensitive to different sound frequencies
_____ Sound's frequency is coded by the activity level of a sensory neuron
_____ Partial or complete inability to hear
_____ Auditory receptor cell of the inner ear
_____ Fluid-filled, snail-shaped structure that contains sensory receptors cells
_____ Eardrum
_____ Sound coming from one side of the body is more intense at the closest ear
_____ Small difference in the time at which a given sound wave arrives at each ear
_____ Electronic device that consists of a microphone, speech processor, an electrode array to directly stimulate the auditory nerve
_____ Deafness from birth
_____ Results in degeneration of inner ear structures that can lead to hearing loss, tinnitus, vertigo, and an increase in pressure within the inner ear
_____ Failure to transmit neural signals from the cochlea to the brain

Lesson 4.5

The Other Senses

OBJECTIVES

- ★ Describe the basic functions of the chemical senses.
- ★ Explain the basic functions of the somatosensory, nociceptive, and thermoceptive sensory systems.
- ★ Describe the basic functions of the vestibular, proprioceptive, and kinesthetic sensory systems.

BIG IDEA

Researchers understand how the chemical (smell and taste) and somatosensory senses communicate information to the brain.

In this lesson, you will learn about the following:

- The Chemical Senses
- Touch, Thermoception, and Nociception
- The Vestibular Sense, Proprioception, and Kinesthesia

The Chemical Senses

Taste (gustation) and smell (olfaction) are called chemical senses, and there is a pronounced interaction between these two senses.

Taste (Gustation)

What are the different taste groupings?

On Your Own

Imagine life if you did not have the ability to taste anything. How would it affect you?

Molecules from food and beverage dissolve in ______________ and interact with taste receptors on the tongue. Taste molecules bind to receptors and cause __________________ changes within the sensory cell that result in neural impulses being transmitted to the brain via different nerves, depending on where the receptor is located.

Taste information is sent to which brain regions?

-
-
-
-

Smell (Olfaction)

Olfactory receptor cells are located in the ______________ membrane at the top of the nose. Once an odor molecule has bound a given receptor, chemical changes within the cell result in signals being sent to the ______________ ____________.

Smell information is sent to which brain regions?

-
-

Label the following figure.

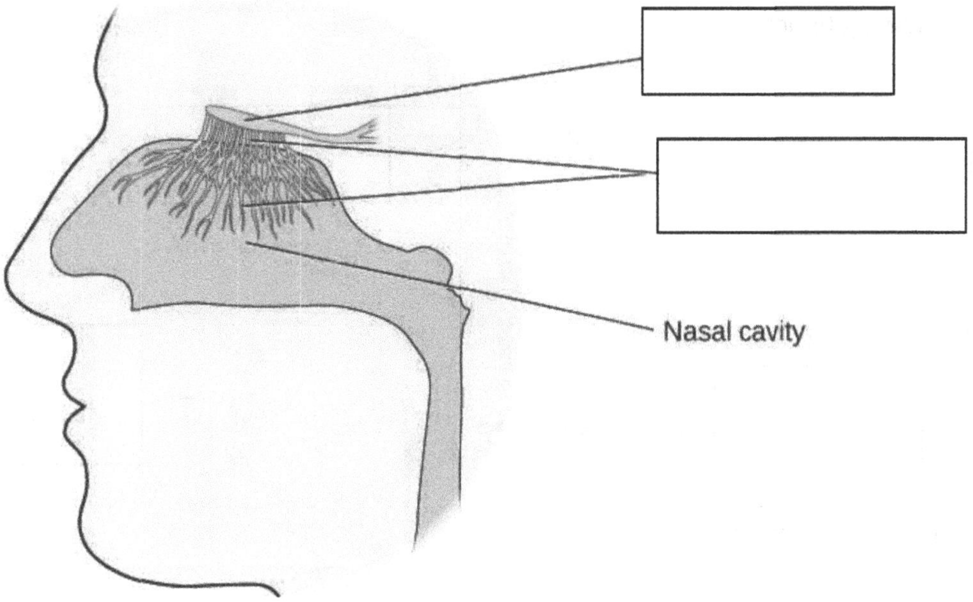

On Your Own

What is your reaction to the idea that humans may communicate via pheromones?

Touch, Thermoception, and Nociception

What are the touch-related receptors?

-
-
-
-

Complete the following chart.

Touch-related Receptor	Responds to...
Pacinian corpuscles	
Ruffini corpuscles	
Meissner's corpuscles	
Merkel's disks	

Label the following figure.

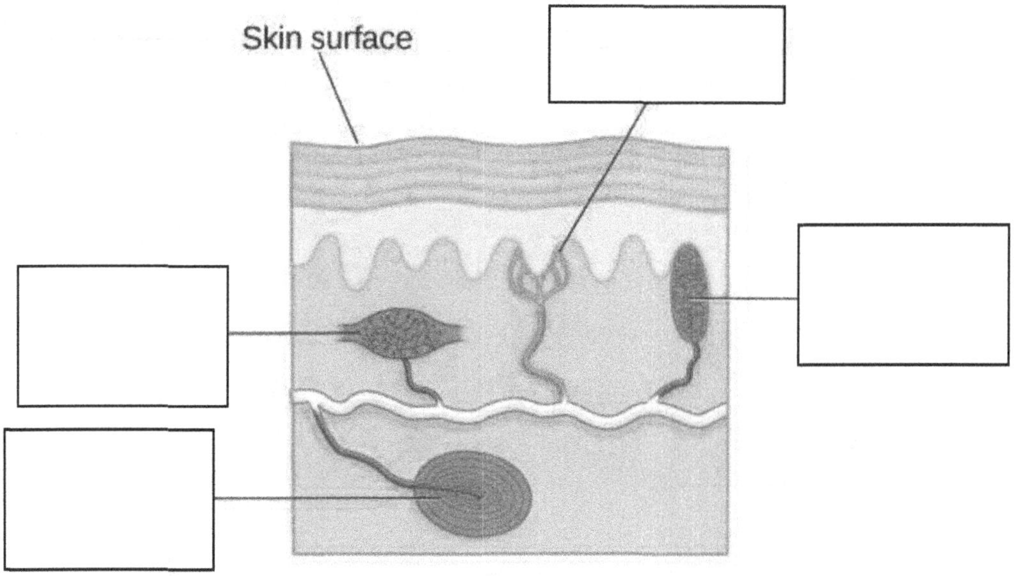

Free nerve endings are responsible for ____________________ (temperature) and ______________ (harm and pain). Information from the free nerve endings travels up the spinal cord to the ____________, thalamus, and ____________________ cortex.

Pain Perception

On Your Own

What is your reaction to the idea that some people cannot feel pain? What negative consequences might they experience?

The Vestibular Sense, Proprioception, and Kinesthesia

The ____________________ sense contributes to our ability to maintain balance and body posture. The vestibular organs are fluid-filled and have hair cells, which respond to movement of the head and ________________________ forces. The major sensory organs of the vestibular system are the utricle, _______________, and the three semicircular canals. This system is also responsible for ________________________ (perception of body position) and ____________________ (perception of body's movement through space).

On Your Own

Why does it make sense that vestibular information is passed to the cerebellum?

Psychology and You

Reflection

What was something about the senses that you were surprised to learn?

Lesson Wrap-up

Say It in a Sentence

In one sentence, describe the vestibular senses.

Test Yourself

Choose the correct answer for each of the following questions. Check your work using the Answer Key in the back of the book.

____ 1. Recent research indicates there may be as many as ____ basic groupings of taste.

- **A.** 4
- **B.** 5
- **C.** 6

____ 2. Humans have fewer than ___ functional genes for olfactory receptors.

- **A.** 400
- **B.** 800
- **C.** 1200

Answer each of the following questions. Check your work using the Answer Key in the back of the book.

3. The brain areas involved in gustation are:

4. The brain areas involved in olfaction are:

Key Terms

For the following key terms, make groupings out of related terms. Be sure to explain how they are related.

Key Terms: congenital insensitivity to pain, inflammatory pain, kinesthesia, Meissner's corpuscle, Merkel's disk, neuropathic pain, nociception, olfactory bulb, olfactory receptor, Pacinian corpuscle, pheromone, proprioception, Ruffini corpuscle, taste bud, thermoception, umami, vestibular sense

Lesson 4.6

Gestalt Principles of Perception

OBJECTIVES

- ★ Explain the figure-ground relationship.
- ★ Define Gestalt principles of grouping.
- ★ Describe how perceptual set is influenced by an individual's characteristics and mental state.

BIG IDEA

Gestalt principles of perception explain how we perceptually group objects together, which sometimes results in optical illusions.

In this lesson, you will learn about the following:

- Gestalt Principles of Perception

Who were the founders of Gestalt psychology?

-
-
-

In Gestalt psychology, the primary theory is that the ______________ is greater than the sum of its parts, which means that the brain creates a __________________ that is more than the sum of all available ______________ inputs.

The first Gestalt principle is figure-______________ relationship. In figure-ground, humans have a tendency to see one aspect as the ______________ (object of interest) and the other as the ________________ (background).

On Your Own

Provide an example of a figure-ground relationship.

A second Gestalt principle that guides perception is the principle of ________________; if objects are close together, they are perceived as a ______________.

On Your Own

Provide an example of a proximity grouping.

The ________________ principle refers to the idea that similar items will be grouped together.

On Your Own

Provide an example of a similarity grouping.

The law of ________________ refers to the idea that individuals are more likely to perceive a continuous, smooth flow compared to jagged, broken lines. ______________ refers to the idea that the brain automatically completes incomplete figures.

Psychology and You

Applying the Gestalt Principle

Describe a time when you had a faulty perception based on a Gestalt principle. For example, people often see visual illusions differently from other people.

Lesson Wrap-up

Say It in a Sentence

In one sentence, define **Gestalt**.

Test Yourself

Choose the correct answer for each of the following questions. Check your work using the Answer Key in the back of the book.

____ 1. When you view the following image as a whole circle, you are using which Gestalt principle?

A. Proximity
B. Closure
C. Similarity
D. Good continuation

____ 2. When you can see circles of the same color as distinct lines, you are using which Gestalt principle?

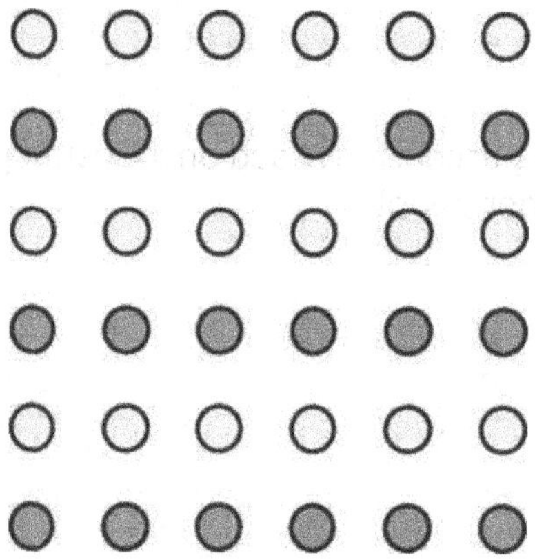

A. Proximity
B. Closure
C. Similarity
D. Good continuation

Answer each of the following questions. Check your work using the Answer Key in the back of the book.

3. If we view a bundle of wires as generally moving from the top to the bottom, this would fit which Gestalt principle?

4. If we looked at a bowling alley and assumed that everyone in a purple shirt was part of a group, we would be using which Gestalt principle?

Key Terms

Use the key terms from the lesson to complete the following crossword puzzle.

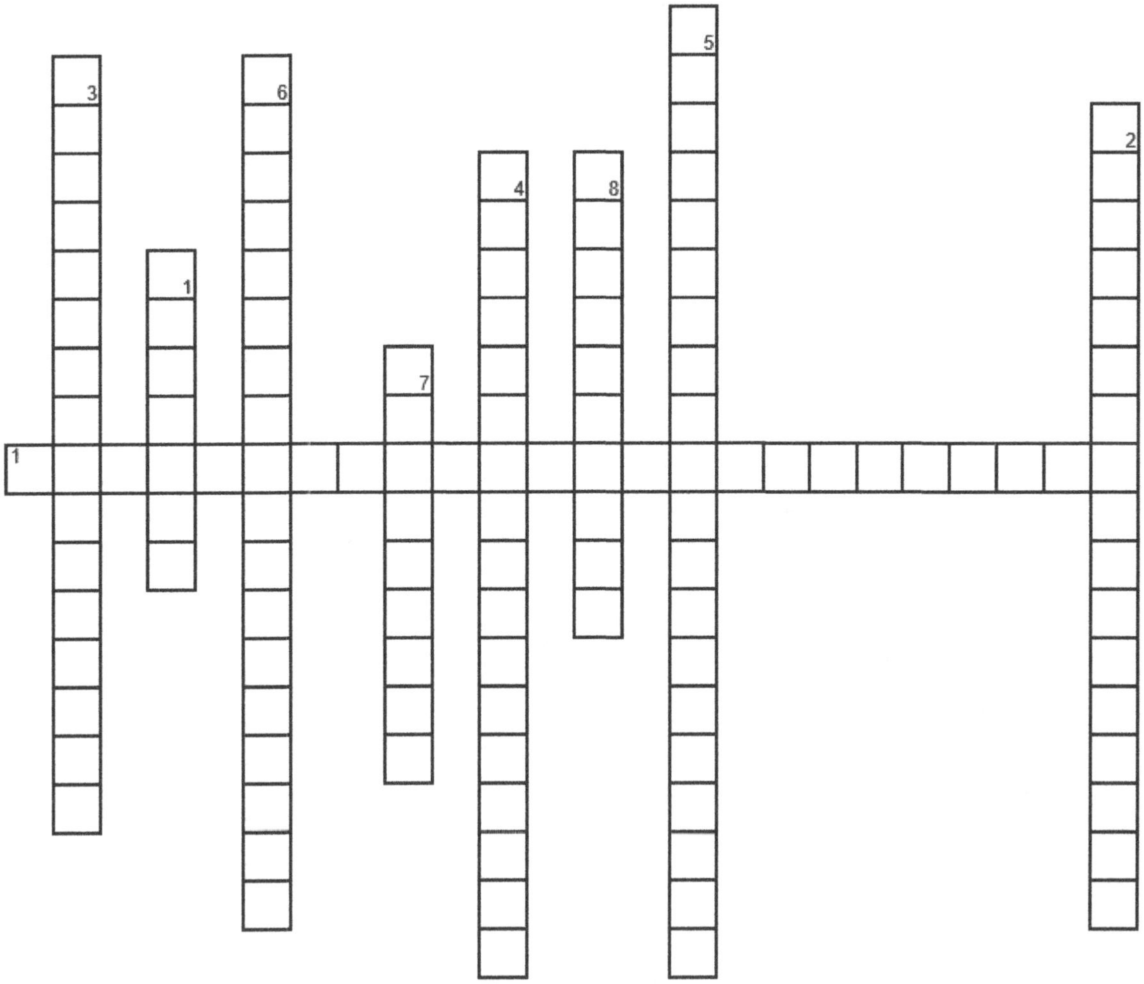

Across

1. Segmenting our visual world into figure and ground

Down

1. Organizing our perceptions into complete objects rather than as a series of parts
2. Field of psychology based on the idea that the whole is different from the sum of its parts
3. We are more likely to perceive continuous, smooth-flowing lines rather than jagged, broken lines (also, continuity)
4. Ability to discriminate among different figures and shapes
5. Educated guess used to interpret sensory information
6. Organize perceptions into complete objects rather than as a series of parts
7. Things that are close to one another tend to be grouped together
8. Things that are alike tend to be grouped together

Chapter 5
Learning

Lesson 5.1
What Is Learning?

OBJECTIVES

★ Explain how learned behaviors are different from instincts and reflexes.
★ Define learning.
★ Recognize and define three basic forms of learning—classical conditioning, operant conditioning, and observational learning.

BIG IDEA

Learning is a change in behavior that comes about as a result of experience. It includes classical and operant conditioning as well as observational learning.

In this lesson, you will learn about the following:

- Learning

_________________ are a motor or neural reaction to a specific stimulus in the environment.

____________________ are innate behaviors triggered by a broader range of events.

Reflexes	Instincts
	Complex
Specific body parts	

List two examples of unlearned behaviors:

1.

2.

Learning allows an organism to ________________ to its environment. It is a ______________________ permanent change in behavior or knowledge that results from ________________________.

On Your Own

Why does the definition of learning include "relatively permanent"?

______________________ learning occurs when an organism makes connections between stimuli or events that occur together in the environment. You will see that associative learning is __________ to all three basic learning processes.

__________ ______________ tends to involve unconscious processes,

__________ ______________ tends to involve conscious processes, and

______________ ______________ adds social and cognitive layers to all the basic associative processes, both ______________ and ______________.

On Your Own

Explain how classical conditioning and operant conditioning are both examples of associative learning.

Provide an example of a time when you utilized observational learning.

On Your Own

Answer each short answer question.

A rat learns that a tone signals that a foot shock is coming. Which type of learning is this, and how do you know?

A dog learns that performing a behavior, like "sit," earns him a tasty treat. Which type of learning is this, and how do you know?

Psychology and You

Operant Conditioning

Discuss a situation in which you experienced operant conditioning. Was that learning permanent?

Lesson Wrap-up

Say It in a Sentence

In one sentence, define learning.

Test Yourself

Choose the correct answer for each of the following questions. Check your work using the Answer Key in the back of the book.

____ 1. While playing video games, Sam learns that screaming at his brother makes him play badly for the rest of the day. This is an example of:

- **A.** Classical conditioning
- **B.** Operant conditioning
- **C.** Observational learning

____ 2. Jonathan learns that dinner is always on the table at 6 p.m. and begins to feel hungry around 5:50 p.m. This is an example of:

- **A.** Classical conditioning
- **B.** Operant conditioning
- **C.** Observational learning

____ 3. When Michael plays with his toys, his younger brother Thomas immediately tries to imitate the behaviors. This is an example of:

- **A.** Classical conditioning
- **B.** Operant conditioning
- **C.** Observational learning

Key Terms

Write the definition for each of the following terms.

Associative Learning:

Instinct:

Learning:

Reflex:

Lesson 5.2

Classical Conditioning

OBJECTIVES

- ★ Explain how classical conditioning occurs.
- ★ Summarize the processes of acquisition, extinction, spontaneous recovery, generalization, and discrimination.

BIG IDEA

Classical conditioning involves the association of a previously reflexive response to a natural stimulus with a new, learned stimulus.

In this lesson, you will learn about the following:

- Real World Application of Classical Conditioning
- General Processes in Classical Conditioning
- Behaviorism

On Your Own

What is your reaction to the idea that Ivan Pavlov surgically implanted tubes on the inside of dog's cheeks to gather saliva?

Provide an example of classical conditioning from one of your own pets or a pet you've known.

Complete the following graphic.

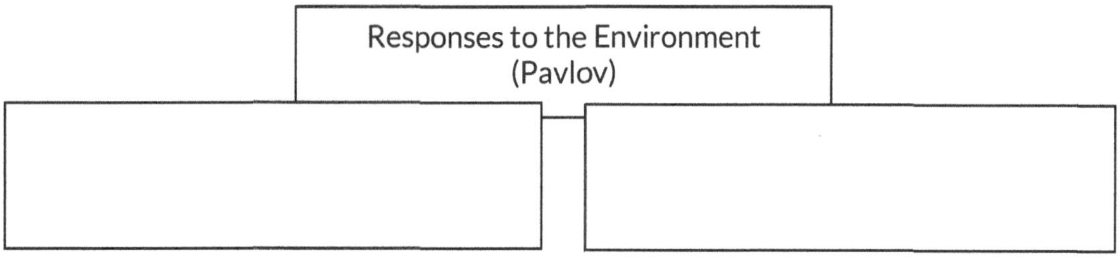

Complete the following graphic by filling in the abbreviations for each component.

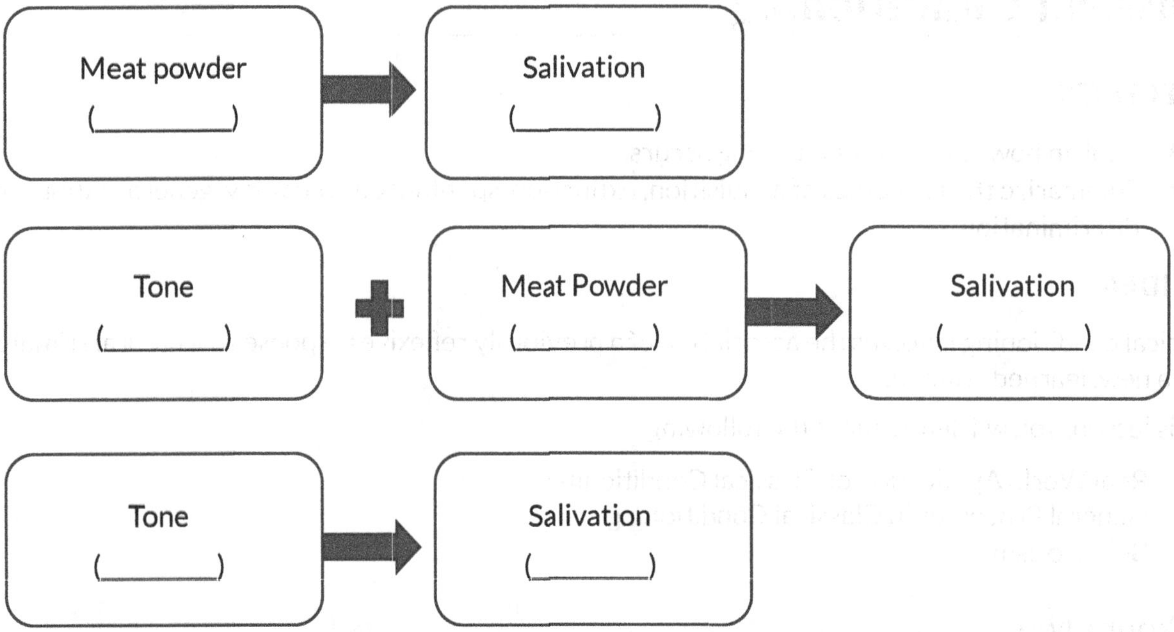

Real World Application of Classical Conditioning

In the example of Tiger and the electric can opener, what are the UCS, CS, UCR, and CR?

- UCS:
- CS:
- UCR:
- CR:

Complete the following graphic:

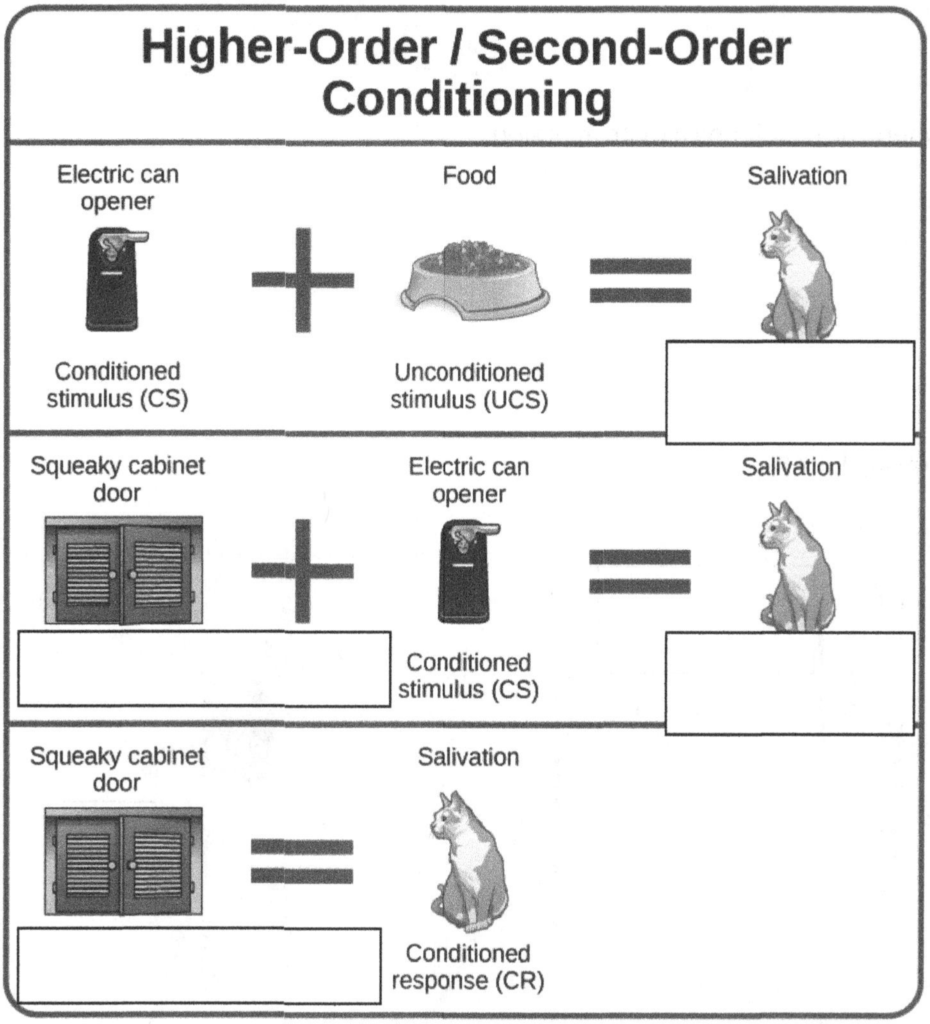

In the Stingray City example, what are the UCS, CS, UCR, and CR?

- UCS:
- CS:
- UCR:
- CR:

On Your Own

Every time someone flushes a toilet, the shower becomes hot and causes you to jump back. Over time, you begin to jump back automatically after hearing the toilet flush before the water temperature changes. In this scenario, what are the UCS, CS, UCR, and CR?

- UCS:
- CS:
- UCR:
- CR:

General Processes in Classical Conditioning

On Your Own

Describe a time when you developed a taste aversion.

Complete the following figure.

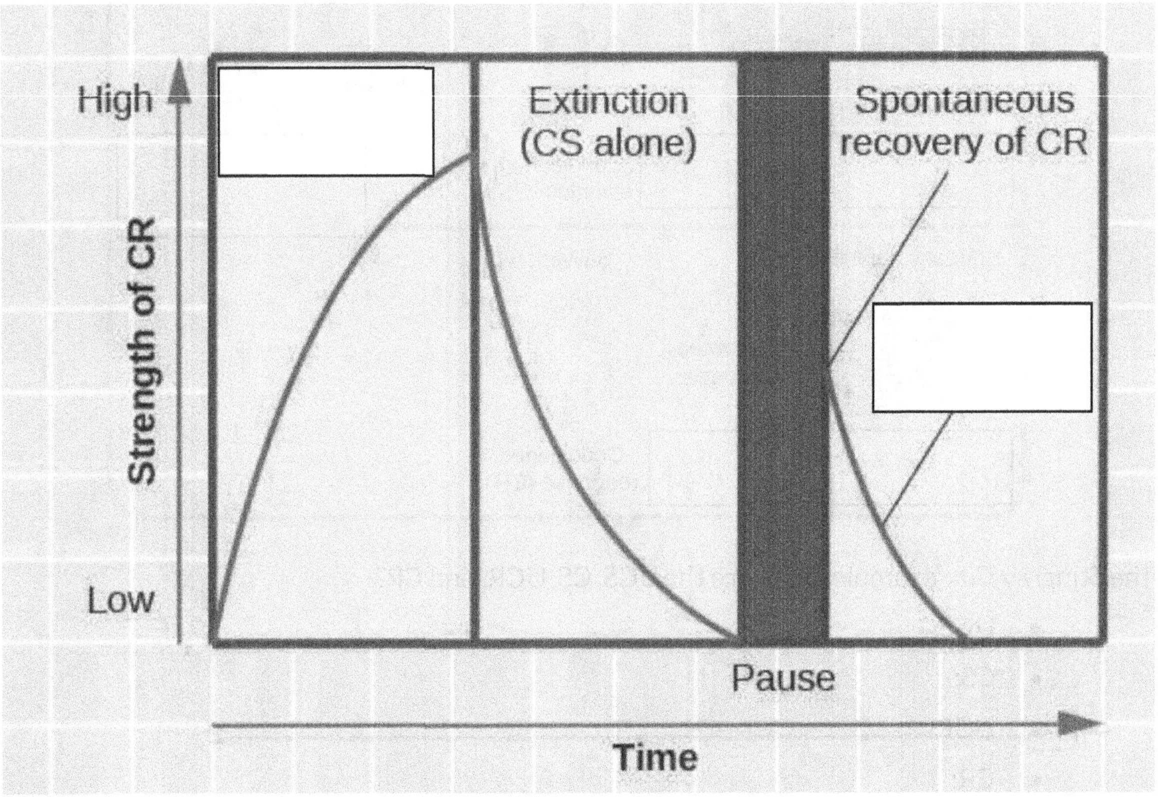

On Your Own

If your nephew has learned that he always gets a piece of candy at the grocery store, how could you extinguish his expectation?

Provide examples of stimulus discrimination and stimulus generalization.

Behaviorism

John B. Watson was the founder of ____________________, which considered human behavior only in terms of __________________ behavior. Watson's famous experiment with _________ ___________ tested whether fear could be conditioned.

Complete the following graphic for the Little Albert study.

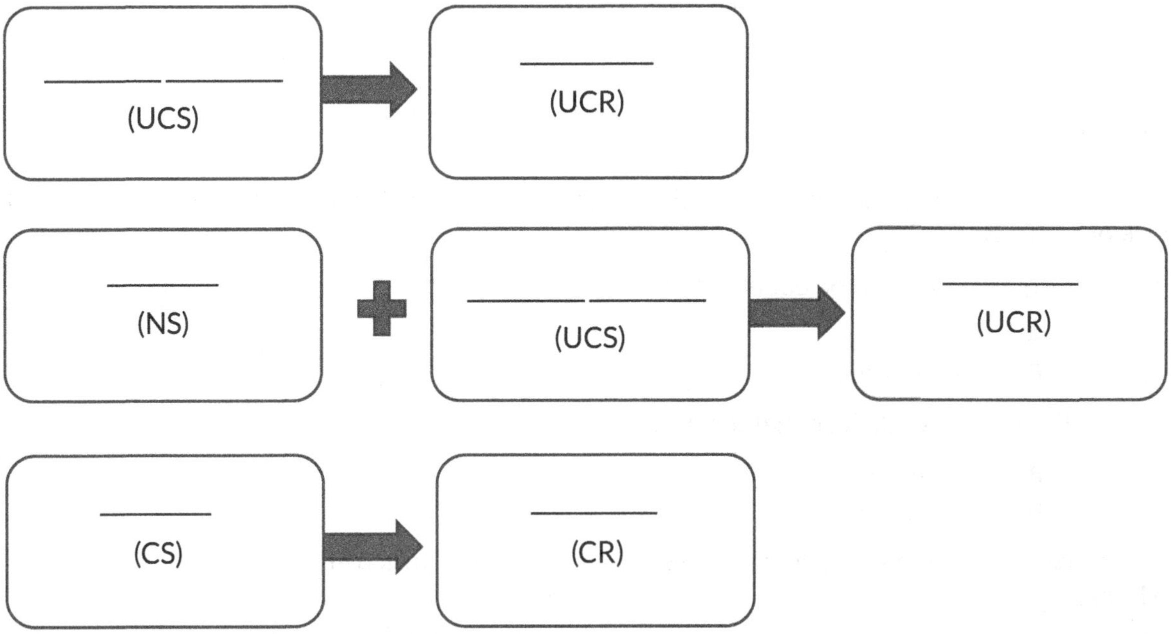

On Your Own

Do you believe that John Watson's experiment with Little Albert was unethical? What ethical standards did it violate, if any?

Psychology and You

Habituation

Describe a time when you experienced habituation.

Lesson Wrap-up

Say It in a Sentence

In one sentence, explain the difference between an unconditioned stimulus and a conditioned stimulus.

Test Yourself

Choose the correct answer for each of the following questions. Check your work using the Answer Key in the back of the book.

____ 1. Acquisition would be equated with:

A. Weakening
B. Strengthening

____ 2. Extinction would be equated with:

A. Weakening
B. Strengthening

Use the scenario to answer the following questions. Check your work using the Answer Key in the back of the book.

A patient gets frequent injections of drugs, which are administered in a small examination room at a clinic. The drug itself causes increased heart rate, but after several trips to the clinic, simply being in a small room causes the patient's heart rate to increase.

____ 3. What is the unconditioned response?

A. Increased heart rate in response to the drugs
B. Increased heart rate in response to the room
C. The waiting room
D. The drugs

____ 4. What is the unconditioned stimulus?

A. Increased heart rate in response to the drugs
B. Increased heart rate in response to the room
C. The waiting room
D. The drugs

____ 5. What is the conditioned response?

A. Increased heart rate in response to the drugs
B. Increased heart rate in response to the room
C. The waiting room
D. The drugs

Answer each short answer question based on the following scenario. Then, check your work using the Answer Key in the back of the book.

The nurse at the doctor's office says, "This won't hurt a bit," just before jabbing you with a needle. The next time you hear, "This won't hurt," you cringe in fear.

6. What is the conditioned stimulus?

7. What is the unconditioned stimulus?

8. What is the conditioned response?

9. What is the unconditioned response?

Key Terms

Match each key term with its definition.

A. Acquisition
B. Classical Conditioning
C. Conditioned Response
D. Conditioned Stimulus
E. Extinction
F. Habituation
G. Higher-Order Conditioning
H. Neutral Stimulus
I. Spontaneous Recovery
J. Stimulus Discrimination
K. Stimulus Generalization
L. Unconditioned Response
M. Unconditioned Stimulus

_____ Stimulus that does not initially elicit a response
_____ When we learn not to respond to a stimulus that is presented repeatedly without change
_____ Response caused by the conditioned stimulus
_____ Ability to respond differently to similar stimuli
_____ Stimulus that elicits a reflexive response
_____ Period of initial learning in classical conditioning in which a human or an animal begins to connect a neutral stimulus and an unconditioned stimulus so that the neutral stimulus will begin to elicit the conditioned response
_____ Learning in which the stimulus or experience occurs before the behavior and then gets paired or associated with the behavior.
_____ Natural (unlearned) behavior to a given stimulus
_____ Demonstrating the conditioned response to stimuli that are similar to the conditioned stimulus
_____ Return of a previously extinguished conditioned response
_____ Using a conditioned stimulus to condition a neutral stimulus

Lesson 5.3

Operant Conditioning

OBJECTIVES

- ★ Define operant conditioning.
- ★ Explain the difference between reinforcement and punishment.
- ★ Distinguish between reinforcement schedules.

BIG IDEA

Operant conditioning involves an organism learning the relationship between a behavior and a consequence, whether pleasant or aversive.

In this lesson, you will learn about the following:

- Reinforcement
- Punishment
- Primary and Secondary Reinforcers
- Reinforcement Schedules
- Cognition and Latent Learning

Operant conditioning involves an organism learning to associate a behavior with its ________________, in which a pleasant consequence makes the behavior ___________ likely and an aversive consequence makes the behavior _________ likely.

On Your Own

Compare classical and operant conditioning. How are they different?

B. F. Skinner built upon the law of __________(Thorndike's work) to propose the idea that reinforcement and ________________ could modify behavior. He tested these effects in rats using a _______________ box, an operant chamber designed to measure lever presses and dispense food.

Provide an example for each type of operant situation.

Positive/Negative	Reinforcement/Punishment	Example
Positive	Reinforcement	

Positive	Punishment	
Negative	Reinforcement	
Negative	Punishment	

Reinforcement

On Your Own

Do you feel that positive reinforcement is manipulative? People are "rewarded" for behavior they should be doing anyway. Is that okay?

Provide two examples of negative reinforcement from your own life.

Punishment

On Your Own

In the popular TV show *The Big Bang Theory*, Sheldon indicates that he can retrain his roommate's girlfriend with "negative reinforcement" by spraying the girlfriend in the face with water when she does an annoying behavior. What is wrong with this example?

A father tells a disobedient child, "You are in trouble, mister! You wait until your mother gets home!" What is wrong with this scenario?

Provide two arguments against the use of physical punishment.

1.

2.

Shaping

In some cases, researchers use shaping to train an animal to perform a particular behavior. Shaping involves rewarding successive approximations of the target behavior.

On Your Own

List the 5 steps used in shaping.

1.

2.

3.

4.

5.

Primary and Secondary Reinforcers

A ____________ reinforcer is innately reinforcing because the need or desire for the reinforcer is not ____________. On the other hand, a ______________ reinforcer has no ____________ value and only has reinforcing qualities when linked to a ____________ reinforcer.

On Your Own

What are some methods for behavioral modification in children? Are they reinforcements or punishments? Positive or negative?

1.

2.

What are important points to remember about the use of time-outs as behavior modification?

1.

2.

3.

4.

5.

Reinforcement Schedules

____________________ reinforcement involves providing a reward each time a person or animal performs a target behavior. In contrast, ________________ reinforcement provides a reward for the target behavior on a particular schedule of reinforcement.

Which schedule of reinforcement fits each example? Complete the following table.

Example	Schedule of Reinforcement
A door-to-door salesman	
Checking your emails for an important email	
Playing slots at the casino	
Getting paid every two weeks	

On Your Own

The lesson discusses the idea that there may be brain differences between compulsive gamblers and non-gamblers. However, it is hard to say whether those differences were there before and contributed to the behavior or are there as a result of the behavior. What do you think?

Cognition and Latent Learning

Edward C. Tolman demonstrated that organisms can learn even if they do not receive ________________ ______________________. In his experiment, some rats were placed into a maze and not provided a food reward. Later, when a food reward was introduced, they demonstrated that they had previously learned the maze and developed a ________________ ____________. This type of learning is referred to as ______________ ________________.

On Your Own

Provide an example of a time when you experienced latent learning.

Psychology and You

Shaping

Describe how you would use shaping to train your dog to fetch his leash.

Lesson Wrap-up

Say It in a Sentence

In one sentence, explain the difference between positive punishment and negative reinforcement.

Test Yourself

Choose the correct answer for each of the following questions. Check your work using the Answer Key in the back of the book.

____ 1. Positive punishment refers to:

- **A.** Decreasing behavior by adding something
- **B.** Increasing behavior by adding something
- **C.** Decreasing behavior by taking something away
- **D.** Increasing behavior by taking something away

____ 2. Negative reinforcement refers to:

- **A.** Decreasing behavior by adding something
- **B.** Increasing behavior by adding something
- **C.** Decreasing behavior by taking something away
- **D.** Increasing behavior by taking something away

____ 3. The most effective way to teach a person or animal a new behavior is through:

- **A.** Positive punishment
- **B.** Positive reinforcement
- **C.** Negative punishment
- **D.** Negative reinforcement

____ 4. The quickest way to teach someone a new behavior is through:

- **A.** Continuous reinforcement
- **B.** Partial reinforcement

____ 5. The best way to produce a behavior that is resistant to extinction is through:

- **A.** Continuous reinforcement
- **B.** Partial reinforcement

Answer each of the following questions. Check your work using the Answer Key in the back of the book.

6. Which reinforcement schedule is the least resistant to extinction?

7. Which reinforcement schedule is easiest to extinguish?

8. Which schedule of reinforcement is in use in this scenario?

   You go fishing and cast your line several times, waiting for a bite.

9. Which schedule of reinforcement is in use in this scenario?

   You place a tray of cookies in the oven and set the timer for 10 minutes.

Key Terms

For the following key terms, make groupings out of the related terms. Be sure to explain how they are related.

Key Terms: cognitive map, continuous reinforcement, fixed interval reinforcement schedule, fixed ratio reinforcement schedule, latent learning, law of effect, negative punishment, negative reinforcement, operant conditioning, partial reinforcement, positive punishment, positive reinforcement, primary reinforcer, punishment, reinforcement, secondary reinforcer, shaping, variable interval reinforcement schedule, variable ratio reinforcement schedule

Lesson 5.4

Observational Learning (Modeling)

OBJECTIVES

- ★ Define observational learning.
- ★ Discuss the steps in the modeling process.
- ★ Explain the prosocial and antisocial effects of observational learning.

BIG IDEA

Humans and other animals learn through observing others and modeling or imitating the observed behaviors. New responses may be learned but not demonstrated, depending on whether the model was punished or rewarded for the behavior.

How would you organize the terms *models*, *observational learning*, and *imitation* in the following organizer?

	involves		of	

In this lesson, you will learn about the following:

- Observational Learning
- Steps in the Modeling Process

Observational Learning

In observational learning, we ____________, or imitate, behavior we see from others.

Unlike the behaviorists, ______________ ___________________ believed that observational learning involved ________________ ______________ and cognition, not simply reinforced behaviors.

On Your Own

Do you remember a time when you were in a new situation and unsure of how to behave? Did you watch others to determine what to do? How successful was the experience?

____________________ would involve simply copying a behavior, whereas ________________________ ___________________ largely involves learning a general rule that can be applied in different situations.

________________ indicated that there were three different ways that observational learning could occur. First, individuals learn a ________ ______________ after watching the results of someone else's behavior. Second, individuals choose whether to ____________ based on consequences for the model. Finally, individuals learn a ____________ ________ that can be applied to other situations.

Observational learning can occur from a variety of models. Label each model as *live*, *verbal*, or *symbolic* in the following table.

Your aunt demonstrates how to change the brake pads on a car.	
You watch a YouTube video about how to replace your iPhone screen.	
Your mom tells you over the phone how to operate your new washing machine.	
You watch a movie in which a stunt man performs several martial arts moves.	

Steps in the Modeling Process

According to Alfred Bandura, what are the necessary steps for modeling to be successful?

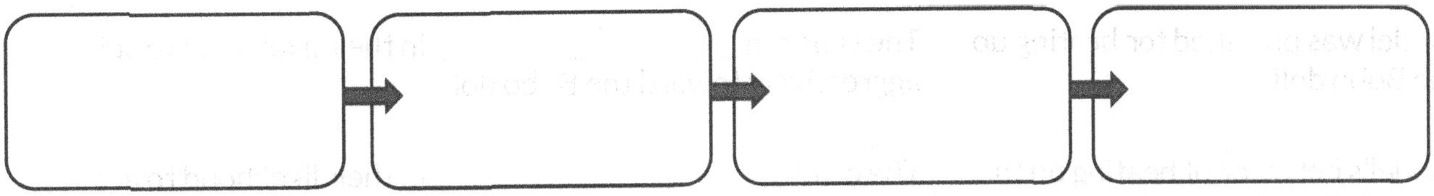

On Your Own

Can you think of a time when you learned a new response or behavior but lacked the motivation to perform the behavior? Describe this experience in terms of attention (to learn the new behavior), retention (memory of the behavior), and the ability to recreate or reproduce the behavior. Although you did not perform the behavior, you still learned it.

____________ ________________ would increase the likelihood of an individual reproducing an observed behavior, whereas ____________ ____________ would decrease the likelihood.

On Your Own

Remember the story in the lesson about Allison and Kaitlyn, who were playing with their mother's make-up? If Allison saw Kaitlyn get in trouble for playing with the cosmetics, Allison would experience vicarious punishment. Can you name a consequence that would be considered vicarious reinforcement?

What are some of your own experiences with vicarious reinforcement and punishment? List some examples.

Vicarious Reinforcement	Vicarious Punishment

Fill in the following table with the results from the Bandura Bobo doll study.

Action	Results
Model was punished for beating up the Bobo doll.	The children ________________ in their likelihood to act aggressively toward the Bobo doll.
Model's behavior of beating up the Bobo doll was ignored.	The children ________________ in their likelihood to act aggressively toward the Bobo doll.
Model was praised for beating up the Bobo doll.	The children ________________ in their likelihood to act aggressively toward the Bobo doll.

On Your Own

What is your reaction to the Bobo doll study? If you could go back and redo the experiment, what would you change?

When a child engages in a positive behavior that has been previously observed, he or she is experiencing a ________________ ________________. Engagement in a negative behavior, on the other hand, would be an ________________ ________________.

On Your Own

Provide an example of a prosocial and antisocial effect of observational learning.

Prosocial	Antisocial

Psychology and You

Observational Learning Reflection

Think of a time when you engaged in observational learning. Did you experience the four steps outlined by Alfred Bandura?

Lesson Wrap-up

Say It in a Sentence

In one sentence, describe observational learning.

Test Yourself

Choose the correct answer for each of the following questions. Check your work using the Answer Key in the back of the book.

____ 1. You watch a video online about how to change an O2 sensor on your car. In this case, who is the model?

A. You
B. The person in the video

____ 2. In the same case where you watch a video online about how to change an O2 sensor on your car, the person in the video is:

A. Live
B. Symbolic
C. Verbal

____ 3. When attending a Zumba class, you imitate the moves of the instructor. The instructor is:

A. Live
B. Symbolic
C. Verbal

Next to each statement, write **T** for True or **F** for False. Check your work using the Answer Key in the back of the book.

1. ______ When you watch your mom cook a turkey so that you can prepare your own at Thanksgiving, you are watching a symbolic model.

2. ______ Alfred Bandura believed that behavior resulted only from rewards or punishments with little to no cognitive involvement.

3. ______ Alfred Bandura considered observational learning more involved than imitation.

Key Terms

Use the key terms from the lesson to complete the following crossword puzzle.

Across

1. Process where the observer sees a model rewarded, making the observer more likely to imitate the model's behavior

Down

1. Type of learning that occurs by watching others
2. Person who performs a behavior that serves as an example
3. Copying an action
4. Psychologist who proposed social learning theory
5. Process where the observer sees a model punished, making the observer less likely to imitate the model's behavior
6. Encourages socially acceptable behavior
7. Encourages socially unacceptable behavior

Chapter 6
Thinking and Intelligence

Lesson 6.1
What Is Cognition?

OBJECTIVES

- ★ Describe cognition.
- ★ Distinguish concepts and prototypes.
- ★ Explain the difference between natural and artificial concepts.

BIG IDEA

Cognitive psychology studies cognition, which is the ability to engage in thought, emotion, creativity, language, and other cognitive or mental processes. These processes, including formation of concepts and schemata, can help people make sense of the world.

What abilities or attributes comprise cognition? Fill in the following graphic.

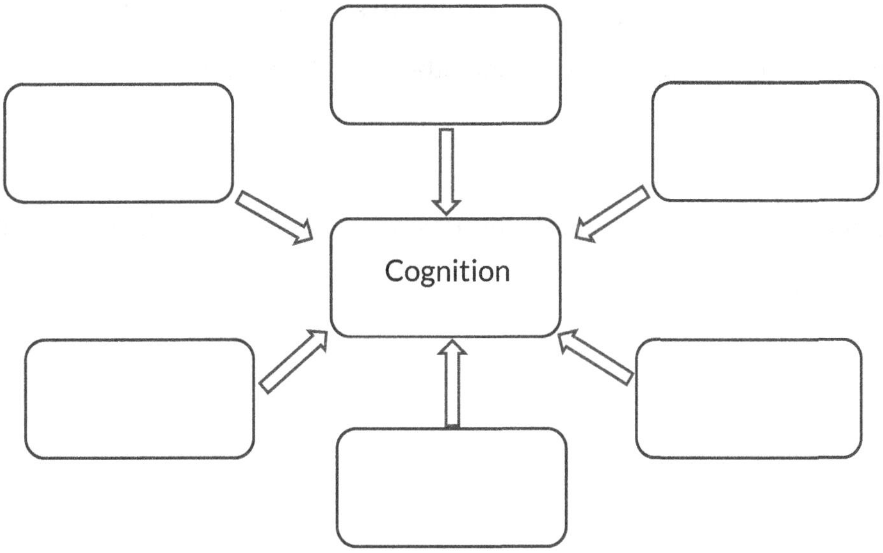

Can you think of any other abilities or attributes that would be included in the concept of cognition?

In this lesson, you will learn about the following:

- Cognition
- Concepts and Prototypes
- Natural and Artificial Concepts
- Schemata

Cognition

Complex cognition is an essential feature of ________________ ________________________, yet not all aspects of cognition are ______________________ experienced.

On Your Own

What are your thoughts upon waking up in the morning? Do you make a plan for the day? What might it look like?

______________________ ______________________ is dedicated to examining how people think by studying emotion, creativity, language, problem solving, and other cognitive processes.

On Your Own

If you were a cognitive psychologist, what are some questions you would want to study scientifically?

1.

2.

3.

Concepts and Prototypes

Place the following terms within the schematic to show the relationship between external and internal environment and the mind.

Thoughts
Memory
Language
Senses

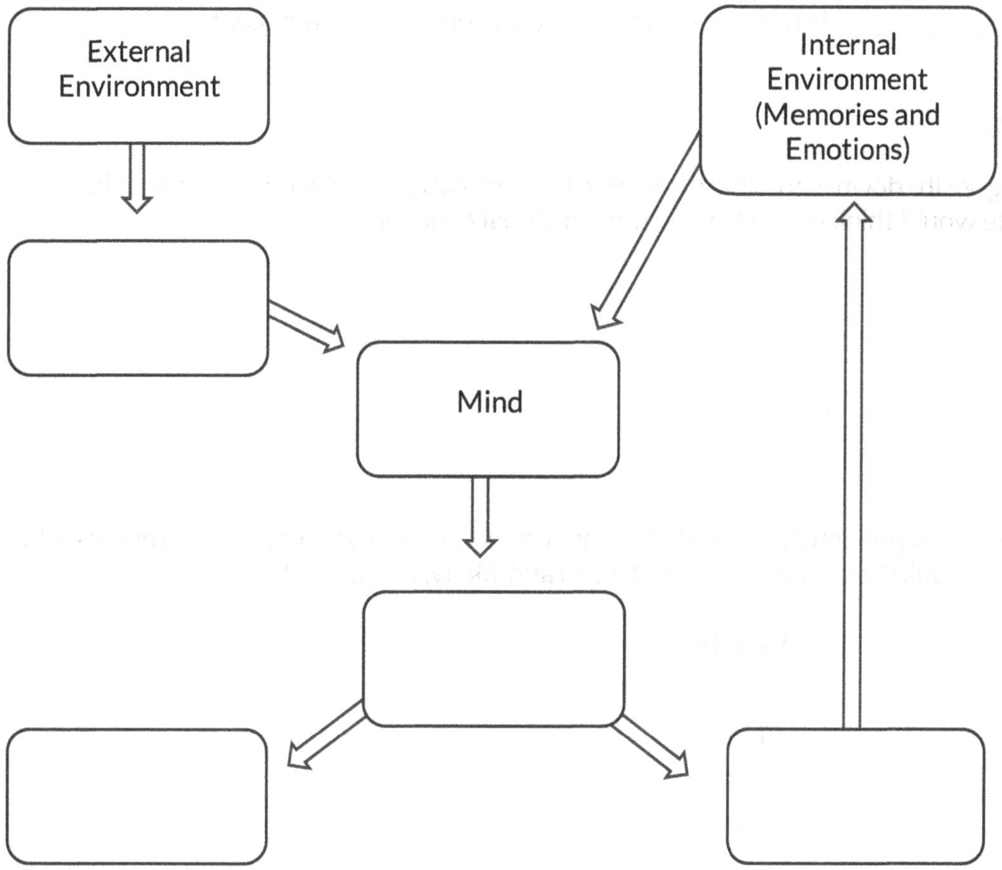

____________________ are categories or groupings of linguistic information, images, ideas, or memories. Concepts are big ideas that are generated by observing ____________________ and categorizing and combining these details into __________________ ______________________.

On Your Own

What are some concepts you can think of? What do they have in common?

For the following list of concepts, label each as *abstract* or *concrete*.

Dachshund	
Truth	
Love	
Chair	

A ______________________ is the best example or representation of a concept.

On Your Own

For the following, write down a possible prototype for each category. Your answers should represent what *most* people would think of when given the individual concept.

Vehicle	
Tree	
Bird	

For the prototypes you previously generated, what *personal answers* would you give for each of the categories? These would be concepts specific to you and, likely, less prototypical.

Vehicle	
Tree	
Bird	

Natural and Artificial Concepts

______________ ________________ are created "naturally" through direct or indirect experiences, whereas ________________ ____________________ are defined by a specific set of characteristics.

Concepts act as ________________ __________________ and can be connected in countless combinations to create complex thoughts.

Schemata

A __________________ is a mental construct consisting of a cluster or collection of related concepts used to ______________________ information to allow the brain to work more efficiently.

A __________ _____________________ makes assumptions about how individuals in certain roles behave, whereas ______ _______________ _____________________ is a set of behaviors that can feel like a routine.

On Your Own

In the following table, create a list of natural and artificial concepts.

Natural	Artificial

Provide examples of role and event schemas that you have witnessed or engaged in.

Role Schemas	Event Schemas

Event schemata are ______________________, so they are often difficult to change. These routines may be the reason many individuals still __________ or __________ on the phone when driving.

On Your Own

What other habits do you have that might be considered event schemata?

How do schemata relate to the idea of prejudice?

Psychology and You

Reflection

How do you prevent yourself from using your phone when driving? If you still use your phone when driving, how could you stop this behavior?

Lesson Wrap-up

Say It in a Sentence

In one sentence, describe what encompasses cognition and why it is important.

Test Yourself

Next to each statement, write **T** for True or **F** for False. Check your work using the Answer Key in the back of the book.

1. ______ An ostrich would be considered a prototypical bird.
2. ______ An oak tree would be considered a prototypical tree.
3. ______ An individual from Arizona believes that sand and dirt are usually red in color, compared to the brown of the Midwest. This belief is an example of an artificial concept.

Choose the correct answer for each of the following questions. Check your work using the Answer Key in the back of the book.

____ 4. Michael's understanding of a triangle, whether it be large and red or small and purple, would best be labeled as a(n):

- **A.** Event schemata
- **B.** Natural concept
- **C.** Role schemata
- **D.** Artificial concept

____ 5. Jamie's understanding of snow, having grown up in Wisconsin, would best be labeled as:

- **A.** Event schemata
- **B.** Natural concept
- **C.** Role schemata
- **D.** Artificial concept

____ 6. When Joseph says, "Policemen are the bravest!" he is using:

- **A.** Event schemata
- **B.** Natural concept
- **C.** Role schemata
- **D.** Artificial concept

____ 7. "The dentist always finds a cavity and has to drill!" is an example of:

- **A.** Event schemata
- **B.** Natural concept
- **C.** Role schemata
- **D.** Artificial concept

Key Terms

For the following key terms, make groupings out of the related terms. Be sure to explain how they are related.

Key Terms: artificial concept, cognition, cognitive psychology, cognitive script, concept, event schema, natural concept, prototype, role schema, schema

Lesson 6.2

Language

OBJECTIVES

- ★ Define language and demonstrate familiarity with the components of language.
- ★ Understand how the use of language develops.
- ★ Explain the relationship between language and thinking.

BIG IDEA

Language is a communication system made up of words and a variety of rules. Children develop language with tremendous ease, suggesting that there is an underlying biological predisposition to learn language.

Complete the following graphic organizer to explain what differentiates language from non-verbal communication.

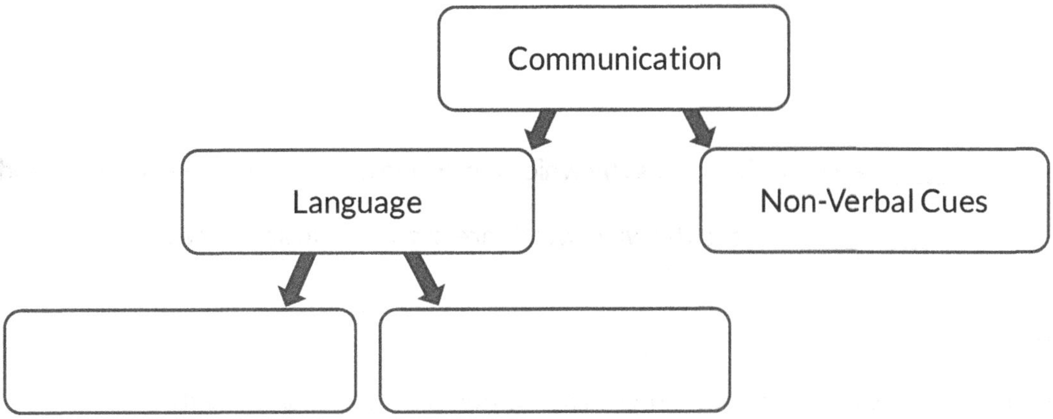

In this lesson, you will learn about the following:

- Components of Language
- Language Development
- Language and Thought

Components of Language

Language has specific components: ____________________ and ____________________. ____________________ refers to the words or vocabulary of a given language, whereas ____________________ refers to the rules that are used to convey meaning through the use of words.

On Your Own

Describe three grammatical rules that you are aware of:

Words are formed by combining various __________________, which are the basic sound units of a given language. ____________________ are combined to form ____________________, which are the smallest units of language that convey some type of meaning.

Generate a list of at least 5 phonemes and 5 morphemes.

Phonemes	Morphemes

__________________ refers to the process by which we derive meaning from morphemes and words, whereas _______________ refers to the ways words are organized in sentences.

On Your Own

In the statement, "The cats won't bake," what is being violated, syntax or semantics?

Language Development

__________ _______________ proposed that language is learned through reinforcement, whereas __________ ________________ theorized that the mechanisms underlying language were biologically determined.

There appears to be a ____________ ______________ for language acquisition, such that proficiency in language is best learned early in life.

On Your Own

What are your thoughts about the experiment that showed newborns prefer the sound of their own mother's voices? What does this experimental result demonstrate?

Describe your experience learning an additional or second language. At what age did you learn? How easy or difficult was it?

Complete the following table.

Stage	Age	Language Development
1	0 to 3 months	
2		Reflexive communication; interest
3	8 to 13 months	
4	12 to 18 months	
5		Simple two-word sentences
6	2 to 3 years	
7		Complex sentences; conversation

On Your Own

React to the story of Genie. Does her story support B.F. Skinner's or Noam Chomsky's theory when it comes to language development? Explain your answer.

Compare and contrast Skinner's and Chomsky's beliefs regarding language development.

Babies can discriminate among the sounds that make up all of the languages of the world until about

_____ __________of age. After that point, they can only discriminate among phonemes that are used in languages in their environment.

Given the previous statement, when should people learn a second language?

The _______________ stage occurs when babies produce various syllables repeatedly.

Children in the __________________ stage tend to use single words to express their wants and needs even though they may know many more words.

On Your Own

Generate a list of 5 possible "first words" that a child may have.

As children learn language, they often make mistakes. One such mistake is _________________________: an extension of a language rule to an exception to the rule.

Language and Thought

Psychologists have long studied if there is a relationship between language and thought such that our language influences how we think, an idea known as _________________ ____________________. Two researchers who believed this to be true were ______________ ___________ and ____________________ ________ ______________.

On Your Own

What do you think of the idea that someone who does not have past-tense words is unable to think about the past?

Psychologists point out the use of words that have more complex meanings than can be expressed in a single English word, such as *saudade*, as evidence that language can influence how individuals think. Do you feel this idea is true? Why or why not?

A study that appears to support the idea of ______________ ________________ investigated Mandarin Chinese speakers and English speakers with regard to how they discuss time. English speakers were best at changes along the ______________ dimension, whereas Mandarin Chinese speakers were faster than English speakers on the _____________ dimension.

On Your Own

The Dani people of Papua New Guinea can still identify differences between 11 different colors even though they only have two color words (i.e., “light” and “dark”). Does this support or refute the idea of linguistic determinism? Explain.

Psychology and You

Language and Cognition

Speakers of multiple languages often report that they think differently depending on which language they speak. For example, when speaking English, some individuals find themselves thinking more about how something might benefit them versus the group. Speaking a language from a more collectivistic country, however, results in a different pattern of thought. Can you think of examples where your language affected your cognition or vice versa?

Lesson Wrap-up

Say It in a Sentence

In one sentence, describe language development.

Test Yourself

Choose the correct answer for each of the following questions. Check your work using the Answer Key in the back of the book.

____ 1. Which of the following would constitute language?

- **A.** A dog growling with its hair standing up
- **B.** A gorilla using sign to signal "water"
- **C.** A sad look on a friend's face

____ 2. In the statement, "The cats won't eating," what is being violated?

- **A.** Syntax
- **B.** Semantics

____ 3. Thomas says, "Me draw with blue marker." What age group is he likely in?

- **A.** 12 to 18 months
- **B.** 18 to 24 months
- **C.** 2 to 3 years
- **D.** 3 to 5 years

____ 4. Your friend says, "Learning language is extremely difficult!" What is the most accurate refute of this claim?

- **A.** Learning language is actually relatively easy provided the individual is learning early in life.
- **B.** Learning language is only difficult for some people.
- **C.** Learning language is actually easy at all stages of life; people are just too lazy to learn.
- **D.** It can't be refuted because this statement is correct.

____ 5. When your nephew says, "Look at all those deers!" what error has he committed?

- **A.** Linguistic determinism
- **B.** Overgeneralization
- **C.** No error

Key Terms

Match each key term with its definition.

A. Grammar	____	Process by which we derive meaning from morphemes and words
B. Language	____	Communication system that involves using words to transmit information from one individual to another
C. Lexicon		
D. Morpheme		

E. Overgeneralization	_____	The words of a given language
F. Phoneme	_____	Set of rules used to convey meaning through the use of a lexicon
G. Semantics	_____	Manner by which words are organized into sentences
H. Syntax	_____	Smallest unit of language that conveys some type of meaning
	_____	Basic sound unit of a given language
	_____	Extension of a rule that exists in a given language to an exception of the rule

Lesson 6.3

Problem Solving

OBJECTIVES

- ★ Describe problem-solving strategies.
- ★ Define algorithm and heuristic.
- ★ Explain some common roadblocks to effective problem solving.

BIG IDEA

When solving a problem, we must identify it, apply a strategy, and sometimes overcome biases or faulty logic.

In this lesson, you will learn about the following:

- Problem-Solving Strategies
- Pitfalls to Problem Solving

Problem-Solving Strategies

Before finding a solution to the problem, the problem must first be clearly ____________________.

A problem-solving strategy is a plan of action used to find a solution. ___________ ________

__________ involves trying different solutions until a solution is found. ____________________ are step-by-step problem-solving formulas. Finally, ___________________ are mental shortcuts used to solve problems.

Which problem-solving strategy does each example represent? Complete the following table.

You follow the instructions to build a bookshelf.	
You calculate when you need to leave the house by working backwards from the time you need to arrive at school that day.	
You try a variety of ways to get your computer to turn on after it crashed.	
You break a 10-page paper into different steps, so you do not become overwhelmed.	

On Your Own

What conditions make it more likely that someone will rely on a heuristic?

1.

2.

3.

4.

5.

Stereotypes are a type of heuristic. Do any of the 5 conditions apply in a situation when someone may use a stereotype to characterize another individual?

________________ __________________ is a useful heuristic in which you begin solving the problem by focusing on the end result.

On Your Own

Can you think of a time when you worked backwards? What was the situation?

Can you think of a time when you broke a larger project into smaller pieces? How did using this heuristic make you feel?

Pitfalls to Problem Solving

A ____________ ________ occurs when you persist in approaching a problem in a way that worked in the past but is clearly not working now. ________________ ________________ is a type of mental set where you cannot perceive an object being used for something other than what it was designed for.

On Your Own

Describe a time when you overcame functional fixedness by using an object in a way it was not designed to be used.

There are quite a few biases or flaws in logic that impede problem-solving ability.

An __________________ __________ occurs when you focus on one piece of information (and ignore others) when making a decision.

A ______________________ __________ is the tendency to focus on information that corresponds with your existing beliefs.

_________________ __________ leads you to believe that an event was predictable.

________________________ _________ is when you unintentionally stereotype someone or something based on what you feel is typical for that group.

An __________________ __________________ is when you use readily available information to make a decision.

Label each situation with the type of bias it demonstrates.

Even though you aren't overly thirsty, you buy the large soda at the movie theater because it is only one dollar more than the medium.	
You believe planes are highly dangerous because you can think of a recent plane crash (even though cars are technically more dangerous than planes).	
You assume that all truck drivers are older Southern men with beards because that seems "typical" to you.	
Uncle Jim thinks certain ethnic groups are lazy. He ignores examples that contradict his belief and only focuses on examples that confirm it.	
When you hear of your best friend's recent break-up, you say, "I knew it! I could see the signs months ago."	

Psychology and You

Problem-Solving Strategy

Identify a problem you faced recently. Which problem-solving strategy did you use to solve the problem? Name and discuss a bias or error of logic that you faced.

Lesson Wrap-up

Say It in a Sentence

In one sentence, explain how biases impede cognition.

Test Yourself

Choose the correct answer for each of the following questions. Check your work using the Answer Key in the back of the book.

____ 1. When you break up your work into smaller chunks, you are using:

- **A.** A heuristic
- **B.** Trial and error
- **C.** An algorithm

____ 2. You assume that your professor never uses foul language because that does not fit your idea of a professor. In this case, you are falling prey to which bias?

- **A.** Anchoring
- **B.** Confirmation
- **C.** Hindsight
- **D.** Representative

____ 3. Research has shown that functional fixedness:

- **A.** Only occurs in industrialized countries
- **B.** Only applies to cultures that have been exposed to highly specialized tools
- **C.** Occurs in both industrialized and non-industrialized countries

____ 4. When a movie theater offers the large bucket of popcorn for a minimal cost compared to the medium, they are using anchoring bias. How does anchoring bias cause people to purchase the large versus the medium?

- **A.** People believe that this is typical of most movie theaters.
- **B.** It causes people to visualize themselves eating the popcorn.
- **C.** People tend to focus only on the perceived savings instead of considering if they actually want a large.

____ 5. Today, individuals have a tendency to follow news programs that fit their personal ideologies. Which bias does this demonstrate?

- **A.** Representative bias
- **B.** Confirmation bias
- **C.** Hindsight bias
- **D.** Anchoring bias

Answer the following question. Check your work using the Answer Key in the back of the book.

6. Which bias is most closely related to racist beliefs? Explain your reasoning.

Key Terms

For each key term, provide an example that expemplifies the meaning of the word.

Algorithm

Anchoring Bias

Availability Heuristic

Confirmation Bias

Functional Fixedness

Heuristic

Hindsight Bias

Mental Set

Problem-Solving Strategy

Representative Bias

Trial and Error

Working Backwards

Lesson 6.4

What Are Intelligence and Creativity?

OBJECTIVES

- ★ Define intelligence.
- ★ Explain the triarchic theory of intelligence.
- ★ Identify the difference between intelligence theories.
- ★ Explain emotional intelligence.

BIG IDEA

Intelligence is typically defined as the ability to learn and retain new skills or knowledge. Over the years, many psychologists have tried to analyze intelligence and break it up into different components, such as emotional, practical, and fluid intelligence.

Complete the following table with the intelligence types that fit each psychologist.

Cattell	Sternberg	Gardner	Spearman

On Your Own

What do you believe intelligence is?

In this lesson, you will learn about the following:

- Classifying Intelligence
- Creativity

Classifying Intelligence

Charles Spearman believed intelligence consisted of one general factor, called _____. Raymond Cattell, on the other hand, believed that intelligence could be broken up into ___________ and ___________________ intelligence.

__________ intelligence is the ability to see complex relationships and solve problems, whereas

______________ intelligence is characterized as acquired knowledge and ability to retrieve it.

On Your Own

Generate examples of crystallized and fluid intelligence from your own life.

Crystallized Intelligence	Fluid Intelligence

Robert Sternberg developed the triarchic theory of intelligence, which was comprised of three parts:

______________, ______________, and ______________.

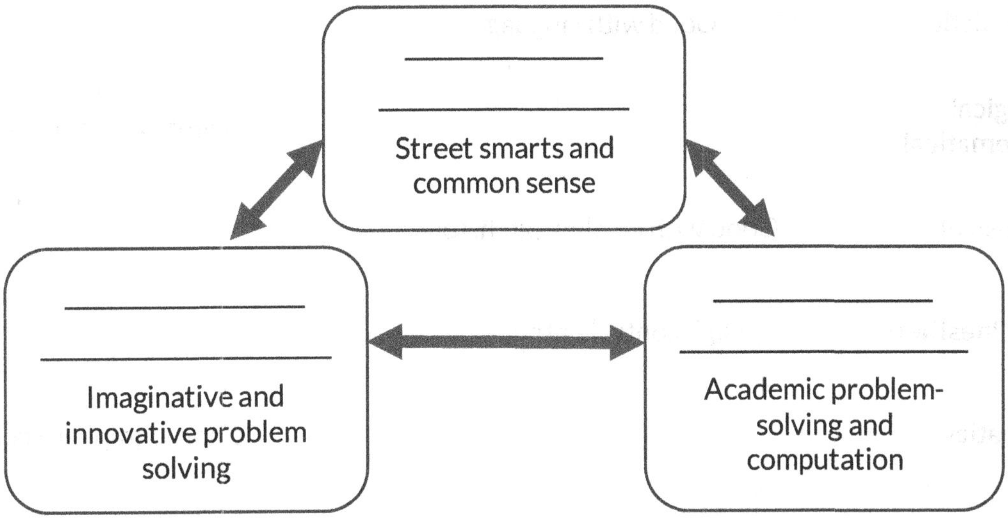

On Your Own

When you think about Sternberg's triarchic theory of intelligence, which of the three components do you feel is more important, and why?

What is your reaction to the story of the Virginia Tech shooting? How might you behave in a similar situation?

_________ _______________ _____________________ _____________, which characterized eight different types of intelligence, was developed by Howard Gardner.

On Your Own

Use the multiple intelligences theory to rank your intelligences from 1 (strongest) to 8 (weakest).

1.
2.
3.
4.
5.
6.
7.
8.

Complete the following table.

Intelligence Type	Characteristics	Representative Career
Linguistic	Good with language	
Logical-Mathematical		Scientist, mathematician
Musical	Good with rhythm, pitch, tone	
Bodily Kinesthetic	High control of the body	
Spatial		Choreographer, sculptor
Interpersonal	Sensitive to others	
Intrapersonal		Good for all careers
Naturalist		Biologist, ecologist

On Your Own

Do you agree that "naturalist" should be an intelligence type? Why or why not?

____________________ ________________________ encompasses the ability to understand the emotions of yourself and others, show empathy, understand social relationships and cues, and regulate your own emotions and respond in culturally appropriate ways.

How well an individual relates to the values of a different culture is an example of __________________ intelligence.

Creativity

_____________________ is the ability to generate, create, or discover new ideas, solutions, and possibilities.

On Your Own

The text indicates five aspects that creative people typically have or do. What are they?

1.
2.
3.
4.
5.

________________________ thinking is thinking that would be considered "outside the box," whereas _______________________ thinking is the ability to generate a correct or well-established answer.

On Your Own

Generate as many ideas as you can for unique ways to travel from New York to California.

Check the box next to the correct answer.

Which theorist only has one aspect of intelligence?

- ☐ Sternberg
- ☐ Spearman
- ☐ Cattell
- ☐ Gardner

Which theorist has eight aspects of intelligence?

- ☐ Sternberg
- ☐ Spearman
- ☐ Cattell
- ☐ Gardner

Whose theory of intelligence included what might be considered "street smarts?"

- ☐ Sternberg
- ☐ Spearman
- ☐ Cattell
- ☐ Gardner

Psychology and You

The Triarchic Theory of Intelligence

Which of the three intelligence types in Sternberg's triarchic theory of intelligence are you best at? Provide an example to support your claim.

Lesson Wrap-up

Say It in a Sentence

In one sentence, define intelligence.

Test Yourself

Answer each of the following questions. Check your work using the Answer Key in the back of the book.

1. When your friend provides a divergent answer to a problem, which aspect of the triarchic theory of intelligence is he or she using?

2. If someone says, "He couldn't find his way out of a paper bag," that person is referring to a lack of which type of intelligence?

Key Terms

Match each key term with its definition.

A. Analytical Intelligence
B. Convergent Thinking
C. Creative Intelligence
D. Creativity
E. Crystallized Intelligence
F. Cultural Intelligence
G. Divergent Thinking
H. Emotional Intelligence
I. Fluid Intelligence
J. Multiple Intelligences Theory
K. Practical Intelligence
L. Triarchic Theory of Intelligence

_____ Ability with which people can understand and relate to those in another culture
_____ Gardner's theory that each person possesses at least eight types of intelligence
_____ Sternberg's theory of intelligence, which includes practical, creative, and analytical intelligence
_____ Aligned with academic problem solving and computations
_____ Characterized by acquired knowledge and the ability to retrieve it
_____ Ability to think "outside the box" to arrive at novel solutions to a problem
_____ Ability to understand emotions and motivations in yourself and others
_____ Providing correct or established answers to problems
_____ Ability to see complex relationships and solve problems
_____ Ability to generate, create, or discover new ideas, solutions, and possibilities
_____ Ability to produce new products, ideas, or inventing a new, novel solution to a problem

Lesson 6.5

Measures of Intelligence

OBJECTIVES

- ★ Explain how intelligence tests are developed.
- ★ Describe the history of the use of IQ tests.
- ★ Describe the purposes and benefits of intelligence testing.

BIG IDEA

Intelligence tests have been created and revised since the late 1800s so that individuals who need additional assistance can be identified. These tests are constantly undergoing revisions to ensure they still represent current intelligence averages across the population.

IQ stands for ____________________ __________________ and describes a score earned on a test designed to measure intelligence.

On Your Own

Psychologists still have not settled on a single definition for intelligence. What does this mean for the realm of intelligence testing?

In this lesson, you will learn about the following:

- Measuring Intelligence
- The Bell Curve
- Why Measure Intelligence?

Measuring Intelligence

In the following chart, the primary psychologists that helped develop IQ testing are listed. Using only a few words, sum up each person's contribution to the field.

Psychologist	Contributions to IQ Testing
Sir Francis Galton	
Alfred Binet	

Louis Terman	
David Wechsler	

When an IQ test has been _______________, it means that the test was administered to a large enough sample of the population such that the scores resemble a distribution where the majority of the scores fall to the middle of the range, with less scores falling to the edges (both high and low) of the range.

When an IQ test has been ________________________, that means the manner of administration, scoring, and interpretation are all consistent.

On Your Own

What are your thoughts about individuals judging which face was prettier as part of the Binet-Simon IQ test?

The _____________ _____________ is the observation that each generation has a significantly higher IQ than the last generation.

On Your Own

James Flynn argued that the Flynn effect may not mean that each successive generation is actually smarter than the last generation. What else might account for the fact that each generation scores better on IQ tests?

The WISC-V tests Verbal Comprehension, Visual Spatial, Fluid Reasoning, Working Memory, and Processing Speed. Which theories of intelligence, from the last lesson, do you see in this list?

What is your reaction to the results of the *Atkins v. Virginia* case? Should individuals who are deemed mentally disabled be protected from execution for their crimes?

The Bell Curve

A ___________ ______________ graph demonstrates a normal distribution of a trait in the human population. More individuals will fall in the average range with fewer individuals to the two extremes. A bell curve depends upon a _____________ sample size to be accurate.

On Your Own

If you consider your psychology class, would you say it is representative of the population in any way? Explain.

The average IQ score on an IQ test is _________. ______________ _______________ describe how the data is dispersed around the mean. One standard deviation is _______ points, such that scores within one standard deviation of the mean (100) would be scores between _______ to _______.

Only _____% of the population has an IQ score below 70. Similarly, only 2% of the population has an IQ score over __________.

Complete the following table.

IQ Score Range	Percentage of Individuals in that IQ Score Range
100 to 115	
Below 70	
115 to 130	
85 to 115	

A score of ________ _____ ______________ indicates significant cognitive delays. When these are combined with major deficits in _______________ ___________________, a person is diagnosed with having an intellectual disability. There are four subtypes: __________, moderate, severe, and ________________.

Complete the following table.

Intellectual Disability Subtype	Percentage of Intellectually Disabled Population	Description
Moderate		
Severe		

On Your Own

What do you think about the move from "mental retardation" to "intellectual disability"? Do you feel the name change helps those who would fall within this category? Why or why not?

Why Measure Intelligence?

What are the benefits of IQ testing?

1.

2.

3.

4.

Psychology and You

WISC-V

If you took the WISC-V (Verbal Comprehension, Visual-Spatial, Fluid Reasoning, Working Memory, and Processing Speed), in which areas do you feel you would excel, and in which would you perform poorly? Explain.

Lesson Wrap-up

Say It in a Sentence

In one sentence, explain the value of intelligence testing.

Test Yourself

Choose the correct answer for each of the following questions. Check your work using the Answer Key in the back of the book.

____ 1. You took an intelligence test and scored a 130. When asked how you did, you reply:

- **A.** "I scored one standard deviation below the mean."
- **B.** "I scored one standard deviation above the mean."
- **C.** "I scored two standard deviations below the mean."
- **D.** "I scored two standard deviations above the mean."

____ 2. The first person to develop an intelligence test was:

- **A.** Alfred Binet
- **B.** David Wechsler
- **C.** Louis Terman
- **D.** Sir Francis Galton

____ 3. You took an intelligence test and scored a 90. You would be considered:

- **A.** Above average
- **B.** Below average
- **C.** Average
- **D.** Intellectually disabled

Next to each statement, write **T** for True or **F** for False. Check your work using the Answer Key in the back of the book.

4. ______ Alfred Binet was asked to test English children to determine who needed additional help in school.

5. _______ An IQ score of 135 is a rare score.

6. _______ An IQ score of 87 is a rare score.

Key Terms

Use the key terms from the lesson to complete the following crossword puzzle.

Across

1. Subset of the population that accurately represents the general population
2. Score on a test designed to measure intelligence

Down

1. Observation that each generation has a significantly higher IQ than the previous generation
2. Administering a test to a large population so data can be collected to reference the normal scores for a population and its groups
3. Measure of variability that describes the difference between a set of scores and their mean
4. Method of testing in which administration, scoring, and interpretation of results are consistent

Lesson 6.6

The Source of Intelligence

OBJECTIVES

- ★ Describe how genetics and environment affect intelligence.
- ★ Explain the relationship between IQ scores and socioeconomic status.
- ★ Describe the difference between a learning disability and a developmental disorder.

BIG IDEA

Both nature (heritability and genetics) and nurture (an individual's environment and upbringing) can contribute to levels of intelligence.

On Your Own

What is your reaction to the Oprah Winfrey story? Given her past, what would you have imagined the result would be?

In this lesson, you will learn about the following:

- High Intelligence: Nature or Nurture?
- What Are Learning Disabilities?

High Intelligence: Nature or Nurture?

The idea that intelligence could be a trait inherited from a person's parents means that intelligence would be considered ____________________.

Rank the following scenarios from 1 (highest degree of correlation) to 4 (lowest degree of correlation).

Relation	Rearing	Degree of Correlation between IQ Scores
Fraternal twins	Raised together	
Siblings	Raised together	
Identical twins	Raised together	
Identical twins	Raised apart	

On Your Own

If a clone of you was created today, would it be similar to you in behavior? Be sure to use *nature* and *nurture* in your answer.

With regard to the primary influence on intelligence, one study suggests that although

_________________ seem to be in control of the level of intelligence, the ______________________

influences provide both stability and change to trigger manifestation of cognitive abilities.

__________ _____ ______________ is the theory that each person responds to the environment in a unique way based on his or her genetic makeup. An individual's genetic potential is a _________ quantity, but whether the person reaches full intellectual potential is dependent on the __________________.

On Your Own

Paraphrase the following statement.

> "The two extremes of optimal and pathological experience are both represented disproportionately in the backgrounds of creative individuals" (Csikszentmihalyi & Csikszentmihalyi, 1993, p. 187).

Past IQ testing has shown a difference in racial performance. Provide a reason that has nothing to do with race as to why this difference may occur.

Arthur Jensen felt that intelligence was made up of two types of abilities. In his theory, Level ____ is responsible for rote memorization, whereas Level ____ is responsible for conceptual and analytical abilities.

According to Arthur Jensen, in which level of intelligence does each example fit?

Solving a mental math problem	
Remembering the definition for *encoding*	
Engaging in solving a Tower of Hanoi problem	

On Your Own

What do you think of the Jensen levels of intelligence compared to the different types of intelligences you have learned about previously?

Do you believe that IQ tests can be fair across socioeconomic circumstances? Explain your answer.

What Are Learning Disabilities?

________________ ________________ are cognitive disorders that affect different areas of cognition, particularly language or reading. These are considered specific neurological impairments rather than global intellectual or developmental disabilities.

____________________ is a learning disability in which individuals struggle to write legibly, whereas ________________ is when individuals have difficulty processing letters.

On Your Own

Why does it make sense that spatial difficulties may accompany dysgraphia?

Psychology and You

Reflection

Imagine that you have dysgraphia. How might your life be different than it is today?

Lesson Wrap-up

Say It in a Sentence

In one sentence, explain the influence of nature and nurture on intelligence.

Test Yourself

Choose the correct answer for each of the following questions. Check your work using the Answer Key in the back of the book.

____ 1. Which level of intelligence did Arthur Jensen believed differed between ethnic groups?

- **A.** Level I
- **B.** Level II
- **C.** Level III

____ 2. This learning disability is characterized by problems processing letters.

- **A.** Dysgraphia
- **B.** Dyslexia

____ 3. Which pair would have the highest correlation in IQ scores?

- **A.** Identical twins
- **B.** Fraternal twins
- **C.** Siblings
- **D.** Parent and child

Next to each statement, write **T** for True or **F** for False. Check your work using the Answer Key in the back of the book.

1. _____ Up to 70% of children with ADHD also have a learning disability.
2. _____ Identical twins have similar IQ scores, regardless of being raised together or apart.
3. _____ Nurture has the sole influence on intelligence levels.

Key Terms

Write a paraphrased definition for each key term.

Dysgraphia:

Dyslexia:

Range of Reaction:

Chapter 7
Memory

Lesson 7.1
How Memory Functions

OBJECTIVES

★ Discuss the three basic functions of memory.
★ Describe the three stages of memory storage.
★ Describe and distinguish between procedural and declarative memory and semantic and episodic memory.

BIG IDEA

Memory is the set of processes used to encode, store, and retrieve information over different periods of time. Like a computer, memory is an information processing system.

What are the three functions of memory?

[______________] ⟹ [______________] ⟹ [______________]

In this lesson, you will learn about the following:

- Encoding
- Storage
- Retrieval

Encoding

Encoding is the ______________ of information into the memory system. We receive ______________ information from the environment, and our brains ______________ or code it. Encoding information occurs through automatic processing and effortful processing.

Automatic processing is the encoding of ____________________ like time, space, frequency, and the meaning of words. It is usually done without any conscious ________________________.

Example:

What did you have for lunch? Where did you last park your car?

These are details that likely took no effort on your part to encode.

Effortful processing requires a lot of ______________________.

Example:

Learning how to drive requires effort and attention to encode important information.

There are three types of encoding. **Semantic encoding** is the encoding of __________________ and their ______________________. **Visual encoding** is the encoding of _________________, and **acoustic encoding** is the encoding of _____________________. We can better remember verbal information that is semantically encoded, especially if we apply the ________________________ _______________. This is the tendency to have better memory for information that relates to us. Have you ever remembered something new by relating it to your own experience?

On Your Own

Write at least one example of something you've remembered using each type of encoding:

Semantic	
Visual	
Acoustic	

Storage

Once the information has been encoded, we must somehow retain it. Our brains take the encoded information and place it in storage. ___________________ is the creation of a permanent record of information.

Memory gets stored by moving through three stages: **sensory memory,** _____________________ memory, and finally, _________________________ memory.

Fill in the missing parts of the following Atkinson-Shiffrin model of memory.

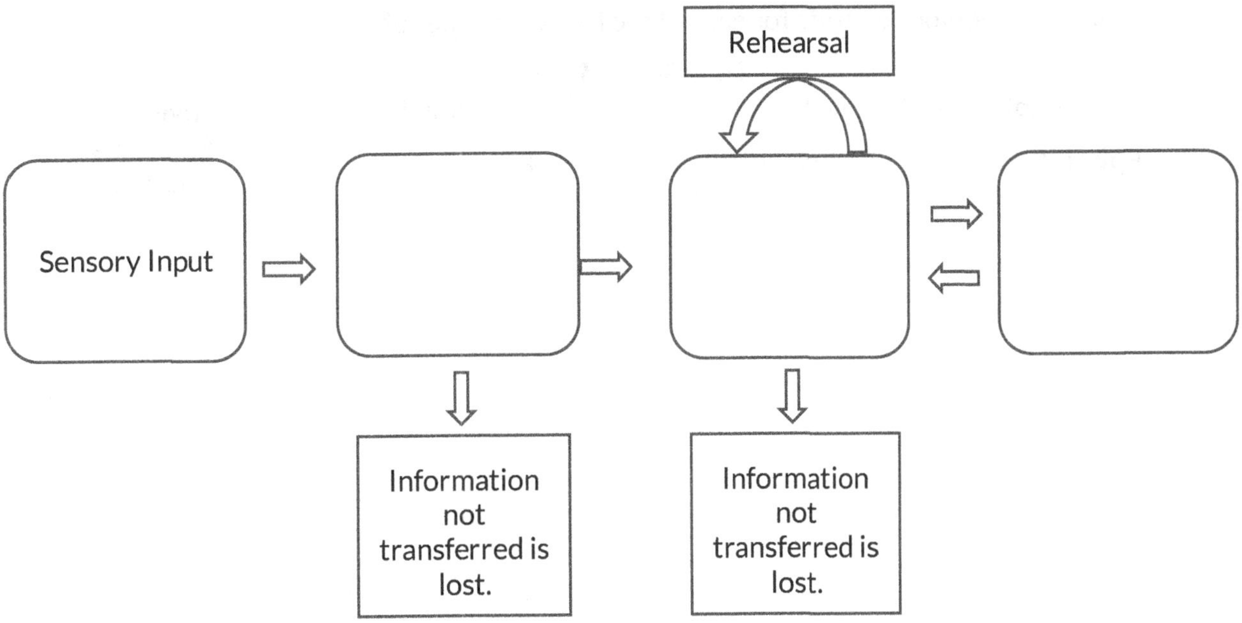

Sensory Memory

In the Atkinson-Shiffrin model, ____________________ from the environment are first stored in **sensory memory**: storage of brief sensory events such as sights, sounds, and tastes. This is very brief—up to a couple of ____________________.

Short-term Memory

Short-term memory (STM) is a temporary storage system that processes incoming sensory information; sometimes it is called ____________________ memory. We consolidate that information into our long-term memory through conscious repetition, or ____________________.

Long-term Memory

Long-term memory (LTM) is the ____________________ storage of information. Unlike short-term memory, LTM has no ____________________. It is divided into two types: ____________________ and implicit.

On Your Own

List some examples from your own life for each of the following types of memory:

Long-Term Memory			
Explicit (declarative)		Implicit (non-declarative)	
Episodic	Semantic	Procedural	Emotional Conditioning

Retrieval

Getting information out of storage is called **retrieval**. We do this in three main ways. Most often, we do this without any cues, a process called ____________________. When we remember information because we're encountering it again, it's called **recognition**. Sometimes, we need to **relearn** information in order to remember it.

Psychology and You

Making Lists

You can help yourself recall things by thinking about them sequentially and spatially. Try making a short list of grocery items by listing them in the order you'd pick them up at your local store.

1.
2.
3.
4.
5.
6.
7.
8.

Lesson Wrap-up

Say It in a Sentence

In only one sentence, summarize how memory functions.

Test Yourself

Next to each statement, write **T** for True or **F** for False. Check your work using the Answer Key in the back of the book.

1. ____ The storage capacity of long-term memory is essentially limitless.
2. ____ The three functions of memory are encoding, storage, and recall.
3. ____ Implicit memory is another name for short-term memory.
4. ____ If we rehearse information in our working memory, it moves into long-term memory for permanent storage.

Identify the type of retrieval illustrated in each of the following scenarios. Check your work using the Answer Key in the back of the book.

____ 5. Liv had not read music in ten years, but when she started taking violin lessons again, she was pleased at how quickly she was able to feel comfortable with it.

- **A.** Recall
- **B.** Recognition
- **C.** Relearning

____ 6. Peyton makes a cake by remembering the recipe her father told her over the phone.

- **A.** Recall
- **B.** Recognition
- **C.** Relearning

____ 7. Kristian has no trouble putting the answers in order once he sees them listed in front of him.

- **A.** Recall
- **B.** Recognition
- **C.** Relearning

Key Terms

Match each key term with its definition.

A. Automatic Processing	____	Input of information into the memory system
B. Declarative Memory	____	Creation of a permanent record of information
C. Encoding	____	Act of getting information out of long-term memory storage and back into conscious awareness
D. Memory	____	Input of words and their meaning
E. Semantic Encoding		

F. Storage	_____	Encoding of informational details like time, space, frequency, and the meaning of words
G. Recognition	_____	Type of long-term memory of facts and events we personally experience
H. Implicit Memory	_____	Identifying previously learned information after encountering it again, usually in response to a cue
I. Retrieval	_____	Memories that are not part of our consciousness
	_____	System or process that stores what we learn for future use

Lesson 7.2

Parts of the Brain Involved with Memory

OBJECTIVES

- ★ Explain the brain functions involved in memory.
- ★ Recognize the roles of the hippocampus, amygdala, and cerebellum.

BIG IDEA

While psychologists are still studying whether the whole brain or specific parts and neurons are involved in memory, we know that the amygdala, hippocampus, cerebellum, and prefrontal cortex play a critical role.

In this lesson, you will learn about the following:

- The Amygdala
- The Hippocampus
- The Cerebellum and Prefrontal Cortex
- Neurotransmitters

Fill in the following diagram.

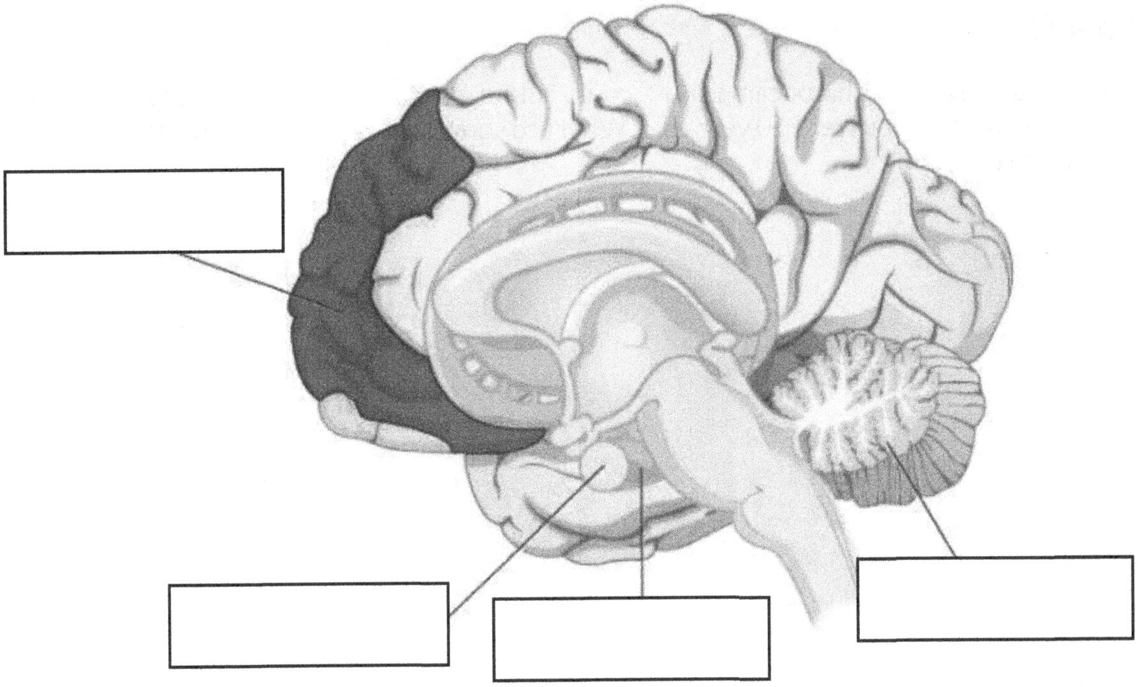

The Amygdala

The main job of the amygdala is to regulate ____________________, such as __________ and

__________________. The amygdala plays a part in how memories are stored because storage is

influenced by stress ____________________.

On Your Own

Design an experiment to test the role the amygdala plays in memory consolidation.

The Hippocampus

The hippocampus is involved in normal ________________ memory as well as ______________ memory. It also plays a role in giving memories ______________ and in memory ________________.

On Your Own

As a result of damage to his hippocampi, H.M. could not form new semantic knowledge. Imagine this happened to you when you were 10 years old. What are some things you know now that you wouldn't have been able to retain?

The Cerebellum and Prefrontal Cortex

The cerebellum plays a role in the creation of ______________ memories (procedural memory, motor learning, classical conditioning). Researchers have found that rabbits with damaged cerebellums were not able to learn a ____________________ eye-blink response when subjected to a puff of air in the eye.

Brain scans (such as PET scans) have shown increased activation in the left __________________ cortex when participants are given ________________ tasks, and __________________ of information is associated with the right frontal region.

Neurotransmitters

Which neurotransmitters appear to be involved with the process of memory?

1.
2.
3.
4.
5.

The _______________ theory posits that _______________ emotions trigger the formation of strong memories, and _____________ emotions form weaker memories. The clearest representation of this theory is the ___________________ memory phenomenon.

Psychology and You

Flashbulb Memories

Think about a memory that is incredibly clear to you because of the emotional state you were in at the time. What details do you remember? Why do you think this event or memory stands out to you?

Lesson Wrap-up

Say It in a Sentence

In one sentence, explain what we don't know about the parts of the brain involved in memory.

Test Yourself

Choose the correct answer for each of the following questions. Check your work using the Answer Key in the back of the book.

____ 1. Olivia's dog Milton doesn't seem to be responding to classical conditioning after an accident. Which part of the brain might have been affected?

A. Cerebellum
B. Amygdala
C. Hippocampus
D. Right prefrontal cortex

____ 2. Alyssa remembers her ride-along with an EMT as part of her nursing program in incredible detail because of the emotional impact of losing a patient. Which of the following does this represent?

A. Engram
B. James-Lange theory
C. Flashbulb memory
D. Equipotentiality hypothesis

Next to each statement, write **T** for True or **F** for False. Check your work using the Answer Key in the back of the book.

3. _____ There is a scientific consensus regarding precisely which parts of the brain are involved in memory.

4. _____ Memory consolidation is the process of transferring new learning into long-term memory.

5. _____ We know exactly which neurotransmitter plays each role in memory.

Key Terms

Match each key term with its definition.

A. Arousal Theory
B. Engram
C. Equipotentiality Hypothesis
D. Flashbulb Memory

_____ Physical trace of memory
_____ Some parts of the brain can take over for damaged parts in forming and storing memories
_____ Strong emotions trigger the formation of strong memories, and weaker emotional experiences form weaker memories
_____ Exceptionally clear recollection of an important event

Lesson 7.3

Problems with Memory

OBJECTIVES

- ★ Compare and contrast the two types of amnesia.
- ★ Discuss the unreliability of eyewitness testimony.
- ★ Discuss encoding failure.
- ★ Discuss the various memory errors.
- ★ Compare and contrast the two types of interference.

BIG IDEA

Although many people feel that their memory is infallible, it is actually relatively fragile and can often be incorrect for a variety of reasons.

On Your Own

How would you characterize your memory? Is it relatively good or bad? Provide an example.

In this lesson, you will learn about the following:

- Amnesia
- Memory Construction and Reconstruction
- Forgetting

Amnesia

Amnesia is the loss of ____________________ memory that occurs as the result of disease, physical trauma, or psychological trauma.

On Your Own

Imagine living life as K.C. How would your life be different than it is today? What would you find most difficult?

Anterograde Amnesia

An individual with anterograde amnesia cannot remember ____________ ____________________ but can still remember information from his or her past. The ________________________ is usually affected, resulting in an inability to move short-term information to long-term memory.

On Your Own

Jim has anterograde amnesia; a rare type of tumor that impacted his hippocampus had to be removed to save his life. What kinds of information might Jim still be able to learn?

Complete the following table based on the abilities of Henry Molaison (H.M.).

New Activity	Could He Remember Later?	Type of Memory Used
Meeting someone new	No	Episodic
Reading a book		
Learning the state capitals		
Solving a spatial puzzle		

Complete the following graphic.

Retrograde Amnesia

An individual with retrograde amnesia has experienced loss of memory for events that occurred

____________ the trauma.

On Your Own

Imagine life with retrograde amnesia. How might your family or close friends help you cope?

Memory Construction and Reconstruction

The formulation of new memories is called ________________, whereas the process of bringing up old memories is called ____________________.

On Your Own

Based on the lesson, would you say that our memories are flawless? Why or why not?

In 2015, Brian Williams, a well-known news anchor, told a story about how he was in a helicopter that was shot down in 2003. However, in 2003, he indicated that he was not in the helicopter that was shot down. Some people thought he deliberately changed the story to make himself seem the victim. Others claimed it was an innocent memory issue that could happen to anyone. What do you think?

Suggestibility

Suggestibility describes the effects of misinformation from external sources that leads to the creation of

_____________ memories.

On Your Own

What is your reaction to the story about the white van? How could so many people report seeing a white van?

Eyewitness Misidentification

On Your Own

Do you support the use of eyewitness testimony? Why or why not?

What were some differences between the way the Jennifer Thompson case and the Elizabeth Smart case were handled?

Thompson Case	Smart Case

The Misinformation Effect

The misinformation effect paradigm occurs when a person may misremember the original event based on exposure to ____________ ____________.

On Your Own

In the Loftus and Palmer (1974) study, individuals were asked to rate the speed of a car that had just been in an accident. The researchers varied the wording and found that the words used could evoke different speeds. How would you change the study? What results would you expect from your manipulations?

Controversies over Repressed and Recovered Memories

The ________ ____________ syndrome, or the recall of false autobiographical memories, has received a great deal of publicity.

On Your Own

In the Ceci and Brucks (1993, 1995) studies, a majority of three-year-old children reported that their doctors had touched their genitals even though that event did not happen. What is your reaction to this study?

Forgetting

Forgetting refers to loss of information from ____________ memory.

Encoding Failure

Sometimes, memory loss happens ______________ the actual memory process begins, which is encoding failure. We cannot remember something if we never stored it in our memory in the first place.

On Your Own

What do you encode about a penny? A quarter?

Memory Errors

Complete the following table of Schachter's memory sins:

Sin	Description
	Accessibility of memory decreases over time
Absentmindedness	
Blocking	Accessibility of information is temporarily blocked
	Source of memory is confused
Suggestibility	
Bias	Memories distorted by current belief system
Persistence	

In which category does each of the 7 memory sins fall?

Forgetting	Distortion	Intrusion

On Your Own

What are the implications of Ebbinghaus' work for your education?

Describe a time when you experienced misattribution.

Which bias is present in the following scenarios (egocentric, stereotypic, or hindsight)?

- ________________: Remembering always getting good grades (when you did not always get good grades)
- ________________: Remembering a fight that supports the fact that you broke up with your significant other even though that fight never actually happened
- ________________: Remembering a student's name as "Deja" because she is African-American when it is actually "Dana"

Interference

Sometimes, information is stored in memory but is inaccessible. For instance, when old information impairs the ability to recall newly learned information, ________________ ________________ has occurred. On the other hand, ________________ ________________ occurs when recently learned information impairs the ability to recall old information.

On Your Own

Check the box next to the type of interference that applies to each of the following scenarios.

You cannot remember your address from ten years ago:

- ☐ Retroactive interference
- ☐ Proactive interference

After getting a new phone number, you continue to tell people your old one:

- ☐ Retroactive interference
- ☐ Proactive interference

You continue to write the wrong year on your papers after the New Year:

- ☐ Retroactive interference
- ☐ Proactive interference

You can only remember your current zip code, not the one for your childhood home:

- ☐ Retroactive interference
- ☐ Proactive interference

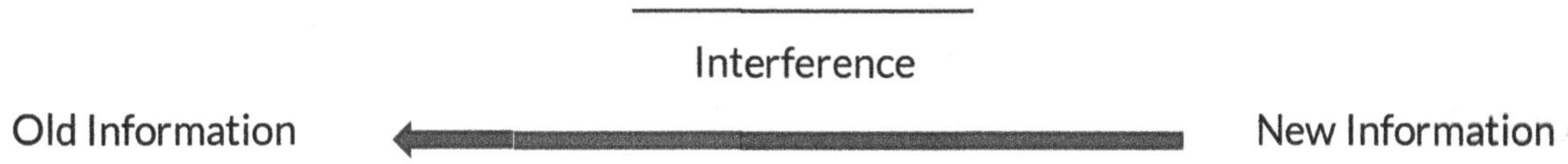

On Your Own

Answer each of the following short answer questions.

Based on what you read in the lesson, would you agree that most people who experience sexual abuse as children remember those experiences? Explain your answer.

Elizabeth Loftus argues that recovered memories are likely incorrect, whereas proponents of the Recovered Memory Project feel that pulling forth repressed memories helps individuals in the healing process. Whom do you believe, and why?

If you were a police officer in charge of questioning a child about a recent crime, how would you handle the situation?

Psychology and You

Retroactive and Proactive Interference Examples

Provide examples of when you experienced retroactive and proactive interference.

Lesson Wrap-up

Say It in a Sentence

In one sentence, explain the seven sins of memory.

Test Yourself

Choose the correct answer for the following questions. Check your work using the Answer Key in the back of the book.

____ 1. In the Loftus and Palmer (1974) study, which verb resulted in the highest speed ratings?

A. Smashed
B. Bumped
C. Contacted
D. Hit

____ 2. After receiving electroconvulsive therapy, Curtis can no longer remember what happened a few days prior to the treatment. He is experiencing:

A. Prograde amnesia
B. Retrograde amnesia
C. Anterograde amnesia

____ 3. When asked how old he is, eight-year-old Joey replies, "Seven! Wait, I'm eight!" Which type of interference occurred?

A. Proactive interference
B. Retroactive interference
C. Anteroactive interference

Key Terms

For each key term, provide an example that exemplifies the meaning of the word.

Absentmindedness:

Amnesia:

Anterograde amnesia:

Bias:

Blocking:

Construction:

False Memory Syndrome:

Forgetting:

Misattribution:

Misinformation Effect Paradigm:

Persistence:

Proactive Interference:

Reconstruction:

Retroactive Interference:

Retrograde Amnesia:

Suggestibility:

Transience:

Lesson 7.4

Ways to Enhance Memory

OBJECTIVES

★ Recognize and apply memory-enhancing strategies.
★ Recognize and apply effective study techniques.

BIG IDEA

Given that our memories are often faulty, there are a variety of ways that individuals can enhance their memories in everyday life.

On Your Own

Do you use any memory-enhancing strategies? What are they?

In this lesson, you will learn about the following:

- Memory-Enhancing Strategies
- How to Study Effectively

Memory-Enhancing Strategies

______________ ______________ can help make sure that information moves from short-term memory to long-term memory. There are a variety of strategies one can use.

______________ involves the conscious repetition of information.

On Your Own

Do you use rehearsal when studying information? How well does it work for you?

______________ is a way to organize information into manageable pieces.

______________ ______________ involves thinking about the meaning of new information and its relation to already stored knowledge.

On Your Own

Give an example of how you use elaborative rehearsal when studying for your classes.

________________ ________________ are memory aids that help us organize information for encoding.

On Your Own

You have likely been taught a number of mnemonic devices over the course your life. For example, children are often taught ROY G BIV for the colors of the rainbow (Red, Orange, Yellow, Green, Blue, Indigo, and Violet). What are three other mnemonics you have been taught or created yourself?

What are the memory-enhancing strategies included in the lesson?

1.
2.
3.
4.
5.
6.

How to Study Effectively

There are a multitude of ways to apply psychological knowledge to enhancing how students study. For instance, Craik and Lockhart (1972) suggest using ________________ ________________ to ensure information goes more deeply into long-term memory. This theory is called ____________ ________ ________________. It would be even more beneficial to memory if students were able to elaborately rehearse in a way that was personally meaningful, as they would benefit from the ____________________ effect.

On Your Own

Imagine that you have a test tomorrow. What 8 methods that the lesson suggests would improve your memory (and hopefully your performance)?

1.
2.
3.
4.
5.
6.
7.
8.

Psychology and You

Study Habits

Using the methods from this lesson, how do you intend to change your study habits? Be sure to incorporate three different methods to help enhance your memory.

Lesson Wrap-up

Say It in a Sentence

In one sentence, describe mnemonic devices.

Test Yourself

Choose the correct answer for each of the following questions. Check your work using the Answer Key in the back of the book.

____ 1. When Brigitte provides her phone number to the credit card company, she says "91-7345-21-42," which confuses the operator. Brigitte violated which rule for memory enhancement?

- **A.** Rehearsal
- **B.** Chunking
- **C.** Elaborative rehearsal
- **D.** Mnemonic devices

____ 2. In a study by Yogo and Fujihara (2008) participants were able to increase their recall for _______ by using expressive writing.

- **A.** vocabulary words
- **B.** traumatic events
- **C.** best-selling novels

____ 3. Students often use catchy sayings or the first letter of words in a list to make a new word to trigger memory during exams. These methods would be considered:

- **A.** Rehearsal
- **B.** Chunking
- **C.** Mnemonic devices

Next to each statement, write **T** for True or **F** for False. Check your work using the Answer Key in the back of the book.

4. ______ When Ryan breaks a long number into smaller groups, he is using a mnemonic device.

5. _____ "Oh, Oh, Oh To Take A Family Vacation! Go Vegas After Hours!" would be considered a mnemonic device because it is used to remember the 12 cranial nerves of the brain.

6. _____ Simply repeating something over and over is an example of elaborative rehearsal.

Key Terms

Match each key term with its definition.

A. Chunking
B. Elaborative Rehearsal
C. Levels of Processing
D. Memory-Enhancing Strategy
E. Mnemonic Device

_____ Technique to help make sure information goes from short-term to long-term memory

_____ Organizing information into manageable bits

_____ Memory aids that help organize information for encoding

_____ Thinking about the meaning of the new information and its relation to knowledge already stored in your memory

_____ Information that is thought of more deeply becomes more meaningful and thus better committed to memory

Chapter 8
Lifespan Development

Lesson 8.1
What Is Lifespan Development?

OBJECTIVES

- ★ Define and distinguish between the three domains of development: physical, cognitive, and psychosocial.
- ★ Discuss the normative approach to development.
- ★ Understand the three major issues in development: continuity and discontinuity, one common course of development or many unique courses of development, and nature versus nurture.

BIG IDEA

Lifespan development examines how individuals grow and develop from birth until death, taking into account not only physical but also psychosocial and cognitive growth.

On Your Own

Are you the same person you were as a child? Has your personality changed or stayed the same? Explain.

In this lesson, you will learn about the following:

- What Is Lifespan Development?
- Issues in Developmental Psychology

____________________ psychologists study how humans change and grow from conception through childhood, adolescence, adulthood, and death. They see development as ________________, and it can be focused on physical, cognitive, or psychosocial development. _________________ development involves growth and changes in the body, brain, sense, motor skills, and health. _________________ development involves learning, attention, memory, language, and thinking. Finally, ___________________ development involves emotions, personality, and social relationships.

Developmental psychologists use a variety of research methods. In ______________________

______________________, individuals are observed in their natural environments. _____________ _________________ involve in-depth investigation into a single individual or a small group of people. The _______________ method asks individuals to self-report important information about their thoughts, feelings, and beliefs. Finally, ___________________ involve significant control over extraneous variables and manipulation of the independent variable.

Complete the following table by naming the type of research method that each example portrays.

Study	Research Method
Children are shown videos of different levels of aggression and then observed to see if they display aggression.	
Child peer interactions are observed on the playground.	
A psychologist spends many hours working with a child with autism to best understand his or her developmental pattern.	
Researchers asks high school students to provide anonymous information about their patterns of drug use.	

The ____________________ approach attempts to determine normal developmental patterns. The goal is to establish _________________, or average ages, where children should be reaching certain _________________________ milestones, such as crawling or walking.

On Your Own

Provide an example of how developmental milestones might differ across cultures.

Issues in Developmental Psychology

On Your Own

What are the three predominant issues in developmental psychology? Provide an example of each.

1.

2.

3.

Is Development Continuous or Discontinuous?

________________ ____________________ views development as a cumulative process, gradually improving on existing skills. On the other hand, __________________ ____________________ posits that development takes place in unique stages.

On Your Own

Provide an example of an aspect of development that fits continuous development and an example of discontinuous development.

Label the following graphics as either continuous or discontinuous.

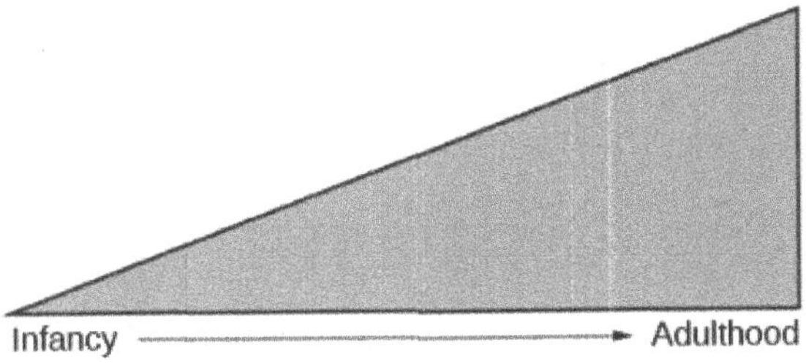

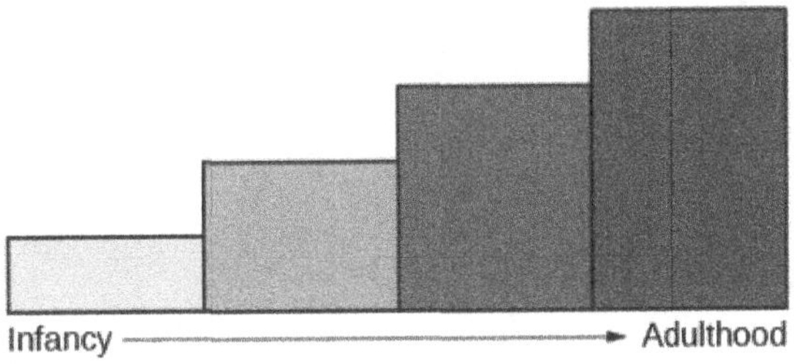

Is There One Course of Development or Many?

Stage theories hold that the sequence of development is ____________________.

On Your Own

Given the impact of culture on developmental milestones, do you feel we should even have milestones that we publish to parents? Explain.

How Do Nature and Nurture Influence Development?

One long-standing question in psychology is the nature versus nurture debate. Specifically, are personalities and traits the product of ________________ through genetic makeup and biological factors, or are they shaped by ________________ via environment?

The ________________ ____________ refers to the persistent difference in grades, test scores, and graduation rates that exist among students of different ethnicities, races, and sexes.

On Your Own

What do you think could be implemented to help eliminate the achievement gap?

Psychology and You

Design an Experiment

Imagine you want to study cognitive development between ages 5 and 7. Describe an experiment that you might conduct to investigate how kids change in the way they think.

Lesson Wrap-up

Say It in a Sentence

In one sentence, describe the nature versus nurture debate.

Test Yourself

Choose the correct answer for each of the following questions. Check your work using the Answer Key in the back of the book.

____ 1. A primary difference between low-income parents and high-income parents was:

- **A.** High-income parents spent more money on necessities for their children.
- **B.** Low-income parents worked more than high-income parents.
- **C.** High-income parents talked to their children more than low-income parents.

____ 2. Before entering kindergarten, children of high-income parents outperformed children of low-income parents by _______ on achievement tests.

A. 60%
B. 50%
C. 40%

____ 3. If a person's intelligence was completely determined by genetics, _________ would be in control.

A. nature
B. nurture

Answer each of the following questions. Check your work using the Answer Key in the back of the book.

4. Your friend says, "People from different cultures learn language in a different sequence than we do." Is that true? Explain your answer.

5. Your friend says, "Babies around the world all start to walk around the same time of life." Is that true? Explain your answer.

Key Terms

For the following key terms, make groupings out of the related terms. Be sure to explain how they are related.

Key Terms: cognitive development, continuous development, developmental milestone, discontinuous development, nature, normative approach, nurture, physical development, psychosocial development

Lesson 8.2

Lifespan Theories

OBJECTIVES

★ Discuss Freud's theory of psychosexual development.
★ Describe the major tasks of children and adult psychosocial development according to Erikson.
★ Discuss Piaget's view of cognitive development and apply the stages to understanding childhood cognition.
★ Describe Kohlberg's theory of moral development.

BIG IDEA

Sigmund Freud, Erik Erikson, Jean Piaget, and Lawrence Kohlberg developed theories to explain how children develop into adults across cognitive, psychosocial, and moral domains.

In this lesson, you will learn about the following:

- Psychosexual Theory of Development
- Psychosocial Theory of Development
- Cognitive Theory of Development
- Theory of Moral Development

Psychosexual Theory of Development

Sigmund Freud believed that personality developed during early childhood. He believed that each of us must pass through a series of ____________________ stages, which best fits with a ____________________ view of development. For Freud, development was based on ____________________ urges that were centered on different ____________________ zones.

What are Freud's psychosexual stages in order?

Psychosocial Theory of Development

Erik Erikson also had a ____________________ view of development and believed that children developed through various ____________________ stages that spanned from birth until death. Erikson suggested that how individuals interact with others is what affects sense of self, or ____________________.

In Erikson's stages, there is a ________________ that individuals need to resolve to successfully navigate out of that stage with a sense of ____________________ and a healthy personality.

Trust vs. mistrust (stage 1) refers to the stage where ____________________ and sensitive caregivers help a child develop trust in the world as a safe and predictable place. On the other hand, unresponsive caregivers can teach children that the world is ________________________.

In ______________________ vs. doubt (stage 2), a toddler must establish independence to gain confidence in his or her own abilities.

On Your Own

Your friend exclaims, "I am so frustrated! My daughter will not let me help her do anything; she always insists that she does it and then ends up making a mess or screaming because she isn't capable!" You know that your friend's daughter is 2 years old. What advice would you give her based on Erikson's theory of development?

During preschool, children are capable of initiating activities and asserting control through ____________ __________________ and play. In order to successfully navigate initiative vs. _____________(stage 3), children must learn to plan and achieve goals while interacting with others.

On Your Own

What can parents do to ensure their children successfully navigate the initiative vs. guilt stage of development?

Between the ages of 6 and 12, children face a conflict of industry vs. ________________. Children begin to develop a sense of pride and accomplishment, or they feel ____________________ based on comparisons with their peers.

On Your Own

When you were younger, do you remember feelings of inadequacy in comparison to your peer group? What were they, and how did you handle them?

In ____________________, children face the task of identity vs. ____________ ____________________.

According to Erikson, an adolescent's main task is developing a sense of __________. Common questions include "Who am I?" and "What do I want to do with my life?"

On Your Own

During your identity vs. role confusion stage, did you try on different selves? Describe. Are you still different people among others in your life (i.e., you act differently with a grandparent than with your best friend)?

People in early adulthood are concerned with _________________ vs. isolation. After we have developed a sense of self, we are ready to share our life with others.

Middle adulthood is centered around generativity vs. ____________________. Individuals want to find their life's work and contribute to the development of others.

The final stage of Erikson's theory encompasses the end of life. As individuals approach death, they will reflect on their lives and either feel __________________ or failure depending on how they lived their lives. This stage is the _______________ vs. _______________ stage.

Complete the following table of Erikson's stages.

Stage	Age	Language Development
1	Birth to 1 year	
2		Autonomy vs. shame/doubt
3	3 to 6 years	
4	7 to 11 years	
5		Identity vs. confusion

6	19 to 29 years	
7		Generativity vs. stagnation
8		Integrity vs. despair

Cognitive Theory of Development

Jean Piaget focused on ________________ growth with his ____________________ view of development. He believed that children do not think and reason like adults; instead, cognitive development grows through ___________ distinct stages.

_________________ are concepts used to categorize and interpret information. When children learn new information, they adjust their schemata. In some cases, the new information is added to a current category of knowledge (a process called __________________). In other cases, the schemata needs to be changed based on the new information (a process called ______________________).

On Your Own

For the following scenarios, identify if Blake is performing accommodation or assimilation.

1. Blake points and says, "Dog!"
   His father says, "No, that is a cat."

   Blake learns the distinction between a dog and a cat.

   ☐ Accommodation
   ☐ Assimilation

2. "Dog?" Blake asks after seeing a Chihuahua.
   His father replies, "Yes, that is a dog."

   Blake adds Chihuahua to his dog category.

   ☐ Accommodation
   ☐ Assimilation

Complete the following table of Piaget's cognitive stages.

Stage	Age	Language Development
	Birth to 2 years	
Preoperational		Use words and images to represent things, but lack logical reasoning

	7 to 11 years	
Formal operational	12+ years	

Piaget's first stage, the ______________________ stage, involved learning about the world through senses and motor behavior. ______________ ______________________, understanding that something out of sight still exists, develops during this stage.

The ___________________________ stage involves the ability to use symbols and engage in _______________ play. However, these children are still cognitively limited as they have difficulty manipulating _________________ ________________________.

On Your Own

The inability to understand conservation can sometimes result in a child getting tricked. An older child or adult might say, "I will give you these two pieces of money for your one piece of money." However, the trade is actually taking a $5 bill from the child and replacing it with two $1 bills. Provide an example of a way that a child can be tricked via lack of conservation abilities.

Egocentrism refers to a child's inability to take the ______________________ of others. A child at this stage thinks that everyone sees, thinks, and feels just as the child does.

On Your Own

Do you believe egocentrism exists at older ages? Explain your answer.

The ___________________ operational stage involves children being able to think logically about real events. They are able to engage in mathematical thinking, are fully capable of conservation, and understand ______________________, or the idea that an object can be changed and then returned to its original state.

The final Piagetian stage, the ________________ operational stage, involves full cognitive reasoning.

Children in this stage can use abstract thinking and deal in ______________________ situations.

Beyond Formal Operational Thought

On Your Own

What are three criticisms of Piaget's cognitive theory of development?

1.

2.

3.

Do you agree that adults beyond age 20 are in the postformal stage? Why or why not?

Theory of Moral Development

Similar to Piaget, Freud, and Erikson, Lawrence Kohlberg also had a ______________________ view of development. He believed that morality developed across a series of stages of moral reasoning.

On Your Own

How would you answer the Heinz dilemma?

Complete the following graphic describing Kohlberg's stages of moral reasoning.

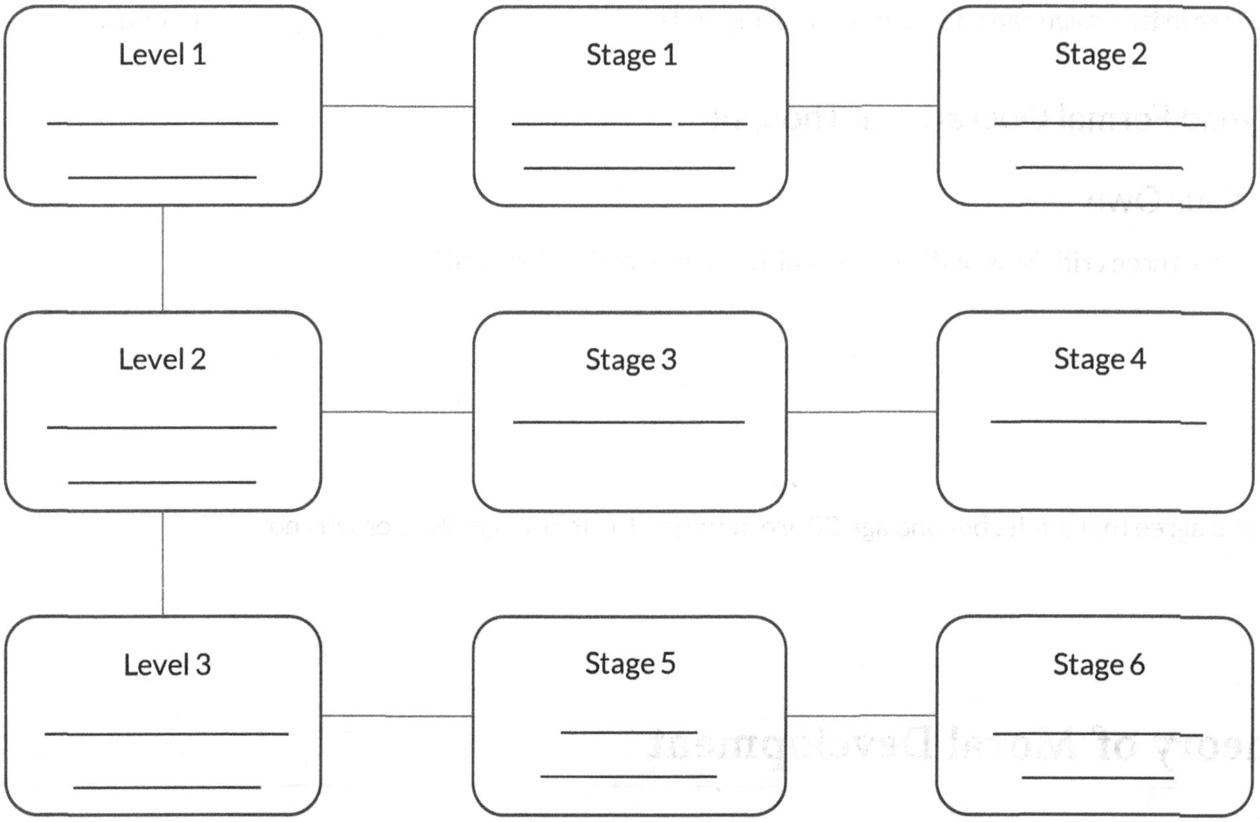

On Your Own

Where do you think you fall in the stages of moral reasoning? Explain your answer.

Psychology and You

Erikson's Stages

Which of Erikson's stages are you currently in? Explain.

Lesson Wrap-up

Say It in a Sentence

In one sentence, explain the difference between assimilation and accommodation.

Test Yourself

Choose the correct answer for each of the following questions. Check your work using the Answer Key in the back of the book.

____ 1. What do Freud's and Erikson's theories have in common?

- **A.** A focus on sexual energy
- **B.** A discontinuous view of development
- **C.** A continuous view of development
- **D.** A focus on social interactions

____ 2. Joe is not really sure what he believes or how to behave in certain situations. Sometimes, he neglects his appearance and acts moody. Other times, he cleans up and is polite and studious. It is likely he is in which of Erikson's stages?

- **A.** Trust vs. mistrust
- **B.** Autonomy vs. shame
- **C.** Identity vs. role confusion
- **D.** Intimacy vs. isolation

____ 3. Chloe, a 2-year-old, is learning that objects can be banged on the table. She bangs a ball, and it makes a great noise. She grabs a nearby bowl and bangs it on the table. Instead of making a great noise, it breaks. Chloe now makes a distinction between things that can be banged on the table and things that cannot. What has occurred?

- **A.** Accommodation
- **B.** Assimilation
- **C.** Equilibrium

Answer each of the following questions. Check your work using the Answer Key in the back of the book.

4. Compare Freud's and Erikson's theories of development.

5. Your friend has an infant who constantly tosses objects off his high chair. Your friend expresses frustration about the baby's behavior. Based on what you have learned about Piaget's theory of cognitive development, what advice would you give your friend?

6. What are Piaget's cognitive stages in order?

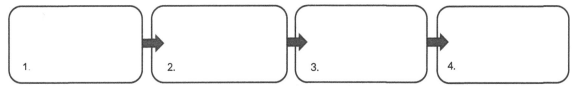

1. → 2. → 3. → 4.

Key Terms

Match each key term with its definition.

A. Assimilation
B. Accommodation
C. Concrete Operational Stage
D. Conservation
E. Egocentrism
F. Formal Operational Stage
G. Object Permanence
H. Preoperational Stage
I. Psychosexual Development
J. Psychosocial Development
K. Reversibility
L. Schema
M. Sensorimotor Stage
N. Stage of Moral Reasoning

_____ The idea that even if you change the appearance of something, it is still equal in size, volume, or number as long as nothing is added or removed

_____ Process proposed by Freud in which pleasure-seeking urges focus on different erogenous zones of the body as humans move through five stages of life

_____ From ages 2 to 7, children learn to use symbols and language but do not understand mental operations and often think illogically.

_____ Process proposed by Kohlberg

_____ From age 11 on, children are able to deal with abstract ideas and hypothetical situations.

_____ Adjustment of a schema by adding information similar to what is already known

_____ From 7 to 11 years, children can think logically about real events.

_____ Principle that objects can be changed but then returned back to their original form or condition

_____ Concept that is used to help categorize and interpret information

_____ Adjustment of a schema by changing a scheme to add new information different from what is already known

_____ Preoperational child's difficulty in taking the perspective of others

_____ Process proposed by Erikson in which social tasks are mastered as humans move through eight stags of life from infancy to adulthood

_____ Idea that even if something is out of sight, it still exists

_____ From birth through age 2, a child learns about the world through senses and motor behavior.

Lesson 8.3

Stages of Development

OBJECTIVES

- ★ Describe the stages of prenatal development and recognize the importance of prenatal care.
- ★ Discuss physical, cognitive, and emotional development that occurs from infancy through childhood.
- ★ Discuss physical, cognitive, and emotional development that occurs during adolescence.
- ★ Discuss physical, cognitive, and emotional development that occurs in adulthood.

BIG IDEA

From birth to death, there are a number of stages individuals go through that impact cognitive, physical, and emotional development.

In this lesson, you will learn about the following:

- Prenatal Development
- Infancy through Childhood
- Adolescence
- Adulthood

Prenatal Development

What are the three stages of prenatal development?

1.

2.

3.

Germinal Stage (Weeks 1–2)

________________ occurs when sperm fertilizes an egg and forms a ________________, a one-cell structure that begins to divide through a process called ________________. In the germinal stage, the mass of cells has yet to attach to the uterus lining.

On Your Own

Henry VIII blamed his wives when they gave birth to daughters instead of sons. Based on the lesson, what was wrong with blaming the women?

Embryonic Stage (Weeks 3–8)

After the ______________ divides and implants into the lining of the uterus, it is now called a(n)

_____________. The _________________, the structure connected to the uterus that provides nourishment and oxygen from the mother to the embryo, forms.

Fetal Stage (Weeks 9–40)

After nine weeks, the embryo is called a ____________. From _____ to _______ weeks, sexual differentiation begins. By around ________ weeks, internal organs, such as the lungs, stomach, heart, and intestines, have formed and could function outside of the mother if necessary. Around ________ weeks, the fetus is almost ready to be born.

Prenatal Influences

________________ ____________, which is medical care received during pregnancy that monitors the health of the baby and the mother, has been shown to reduce complications. It is important that mothers watch their exposure to harmful substances because they can pass through the _______________ to the fetus.

Complete the table about teratogens and their likely effects.

Teratogen	Effects on Fetus
	Poor judgement, impulse control, higher rates of ADHD and learning issues
	Addiction, seizures

On Your Own

If you saw an obviously pregnant woman at a bar with a beer in her hand, would you say anything? Why or why not?

Do you believe that women who use drugs or alcohol during pregnancy should be punished in some way? Explain your answer.

Infancy through Childhood

Although small, a newborn is not completely helpless because of newborn _______________, inborn automatic responses to particular forms of stimulation.

Complete the table of reflexes.

Reflex Name	Infant Behavior
	Turns head towards touched cheek
	Spread arms out, pull them back in, and cry

On Your Own

Newborn infants show a variety of preferences shortly after birth. List those preferences that have been shown experimentally.

1.
2.
3.
4.

Physical Development

On average, newborns weigh between 5 and 10 pounds, and a newborn's weight typically _______________ in six months and _______________ in one year. By 2 years old, the weight will have ______________________.

When it comes to brain development, individuals undergo a period of _____________________, when thousands of new connections are formed during the first few years of life. On the other hand, ________________, during which neural connections are reduced, occurs through childhood and into adolescence.

Motor development occurs in an orderly sequence as infants move from ______________________ ___________________ to more advanced motor functioning. _______________ skills refer to our ability to move our bodies and manipulate objects. _______________ motor skills focus on muscles in our fingers, toes, and eyes and enable coordination of small actions. _______________ motor skills focus on large muscle groups that control our arms and legs and involve larger movements.

Consider the following activities and label each as *fine* or *gross* based on the type of motor skills required.

- Drawing a picture of a tree:
- Kicking a ball as far as possible:
- Counting quarters:
- Walking along a curb without falling off:

Are the following milestones realistic? Label each with *yes* or *no*.

Realistic Milestone	Child's Age	Behavior
	2 years	Using 2 to 4 words in short sentences
	3 years	Playing make-believe
	2 years	Catching a ball successfully
	3 years	Understanding the difference between real and pretend

Cognitive Development

Piaget thought that children's ability to understand objects was a cognitive skill that develops slowly as a child matures and ________________ with the environment. Today, developmental psychologists think children understand objects ________________ they get a chance to interact with them.

On Your Own

What do you think about Baillargeon's assertion that 3-month-old infants know solid objects cannot pass through each other? Is this assertion reasonable?

Between 3 and 5 years of age, children develop ________________________, which is the understanding that people have thoughts, feelings, and beliefs that are different from their own.

Cognitive skills continue to expand into middle and late childhood as thought processes become more ________________ and organized when dealing with __________________ information.

When it comes to language development, babies begin this process ________________ birth. At birth, babies can recognize their mother's voice and discriminate between languages spoken in their home.

Children communicate via ____________ before they can speak.

What is the progression of spoken language development?

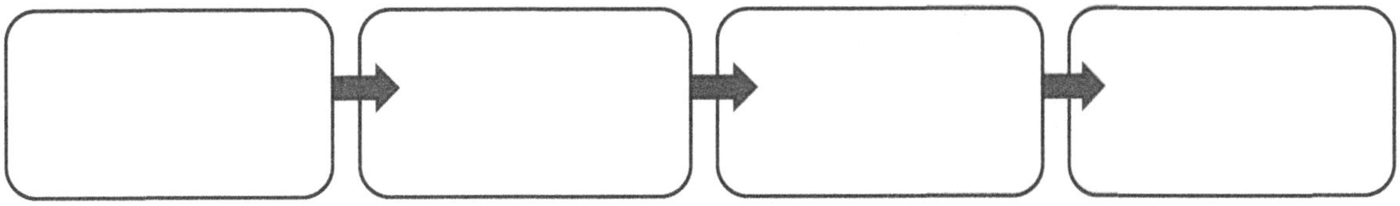

________ ____________ thought that individuals learn language in response to reinforcement and punishment, whereas ____________ ______________ felt that individuals have an inborn capacity to learn language via a mechanism called a ____________ ______________ ____________. Both men are probably correct since there is likely an interplay between nature and nurture when it comes to language development.

Attachment

______________ development occurs as children form relationships, interact with others, and understand and manage their feelings. ________________ is a long-standing connection or bond with others.

On Your Own

A new father feels he cannot form an attachment with his new baby because the baby is breastfed. Using the study performed by Harry Harlow, educate the new father about attachment.

________ __________ developed the concept of attachment theory. He defined attachment as the affectional bond or tie that an infant forms with the ____________. He felt that parents served as a ____________ __________, which provided children with a sense of safety as they explore the world.

On Your Own

What are the two things that John Bowlby said were essential for healthy attachment? After listing them, provide an example of a healthy attachment.

__________ ________________, another attachment researcher, studied whether attachment could vary. She developed and used the ______________ __________________ task to study attachment between others and their infants.

On Your Own

What was the Strange Situation procedure?

Identify the attachment styles demonstrated by the following scenarios.

- __________________: Caregiver used as secure base; infant distressed when caregiver leaves, happy upon caregiver's return
- __________________: Clingy but rejecting toward caregiver; too fearful to explore; angry at caregiver when left with stranger
- __________________: Freeze, run erratically around the room, or run away when caregiver returns
- __________________: Infant unresponsive to caregiver, does not care if caregiver leaves

Self-Concept

The primary psychosocial milestone of childhood is the development of a positive ________________ _______ ________________. Children must develop a ________________________, which is an understanding of who they are.

Once a self-concept has been established, children show an increase in _______________ behavior, and _________________ roles develop. By ______ years of age, children can cooperate with others, share when asked, and separate from their parents. By ______ years of age, children identify themselves as members of groups, such as which grade they are in. As these children age, they better realize their characteristics in comparison to their peers.

On Your Own

What are the benefits of a positive self-concept?

1.

2.

3.

4.

Diana Baumrind described four __________________ styles that may influence a child's self-concept. Identify the parenting style each scenario demonstrates.

- ______________________: Shayla has no curfew and no real rules. She knows her mom and dad lover her unconditionally, but she has little guidance.
- ______________________: When asked if Clay can stay out later, Clay's father responds, "Absolutely not. Curfew is 9 p.m., and that is final."
- ______________________: Tyler's parents generally have little idea where he is on any given day. He largely takes care of himself.
- ______________________: Carrie's parents agree to flex the curfew rules on Saturday to accommodate the school dance.

Children can differ based on the types of parenting styles they experienced. Those with ______________________ parents tend to have _____________ self-esteem and social skills. ________________________ parenting, on the other hand, leads to anxious, withdrawn, and unhappy children. _____________________ parenting tends to result in children with a lack of self-discipline. Naturally, there are poor consequences for ___________________ parenting; these children tend to be emotionally withdrawn, fearful, and anxious. It is important to remember that research shows benefits for certain styles, but these benefits may vary depending on the culture in which they are applied.

____________________ refers to innate traits that influence how one thinks, behaves, and reacts with the environment. Children with ____________ temperaments demonstrate positive emotions, adapt well to change, and are capable of regulating emotion. ________________ children, on the other hand, show negative emotions and have difficulty with change and regulation of emotions.

On Your Own

Some schools have made it a recent trend to eliminate recess in favor of more class time. What is your reaction to this change?

Adolescence

On Your Own

What does it mean that adolescence is a socially constructed concept? Do you agree?

Adolescence is the period of development that beings at _______________ and ends at emerging ____________________. In the United States, adolescence is seen as a time to develop ______________________ from parents while remaining connected to them.

Physical Development

Several physical changes occur during puberty, including __________________ (maturing of adrenal glands) and ____________________ (maturing of the sex glands). Primary (those involving the sex organs themselves) and secondary sexual characteristics develop. Girls experience ________________, the beginning of menstruation, whereas boys experience _____________________, the first ejaculation.

Cognitive Development

More complex thinking abilities emerge during adolescence. Some researchers suggest this is due to increases in ______________ ______________. These individuals are in the Piagetian stage of ______________ ______________ ______________, where they can imagine hypothetical situations and debate ideas.

______________ ______________ is the ability to take the perspective of others and feel concern for others.

Psychosocial Development

As adolescents work to form their identities, they pull away from their ______________.

Contrary to the idea of "storm and stress," most adolescents still like their parents.

On Your Own

Was your adolescence a period of "storm and stress?" Explain.

Emerging Adulthood

On Your Own

When do you feel a child becomes an adult?

Today, there appears to be a great disparity in understanding between the so-called Baby Boomers and the younger generations. Does the lesson support the idea that these generations come from two wholly different worlds? Explain.

Adulthood

Adulthood begins around ________ years of age and has three distinct stages: early, middle, and late.

Physical Development

By the time people reach _____________ ________________ (20s to early 40s), physical maturation is complete although height and weight may increase slightly. In young adulthood, ________________ ________________ are at their peak, including muscle strength, reaction time, sensory abilities, and cardiac functioning. ________________ adulthood (40s to 60s) involves gradual ________________ decline.

_____________ adulthood (60s onward) involves continued ________________ decline.

Cognitive Development

Cognitive abilities remain ________________ through early and middle adulthood.

_____________________ intelligence (information gathered through life) remains stable, whereas _____________ intelligence (processing abilities) becomes slower.

On Your Own

Research has shown that remaining physically and mentally active can help preserve cognitive functioning with age. What will you do to maintain your cognitive skills as you age?

Psychosocial Development

Aspects of healthy aging include activities, social _________________________, and the role of a person's _________________. It is important to continue to find meaning in life, which may come from work and family. Job satisfaction is closely related to work that involves ________________ with others, is interesting, provides ________________________ opportunities, and allows independence.

_______________ appears to be less important.

According to the lesson, what contributes to positive well-being?

1.

2.

3.

4.

5.

6.

_______________ _______________ theory suggests that our social support and friendships dwindle in number but remain as close, if not closer, as in our early years.

Psychology and You

Mirror Test

The lesson describes the mirror test, based on mirror self-recognition, for determining if children have a concept of self. How would you modify the study if you were the researcher?

Lesson Wrap-up

Say It in a Sentence

In one sentence, describe the Strange Situation procedure.

Test Yourself

Choose the correct answer for each of the following questions. Check your work using the Answer Key in the back of the book.

____ 1. The brain starts to develop in the ________ stage.

- **A.** germinal
- **B.** embryonic
- **C.** fetal

____ 2. The heart begins to beat before _______ weeks.

- **A.** three
- **B.** four
- **C.** nine

____ 3. Newborns can distinguish their mothers by:

- **A.** Sound
- **B.** Smell
- **C.** Sound and smell

____ 4. The size of a 2-year-old's brain is ______ of its adult size.

- **A.** 20%
- **B.** 45%
- **C.** 55%
- **D.** 90%

____ 5. Who tends to have more confidence?

- **A.** Early maturing girls
- **B.** Late maturing boys
- **C.** Early maturing boys

Next to each statement, write **T** for True or **F** for False. Check your work using the Answer Key in the back of the book.

6. _______ A zygote implants during the embryonic stage.
7. _______ A 37-week-old pregnancy will likely not result in effects of preterm birth if the baby was born at this juncture.
8. _______ Reflexes tend to remain until an infant is 9 months of age.
9. _______ Babies are able to generate new brain cells for years after birth.
10. _______ When babies are about 12 months old, they will likely say their first word.

Key Terms

Match each key term with its definition.

A.	Adolescence	_____	Characterized by child's unresponsiveness to parent, does not use parent as secure base and does not care if parent leaves
B.	Adrenarche	_____	Medical care during pregnancy
C.	Attachment	_____	Organs specifically needed for reproduction
D.	Authoritarian Parenting	_____	Parents give children reasonable demands and consistent limits
E.	Authoritative Parenting	_____	Long-standing connection or bond with others
F.	Avoidant Attachment	_____	Newly defined period from 18–20 years of age
G.	Cognitive Empathy	_____	When a sperm fertilizes an egg and forms a zygote
H.	Conception	_____	Use of large muscle groups for large actions
I.	Critical Period		
J.	Disorganized Attachment		
K.	Embryo		
L.	Emerging Adulthood		
M.	Fine Motor Skills		
N.	Gonadarche		

O. Gross Motor Skills
P. Menarche
Q. Mitosis
R. Motor Skills
S. Newborn Reflexes
T. Permissive Parenting
U. Placenta
V. Prenatal Care
W. Primary Sexual Characteristics
X. Resistant Attachment
Y. Secondary Sexual Characteristics
Z. Secure Attachment

_____ Characterized by the child's odd behavior when faced with the parent
_____ Period of development from puberty to early adulthood
_____ Ability to move our body and manipulate objects
_____ Maturing of the adrenal glands
_____ Inborn automatic response to a particular form of stimulation
_____ Beginning of the menstrual period
_____ Parents place a high value on conformity and obedience
_____ Ability to take the perspective of and feel concern for others
_____ Time during fetal growth when specific parts and organs develop
_____ Multi-cellular organism in its early stages of development
_____ Maturing of sex glands
_____ Process of cell division
_____ Parents make few demands and rarely use punishment
_____ Characterized by child's tendency to show clingy behavior
_____ Characterized by child using the parent as a secure base
_____ Physical signs of sexual maturation that do not directly involve sex organs
_____ Structure connected to the uterus that provides nourishment to developing baby
_____ Use of muscles in fingers, toes, and eyes for small actions

Lesson 8.4

Death and Dying

OBJECTIVES

★ Discuss hospice care.
★ Describe the five stages of grief.

BIG IDEA

Approaching death has changed in the past 50 years, moving from in-hospital to in-hospice care.

In this lesson, you will learn about the following:

- Hospice Care
- Stages of Grief

Our ______________ and individual backgrounds influence how we view death. In some cultures, death is accepted and embraced.

In 1967, Cicely Saunders created the first modern ______________ in England. It was not until ____________ that Florence Wald began a similar institution in the United States.

On Your Own

What are the benefits of hospice care for the patient?

1.

2.

3.

4.

5.

6.

What are the benefits of hospice care for the family of the patient?

1.

2.

3.

4.

5.

6.

_________ __________ described a process of an individual accepting his own death. She proposed ________ stages of grief that could occur in different orders, depending on the person.

What are the stages of grief?

1.
2.
3.
4.
5.

On Your Own

Some psychologists believe that fighting death is unhealthy, but others believe that not facing death until the end is an adaptive coping mechanism. Which do you believe, and why?

People with __________ or __________ beliefs are better able to cope with death because of their hope of an afterlife and because of social support from various associations.

Psychology and You

Hospice Care

Would you want to live in hospice care at the end of your life? Why or why not?

Lesson Wrap-up

Say It in a Sentence

In one sentence, explain the benefits of hospice care.

Test Yourself

Choose the correct answer for each of the following questions. Check your work using the Answer Key in the back of the book.

____ 1. In what year was hospice care started in the United States?

- **A.** 1967
- **B.** 1974
- **C.** 1986

____ 2. Today, how many indiviuduals receive hospice care?

- **A.** 1 million
- **B.** 1.65 million
- **C.** 2 million
- **D.** 2.65 million

Next to each statement, write **T** for True or **F** for False. Check your work using the Answer Key in the back of the book.

3. ______ According to Elizabeth Kübler-Ross, the five stages of grief are denial, anger, bargaining, depression, and acceptance.

4. ______ An individual always goes through all of the stages of grief in order.

Key Terms

Write the definition of the following term.

Hospice:

Chapter 9
Emotion and Motivation

Lesson 9.1
Motivation

OBJECTIVES

- ★ Define intrinsic and extrinsic motivation.
- ★ Understand that instincts, drive reduction, self-efficacy, and social motives have all been proposed as theories of motivation.
- ★ Explain the basic concepts associated with Maslow's hierarchy of needs.

BIG IDEA

Multiple theories of motivation have been proposed that draw on internal, external, psychological, and biological components.

In this lesson, you will learn about the following:

- Motivation
- Theories of Motivation

Motivation

____________________ describes the wants or needs that direct behavior toward a goal. Motivation can be ____________________ (stemming from internal factors like personal satisfaction) or ____________________ (stemming from external factors like monetary payment).

On Your Own

What are your intrinsic and extrinsic motivations for being in school?

Research shows that receiving ____________________ rewards for activities that individuals find ________________________ rewarding can make the particular task less enjoyable. For example, individuals may enjoy helping the needy. However, once that person is paid to help the needy, the task is less enjoyable. This situation is the ______________________________ effect.

______________ __________________ appears to have ______________ negative impact on intrinsic motivation than monetary rewards. In addition, intrinsic motivation can persist if the tangible reward is a ___________________ rather than expected.

What aspects contribute to higher intrinsic motivation in the classroom?

1.

2.

3.

4.

On Your Own

Think of one of your classes where you do not feel a high level of intrinsic motivation. What could be improved?

Theories about Motivation

______________ ______________, the father of psychology in the United States, theorized that behavior was driven by a number of _________________, or species-specific patterns of behavior that are not learned.

On Your Own

What is your definition of an instinct? Would you consider "a mother's protection of her baby" an instinct? Why or why not? Would you consider "the urge to lick sugar" an instinct? Why or why not?

Another early theory of motivation focused on the idea of ____________________, or the body's tendency to maintain an optimal level within a biological system. In a body system, a control center receives input from ________________. The control center then directs ________________ to correct any imbalance detected by the control center.

On Your Own

Describe how homeostasis would work for ingestive (eating) behavior.

According to ____________ theory, deviations from homeostasis create ______________________ needs, which then result in ______________________ drive states.

A ____________ is a pattern of behavior in which people regularly engage. Once individuals have engaged in a behavior that successfully reduces a drive, they are more likely to engage in that behavior again.

On Your Own

Have you had a class in which you felt underaroused? Overaroused? What contributed to each of those feelings, and how did you ultimately perform in the classes?

Explain the difference between the following two figures.

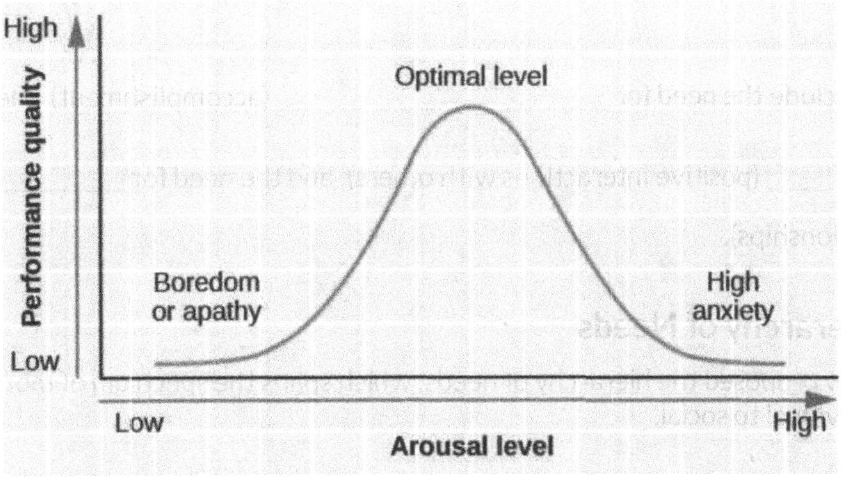

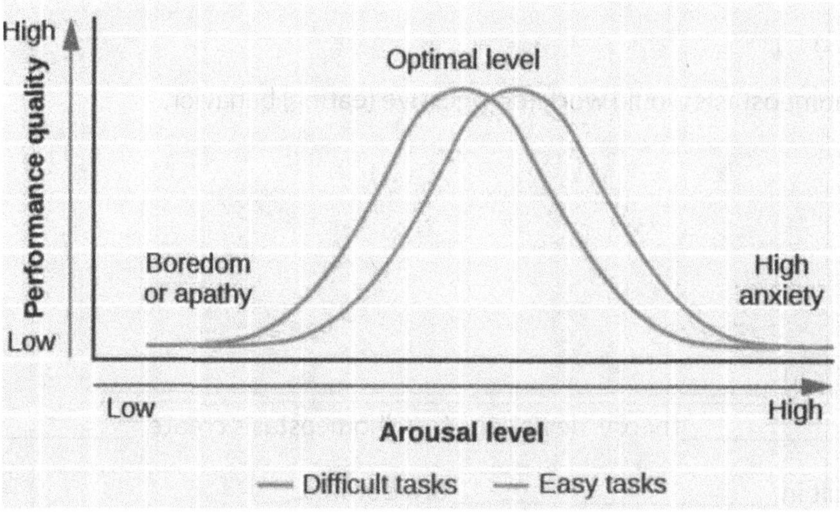

Self-Efficacy and Social Motives

____________ ______________ theorized that _________________, an individual's belief in his or her own capability to complete a task, determined our motivation to engage in a given behavior.

On Your Own

What are your thoughts when you face a challenging task? How would you describe your level of self-efficacy?

Social motives include the need for ___________________ (accomplishment), the need for ________________ (positive interactions with others), and the need for _______________ (deep, meaningful relationships).

Maslow's Hierarchy of Needs

Abraham Maslow proposed the hierarchy of needs, which spans the spectrum of motives ranging from biological to individual to social.

Complete Maslow's Hierarchy:

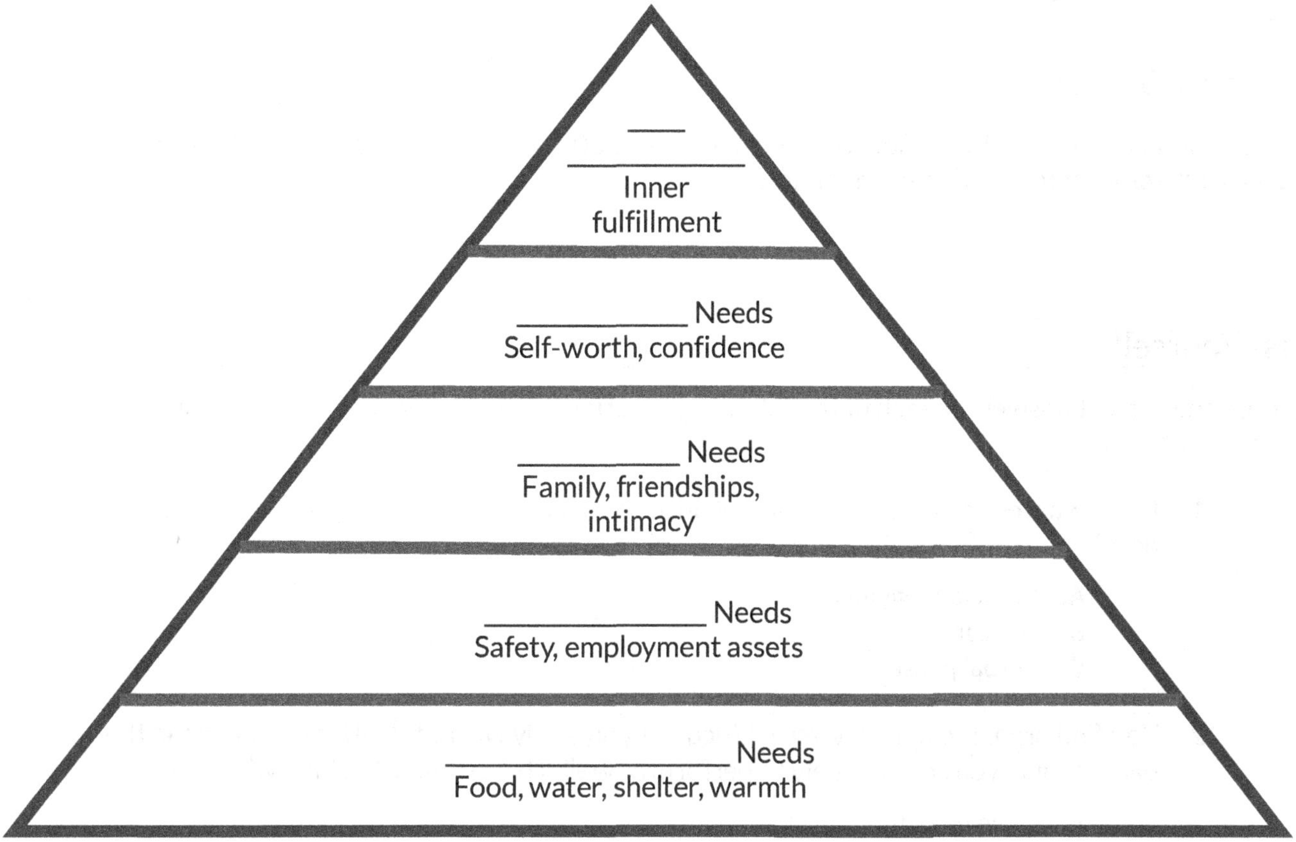

On Your Own

Some researchers feel that men and women travel through Maslow's hierarchy in a different sequence. Specifically, women follow the typical sequence, whereas men put esteem needs before social needs. Do you agree that there are gender differences with regard to the hierarchy? Why or why not?

Where are you on Maslow's hierarchy of needs? Explain.

Psychology and You

Extrinsic Rewards

Research shows that receiving extrinsic rewards for activities that individuals find intrinsically rewarding can make the particular task less enjoyable. Describe a situation in which this happened to you.

Lesson Wrap-up

Say It in a Sentence

In one sentence, explain why an individual might desire to attend college. Your answer should utilize at least two theories of motivation from this lesson.

Test Yourself

Choose the correct answer for each of the following questions. Check your work using the Answer Key in the back of the book.

____ 1. If you wanted to ensure that your intrinsic motivation did not wane, which reward would be best?

- **A.** Monetary payment
- **B.** Gift cards
- **C.** Verbal praise

____ 2. You find organic chemistry very difficult. If you study with a talkative roommate in the background, you are not likely to perform as well. This example best fits which theory?

- **A.** Drive reduction
- **B.** Need for achievement
- **C.** Maslow's hierarchy
- **D.** Yerkes-Dodson law

____ 3. Your dorm room is in bad shape; there are bugs, and you are fairly certain the floor has water damage. You sometimes fear you might fall through as you walk across! You are struggling with which level of Maslow's hierarchy?

- **A.** Physiological needs
- **B.** Safety needs
- **C.** Esteem needs
- **D.** Social needs

Next to each statement, write **T** for True or **F** for False. Check your work using the Answer Key in the back of the book.

4. ______ The Yerkes-Dodson law indicates that an easy task is typically performed better at lower levels of arousal.

5. ______ Classical conditioning shows that motivation is not always dictated by instincts.

Key Terms

Use the key terms from the lesson to complete the following crossword puzzle.

Across

1. Motivation based on internal feelings rather than external rewards

Down

1. Deviations from homeostasis create psychological needs that result in psychological drive states that direct behavior to meet the need and ultimately bring the system back to homeostasis
2. Motivation that arises from external factors or rewards
3. Pattern of behavior in which we regularly engage
4. Spectrum of needs ranging from basic biological needs to social needs to self-actualization

5. Species-specific pattern of behavior that is unlearned
6. Wants or needs that direct behavior toward some goal
7. Individual's belief in his own capabilities or capacities to complete a task
8. Simple tasks are performed best when arousal levels are relatively high, while complex tasks are best performed when arousal is lower

Lesson 9.2

Hunger and Eating

OBJECTIVES

- ★ Describe how hunger and eating are regulated.
- ★ Differentiate between levels of overweight and obesity and the associated health consequences.
- ★ Explain the health consequences resulting from anorexia and bulimia nervosa.

BIG IDEA

The human body is designed to maintain a fairly stable weight; however, eating choices can result in excessive weight gain or loss that can impact health outcomes.

In this lesson, you will learn about the following:

- Physiological Mechanisms
- Metabolism and Body Weight
- Obesity
- Eating Disorders

Physiological Mechanisms

There are a variety of signals that trigger ______________ when there is no food in the digestive tract.

______________, or fullness and satisfaction, typically occurs once an individual has eaten. There are a variety of satiety signals, including ______________, which comes from the fat cells and reduces eating behavior.

List the mechanisms that start and stop a meal.

Start a Meal	Stop a Meal
1.	1.
2.	2.
3.	3.
	4.

Metabolism and Body Weight

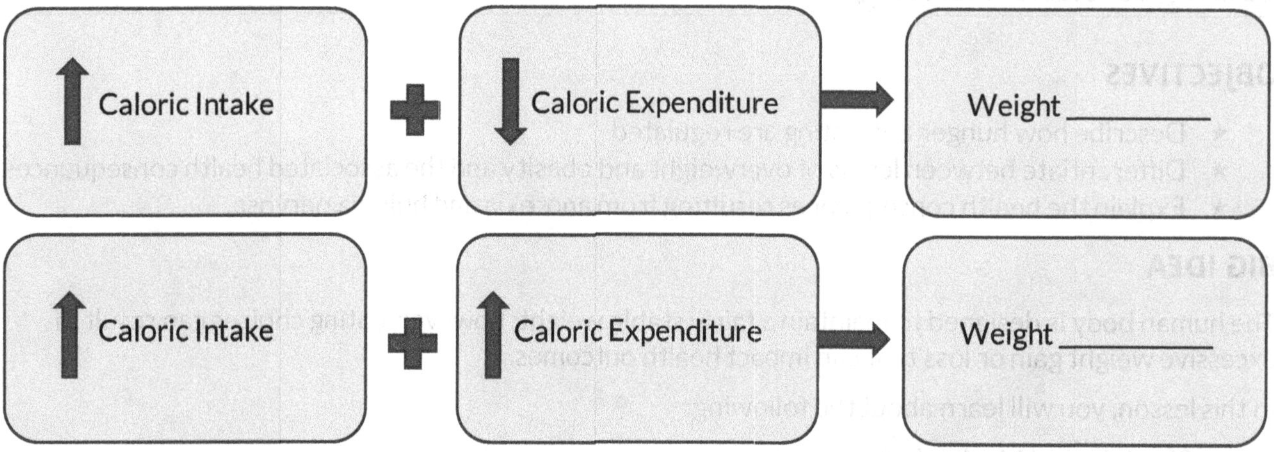

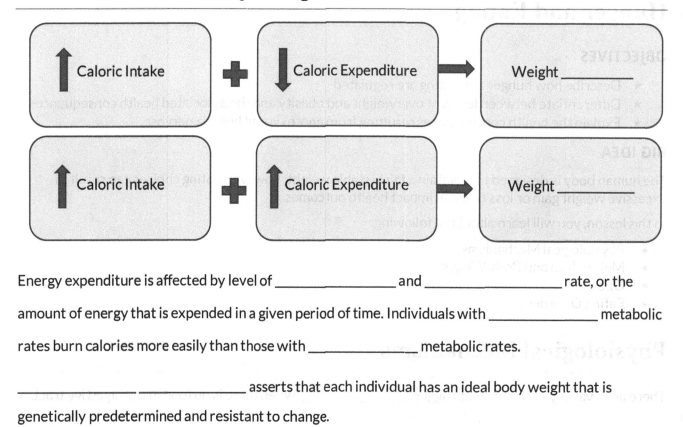

Energy expenditure is affected by level of ________________ and ________________ rate, or the amount of energy that is expended in a given period of time. Individuals with ______________ metabolic rates burn calories more easily than those with ______________ metabolic rates.

________________ ________________ asserts that each individual has an ideal body weight that is genetically predetermined and resistant to change.

On Your Own

According to the lesson, set-point theory was not empirically supported in a study comparing those who recently lost a great deal of weight and a control group (Weinsier et al., 2000). In recent years, the contestants of *The Biggest Loser* have been tested, and their metabolic rates do appear to differ. They need to work even harder to maintain their lower weights. What does this recent finding say about the set-point theory?

Obesity

Based on the Body Mass Index (BMI), what group would each person be classified as?

BMI	Characteristics
17	
20	
24.9	
26	
31	
39	
41	

On Your Own

What are the health consequences of being overweight or obese?

1.
2.
3.
4.
5.
6.
7.
8.
9.

In addition to genetic and metabolic factors, ______________________ status and physical environment must also be considered as contributing factors to obesity. The environment may limit the extent to which an individual can safely engage in _________________ _____________ or obtain healthy food.

For individuals who are unsuccessful at using diet and exercise to lose weight, _______________

_________________ may be an option. This procedure involves modifying the gastrointestinal system to reduce the amount of food that can be eaten or limit how it is absorbed.

On Your Own

If you were obese and had tried to lose weight for an extended period of time, would you consider bariatric surgery? Why or why not?

Imagine you had a child with Prader-Willi syndrome. What would you do to help your child?

Eating Disorders

People suffering from __________________ __________________ engage in binge eating behavior followed by compensatory behaviors to correct for the consumed food. They may engage in vomiting, laxatives, or excessive __________________ to compensate.

Binge eating disorder involves binge eating __________________ compensatory behavior afterwards.

Anorexia nervosa is characterized by starvation and excessive __________________. These individuals usually suffer from __________________ body image and view themselves as overweight when they are, in fact, normal or underweight.

What do the following eating disorders have in common?

Bulimia Nervosa + Binge Eating Disorder	Bulimia Nervosa + Anorexia Nervosa

How do the eating disorders differ?

Bulimia Nervosa + Binge Eating Disorder	Bulimia Nervosa + Anorexia Nervosa

Psychology and You

Healthy Choices

Imagine that someone you love dearly is classified as morbidly obese. What might you say to this individual to help them make healthy choices?

Lesson Wrap-up

Say It in a Sentence

In one sentence, explain the severity of the fact that two-thirds of adults in the United States are overweight.

Test Yourself

Choose the correct answer for each of the following questions. Check your work using the Answer Key in the back of the book.

____ 1. It is currently estimated that _______ of adults in the United States are obese.

- **A.** 1/3
- **B.** 1/2
- **C.** 2/3

____ 2. If your leptin level is high, you should feel:

- **A.** Hungry
- **B.** Happy
- **C.** Satiated

____ 3. It is currently estimated that _______ of children in the United States are overweight.

- **A.** 1/6
- **B.** 1/3
- **C.** 1/2
- **D.** 2/3

Next to each statement, write **T** for True or **F** for False. Check your work using the Answer Key in the back of the book.

4. ______ Ensuring that children get recess at school and adequate play time at home is one way to reduce the number of overweight children.

5. ______ Individuals with anorexia have an increased risk for kidney failure and heart failure, but those with bulimia do not.

Key Terms

Match each key term with its definition.

A. Anorexia Nervosa
B. Bariatric Surgery
C. Binge Eating Disorder
D. Bulimia Nervosa
E. Distorted Body Image
F. Leptin
G. Metabolic Rate
H. Morbid Obesity
I. Obese
J. Overweight
K. Satiation
L. Set-Point Theory

_____ Adult with BMI over 40
_____ Assertion that each individual has an ideal body weight that is resistant to change
_____ Eating disorder characterized by body weight that is well below average through starvation and excessive exercise
_____ Satiety hormone
_____ Type of eating disorder characterized by binge eating and associated distress
_____ Fullness
_____ Type of surgery that modifies the gastrointestinal system to reduce the amount of food that can be eaten or limits how the food can be digested
_____ Amount of energy that is expended over a given period of time
_____ Individuals view themselves as overweight even though they are not
_____ Type of eating disorder characterized by eating followed by purging
_____ Adult with a BMI of 30 to 39.9
_____ Adult with a BMI of 25 to 29.9

Lesson 9.3

Sexual Behavior

OBJECTIVES

- ★ Understand basic biological mechanisms regulating sexual behavior and motivation.
- ★ Appreciate the importance of Alfred Kinsey's research on human sexuality.
- ★ Recognize the contributions that William Masters and Virginia Johnson's research made to our understanding of the sexual response cycles.
- ★ Define sexual orientation and gender identity.

BIG IDEA

Research on healthy sexuality has led to an understanding of sexual motivation, sexual ability, gender identity, and sexual orientation.

In this lesson, you will learn about the following:

- Physiological Mechanisms of Sexual Behavior and Motivation
- Kinsey's Research
- Masters and Johnson's Research
- Sexual Orientation
- Gender Identity
- Cultural Factors in Sexual Orientation and Gender Identity

Physiological Mechanisms of Sexual Behavior and Motivation

Research suggest that neural control of sexual ability and sexual motivation are separate.

List the brain structures that impact sexual ability and motivation.

Sexual Ability	Sexual Motivation

Label the brain areas in the following diagram.

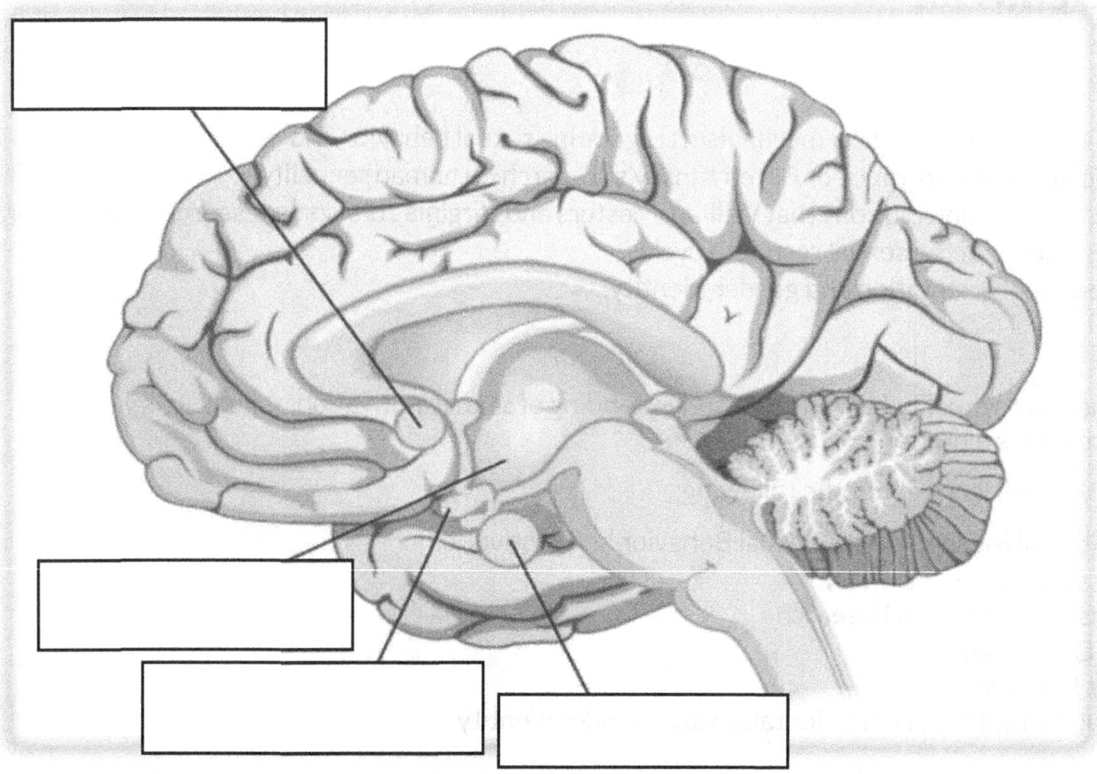

On Your Own

How are rats and humans similar when it comes to the physiological control of sexual behavior and motivation?

Kinsey's Research

Several keystone studies led to a more open exploration of healthy sexual behavior. The first was done by Dr. ________________ ________________, who initiated a large-scale ________________ on sexual behavior. Controversial results led to Dr. Kinsey losing his research funding. Although criticized for ________________ and statistical errors, the research was influential in shaping the future of research in this area.

On Your Own

The Kinsey study used a survey technique to gather the data. What are some potential problems with this method of inquiry?

The results of Kinsey's survey demonstrated that women were ________ interested in sex as men, that both men and women masturbated __________________ negative health consequences, and that ______________________ acts were not a rarity.

Masters and Johnson's Research

On Your Own

What is your reaction to the idea that William Masters and Virginia Johnson observed approximately 700 people as they engaged in sexual behavior, so they could measure what occurred during the process?

Comparing the Kinsey study and the Masters and Johnson study, which do you feel had the more reliable and valid testing procedures? Explain your answer.

What are the four stages of the sexual response cycle?

1.
2.
3.
4.

After a completed sexual response cycle, individuals enter a ________________ period, which is a period of time during which an individual is ________________ of experiencing another orgasm.

__________ appear to be more impacted by the refractory period, with some individuals being affected for as long as a day.

Sexual Orientation

A person's __________ ______________ is his or her emotional and erotic attraction toward another individual. Estimates of homosexuality in the United States range between _____ to _____%.

Why do you think we have estimates of homosexuality between 3 and 10% instead of a single percentage? Why does the variability exist?

Although once subject to the nature vs. nurture debate, research on the issue of homosexuality has consistently demonstrated that sexual orientation has an underlying ________________ component.

Misunderstandings about Sexual Orientation

The lesson states that "research has made clear that sexual orientation is not a choice." What is your reaction?

Do you feel that reparative therapy for homosexuality is ethical? Why or why not?

List the biological components that underlie sexual orientation.

-
-
-

Gender Identity

Gender ________________ refers to one's sense of being male or female. When individuals do not feel comfortable identifying with the gender associated with their biological sex, they experience gender ________________.

Many people with gender dysphoria attempt to live their lives as the gender they identify with by dressing in ________________ clothing, assuming an opposite-sex identity, taking ________________, or pursuing surgery options.

Cultural Factors in Sexual Orientation and Gender Identity

On Your Own

What is your reaction to the idea that some cultures expect exclusively homosexual behavior from youth as part of normal development? Would such a practice be acceptable in the United States?

What is your reaction to the idea that other cultures have a third gender, such as the kathoey?

In cases of so-called ambiguous genitalia (when there has been abnormal development of the external genitalia such that the clitoris is elongated or more penis-like), doctors have urged parents to surgically correct the child to resemble a female. Do you believe this is a good practice? Why or why not?

Psychology and You

Sexology Study

If you were a sexologist (someone who studies sexual behavior), what would you want to study? Describe a study you might actually conduct in this field.

Lesson Wrap-up

Say It in a Sentence

In one sentence, explain the story of David Reimer.

Test Yourself

Choose the correct answer for each of the following questions. Check your work using the Answer Key in the back of the book.

____ 1. If a male rat has the ability to mate but lacks the motivation, which part of the brain might be affected?

- **A.** Medial preoptic area
- **B.** Amygdala
- **C.** Nucleus accumbens
- **D.** Either nucleus accumbens or amygdala

____ 2. Over the course of their study, Masters and Johnson observed over ______ sexual acts.

- **A.** 5,000
- **B.** 10,000
- **C.** 15,000

____ 3. During the ______ phase of the sexual response cycle, men and women experience increases in muscle tone and increased blood flow to the genital areas.

- **A.** excitement
- **B.** plateau
- **C.** orgasm
- **D.** resolution

Next to each statement, write **T** for True or **F** for False. Check your work using the Answer Key in the back of the book.

4. ______ Dr. Alfred Kinsey established The Kinsey Institute for Research, Sex, Gender, and Reproduction in 1947.

5. _______ There is credible evidence that an individual can change his or her sexual orientation through willpower, prayer, or therapy.

6. _______ Gender dysphoria must last for at least three months to meet the DSM-5 criteria.

Key Terms

Write a paraphrased definition of each key term.

Bisexual:

Excitement:

Gender Dysphoria:

Gender Identity:

Heterosexual:

Homosexual:

Orgasm:

Plateau:

Refractory Period:

Resolution:

Sexual Orientation:

Sexual Response Cycle:

Transgender Hormone Therapy:

Lesson 9.4

Emotion

OBJECTIVES

★ Explain the major theories of emotion.
★ Describe the role that limbic structures play in emotional processing.
★ Understand the ubiquitous nature of producing and recognizing emotional expression.

BIG IDEA

Various theories have tried to explain how emotions are comprised of physiological arousal and cognitive appraisal. In general, interpretation of emotions appears to be universal even if there are cultural rules regarding which emotions are acceptable to display in public.

In this lesson, you will learn about the following:

- Theories of Emotion
- The Biology of Emotion
- Facial Expression and Recognition of Emotions

An __________________ is a subjective, relatively intense state of being that individuals usually describe as their feelings. ________________, in contrast, refers to a prolonged, less intense affective state.

Theories of Emotion

What are the components of emotion?

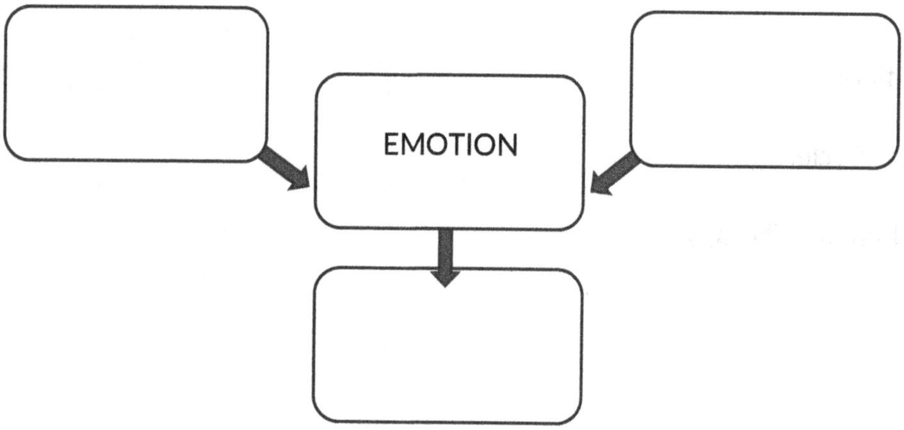

Complete the following graphic using these terms: *physiological arousal*, *cognitive appraisal*, and *cognitive label*.

Schachter-Singer Two-Factor Theory

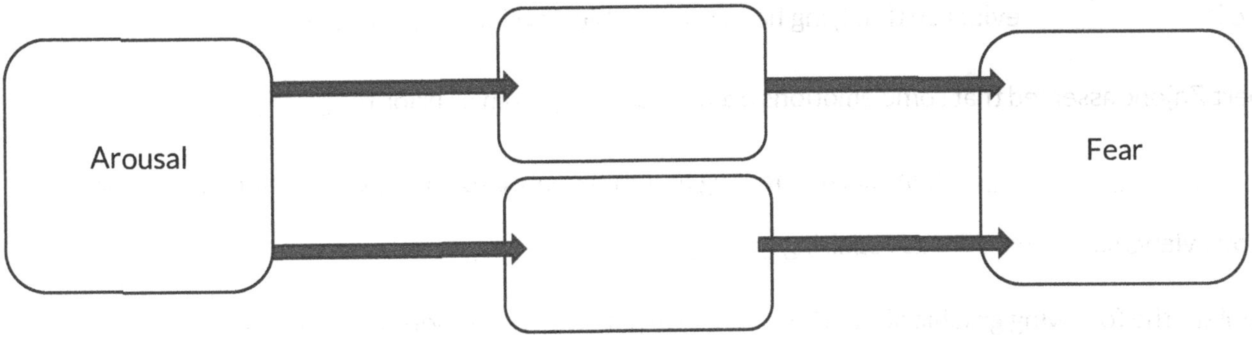

James-Lange Theory

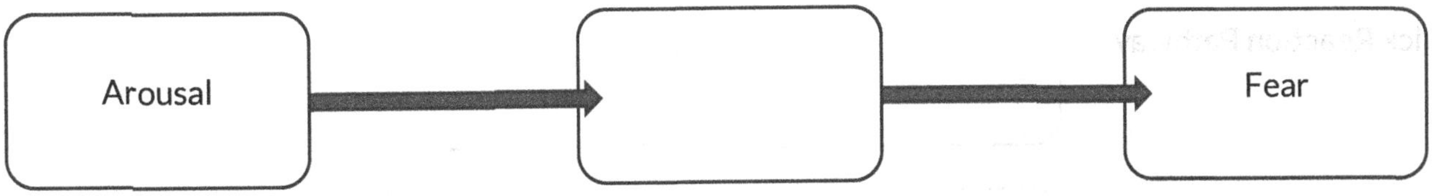

Lazarus' Cognitive-Mediational Theory

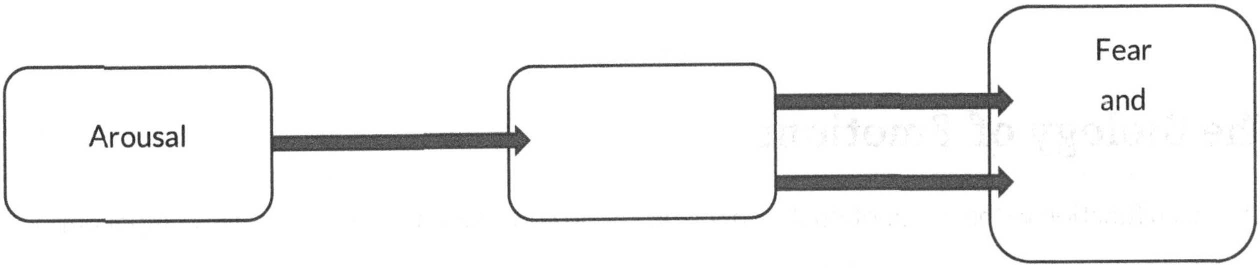

Cannon-Bard Theory

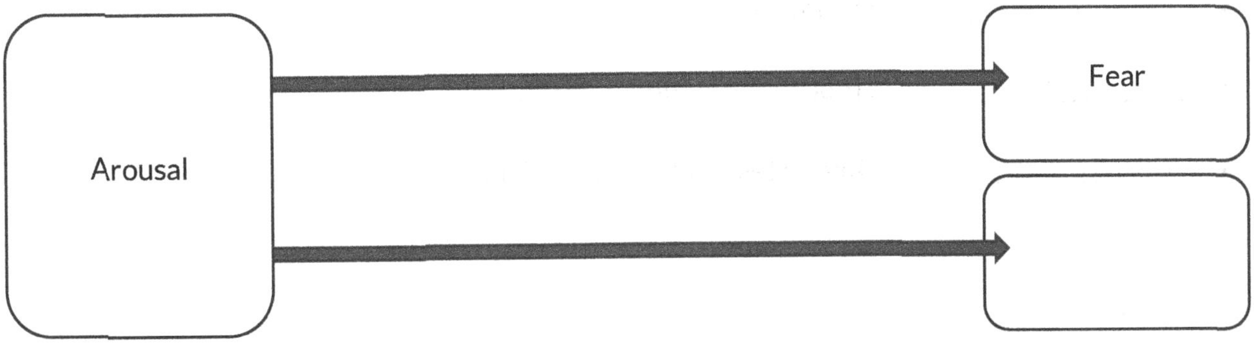

On Your Own

How would you modify the Schachter and Singer epinephrine experiment? What do you hypothesize your results would be after your modification?

Strong emotional responses are associated with ____________ physiological arousal. This correlation has led to individuals proposing the use of a ________________, or lie detector test, to measure physiological changes as a measure of guilt. These tests, however, are highly controversial given that there is __________ evidence that lying has a predictable physiological pattern.

Robert Zajonc asserted that some emotions occur separately from or prior to ________________ ________________ of them, such as feeling fear in response to an unexpected loud sound. Joseph LeDoux views some emotions as requiring ______ ________________.

Complete the following graphic about the two neural pathways for emotional response.

Quick Reaction Pathway

Detail Processing Pathway

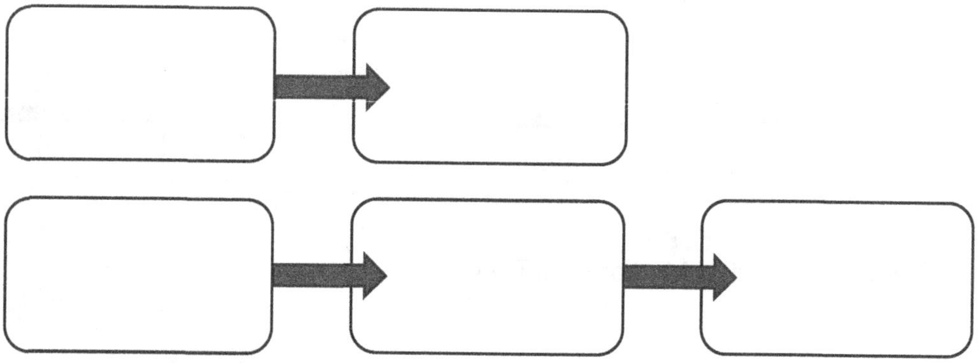

The Biology of Emotions

Label each function within an emotional response with the corresponding limbic system component.

- ____________________: Activates sympathetic nervous system
- ____________________: Sensory relay center
- ____________________: Processes emotional information
- ____________________: Integrates emotional experience with cognition

Label the following diagram of the brain.

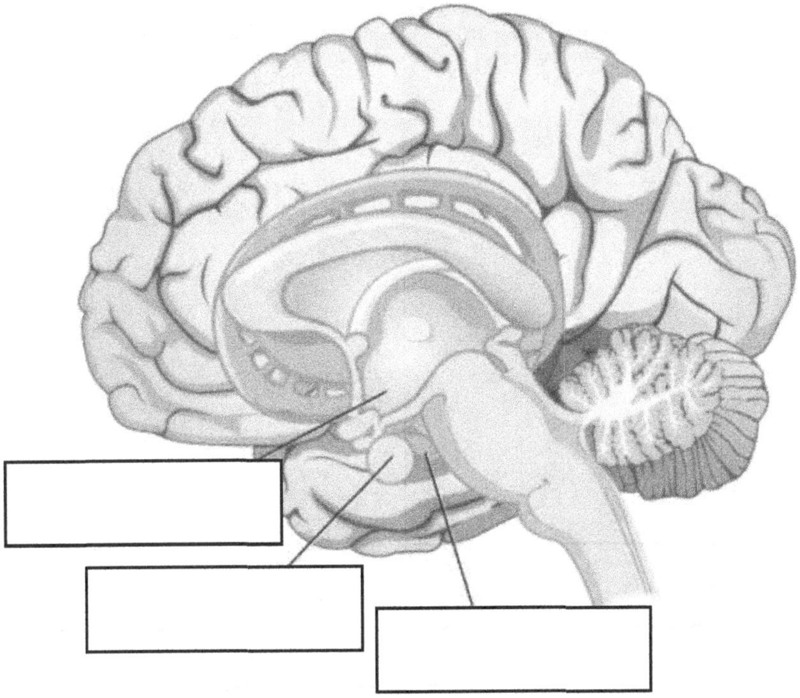

Amygdala

The amygdala is comprised of various subnuclei, including the ____________________

_________________ (responsible for attaching emotional value to learning and memory) and the

______________ _______________ (responsible for attention).

Label the following diagram of the amygdala.

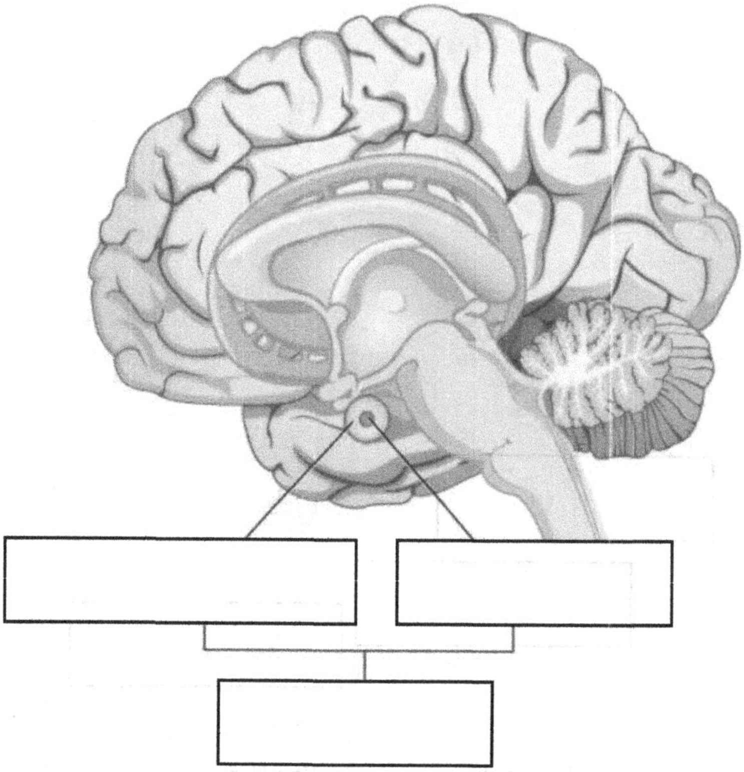

Animal research has demonstrated that there is increased activation of the ________________ in rat pups that have odor cues paired with electrical shock when their mother is ______________. This leads to an ________________ to the odor cue, which suggests the rats learned to fear the odor cue. However, they also learned ________________ and did not demonstrate fear when their mother was present.

Negative early life experience can alter the function of the ________________. In a study in which rat pups experienced different levels of ______________, the rats were more likely to exhibit depression-like symptoms during adolescence.

On Your Own

What are the implications of the Raineki, Cortes, Belnoue, and Sullivan (2012) study for humans?

Hippocampus

The hippocampus is involved in ________________ processing. Individuals suffering from

________________ ____________ ________________ show reductions in volume of several parts of the hippocampus.

Facial Expression and Recognition of Emotions

A ______________ ______________ rule is one of a collection of culturally specific standards that govern the types and frequencies of displays of emotion that are acceptable.

Our ability to recognize and produce facial expressions of emotion appears to be ______________. Even congenitally blind individuals make appropriate facial expressions.

What are the seven universal emotions?

-
-
-
-
-
-
-

The facial ________________ hypothesis asserts that facial expressions are capable of influencing our emotions.

On Your Own

How can you apply the facial feedback hypothesis to your life?

Autism Spectrum Disorder and Expression of Emotions

____________ __________________ disorder is a set of neurodevelopmental disorders characterized by __________________ behaviors and communication and ______________ problems. These individuals have difficulty recognizing ________________ states of others, which may stem from an inability to distinguish various nonverbal expressions of emotion. Individuals with autism also have difficulty expressing emotion through __________ _____ ____________ and facial expressions.

Psychology and You

Autism Spectrum Disorder

Imagine that you have autism spectrum disorder. How might your life be impacted by this diagnosis?

Lesson Wrap-up

Say It in a Sentence

In one sentence, explain the facial feedback hypothesis.

Test Yourself

Choose the correct answer for each of the following questions. Check your work using the Answer Key in the back of the book.

____ 1. If, in order to feel fear, you must cognitively label that you are feeling fear, the __________ theory is supported.

- **A.** Cannon-Bard
- **B.** James-Lange
- **C.** Schachter-Singer two-factor
- **D.** Lazarus' cognitive-mediational

____ 2. The theory that physiological arousal and fear occur at the same time in the absence of cognitive appraisal is the _________ theory.

- **A.** Cannon-Bard
- **B.** James-Lange
- **C.** Schachter-Singer two-factor
- **D.** Lazarus' cognitive-mediational

____ 3. If you responded to a fear stimulus without overthinking the situation, it is likely your thalamus sent information directly to:

- **A.** The amygdala
- **B.** The nucleus accumbens
- **C.** The cortex

____ 4. According to cultural display rules, a Japanese individual would be _______ likely to display negative emotion in the presence of others compared to an American individual.

A. more
B. less
C. as

Next to each statement, write **T** for True or **F** for False. Check your work using the Answer Key in the back of the book.

1. _______ The Schachter-Singer two-factor theory and the Lazarus cognitive-mediational theory both draw on cognitive components.
2. _______ The James-Lange and Cannon-Bard theories both assert that physiological arousal occurs before the emotion of fear.

Key Terms

Match the key term with its definition.

A. Basolateral Complex
B. Body Language
C. Cannon-Bard Theory of Emotion
D. Central Nucleus
E. Cognitive-Mediational Theory
F. Components of Emotion
G. Cultural Display Rule
H. Emotion
I. Facial Feedback Hypothesis
J. James-Lange Theory of Emotion
K. Polygraph
L. Schachter-Singer Two-Factor Theory of Emotion

_____ One of the specific standards that governs the types and frequencies of emotions that are acceptable
_____ Physiological arousal, psychological appraisal, and subjective experience
_____ Part of the brain involved in attention and has connections with the hypothalamus and various parts of the brainstem
_____ Physiological arousal and emotional experience occur at the same time
_____ Facial expressions are capable of influencing our emotions
_____ Part of the brain with dense connections with a variety of sensory areas of the brain; critical for classical conditioning and attaching emotional value to memory
_____ Emotions arise from physiological arousal
_____ Our emotions are determined by our appraisal of the stimulus
_____ Emotions consist of two factors: physiological and cognitive
_____ Subjective state of being often described as feelings
_____ Emotional expression through body position or movement

Chapter 10
Personality

Lesson 10.1
What Is Personality?

OBJECTIVES

★ Define personality.
★ Describe early theories about personality development.

BIG IDEA

Personality, or the traits that make individuals behave in certain ways, has been studied by a variety of theorists who have attempted to explain why humans act as they do.

In this lesson, you will learn about the following:

- Introduction to Personality
- Historical Perspectives

Personality refers to the long-standing __________ and patterns that propel individuals to consistently think, feel, and behave in specific ways. Our personalities are thought to be long-term, __________, and not easily changed.

Historical Perspectives

Hippocrates was the first to examine personality, and he felt that personality traits and behaviors were based on ________ different __________________.

What are the four temperaments, according to Hippocrates?

1.
2.
3.
4.

Adding to Hippocrates' original idea, Galen theorized that different ______________ and personality differences could be explained by __________________ in the humors (fluids) upon which the temperaments were based.

Complete the following table.

Temperaments	Personality Description
	Joyful, eager, optimistic
Melancholic	
Choleric	
	Calm, reliable, thoughtful

____________ ____________ proposed the practice of ____________________, which involved measuring the distances between bumps on the skull to reveal a person's personality traits, character, and mental abilities. Due to the lack of empirical evidence, this approach has been deemed a ____________________.

_______________ __________ developed a list of traits that would describe individuals in the four temperaments. Wilhelm Wundt proposed that these traits be ordered along ________ ________: emotional/non-emotional and changeable/unchangeable.

Based on Wundt's theory, label the following temperaments as *strong* or *weak*.

- Melancholic:
- Choleric:
- Phlegmatic:
- Sanguine:

Based on Wundt's theory, label the following temperaments as *changeable* or *unchangeable*.

- Melancholic:
- Choleric:
- Phlegmatic:
- Sanguine:

Psychology and You

Temperament Spectrum

Reference Figure 3 in the lesson. Where would you fall on the graphic? Be sure to explain your reasoning.

Lesson Wrap-up

Say It in a Sentence

In one sentence, explain the concept of personality.

Test Yourself

Choose the correct answer for each of the following questions. Check your work using the Answer Key in the back of the book.

____ 1. If a person is calm and reliable, this person would fit which of the four humor-based temperaments?

- **A.** Sanguine
- **B.** Phlegmatic
- **C.** Choleric
- **D.** Melancholic

____ 2. If a person is passionate and ambitious, this person would fit which of the four humor-based temperaments?

- **A.** Sanguine
- **B.** Phlegmatic
- **C.** Choleric
- **D.** Melancholic

____ 3. Franz Gall proposed the idea of ________, in which individual personalities could be analyzed by the bumps on the head.

- **A.** phrenology
- **B.** parapsychology
- **C.** pseudoscience
- **D.** epistemology

Answer the following short answer question. Check your work using the Answer Key in the back of the book.

4. Compare the approaches to the concept of personality by Freud and the Neo-Freudians.

Key Terms

Using the following definition as a reference, describe the personality of someone you know or a fictional character.

Personality: Long-standing traits and patterns that propel individuals to consistently think, feel, and behave in specific ways

Lesson 10.2

Freud and the Psychodynamic Perspective

OBJECTIVES

- ★ Describe the assumptions of the psychodynamic perspective on personality development.
- ★ Define and describe the nature and function of the id, ego, and superego.
- ★ Define and describe the defense mechanisms.
- ★ Define and describe the psychosexual stages of personality development.

BIG IDEA

Sigmund Freud proposed a theory of personality based on the belief that individuals are largely driven by unconscious desires that guide personality development.

In this lesson, you will learn about the following:

- Levels of Consciousness
- Defense Mechanisms
- Stages of Psychosexual Development

Sigmund Freud was the first to systematically study and theorize the workings of the ________________

mind in the manner that people associate with modern psychology.

Levels of Consciousness

Complete the following figure.

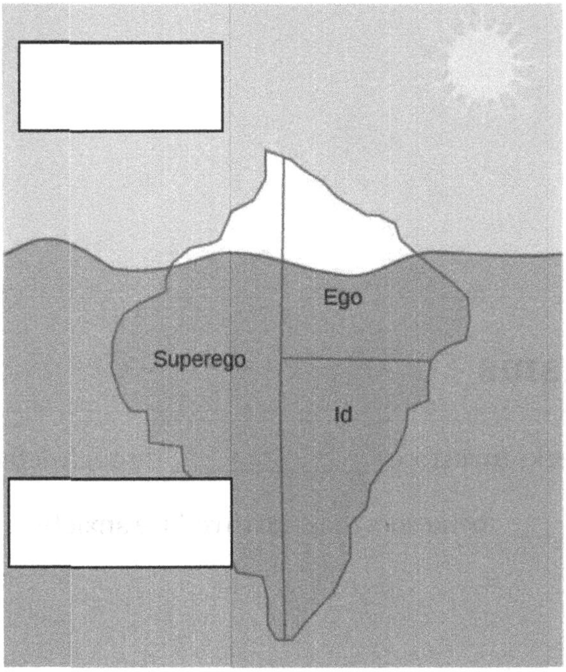

Complete the following graphic.

____
"I want to do that now!"

____
"It's not right to do that."

____
"Maybe we can compromise."

The id is ____________________, contains primitive urges and desires, and operates on the "________________ principle." The superego, on the other hand, is an individual's ________________ that strives for perfection and judges the individual's behavior. Finally, the ego is the ________________ part of personality that operates on the "________________ principle."

On Your Own

Provide an example of an internal struggle that clearly depicts the contribution of the id, ego, and superego.

Defense Mechanisms

Freud believed that the ego seeks to restore _______________ through defense mechanisms, which are unconscious ____________________ behaviors that aim to reduce anxiety.

Complete the following graphic of the defense mechanisms.

__________ Refusing to accept real events because they are unpleasant	__________ Transferring inappropriate urges onto a more acceptable target
__________ Redirecting unacceptable desires through socially acceptable channels	__________ __________ Reducing anxiety by adopting beliefs contrary to your own beliefs
__________ Returning to coping strategies for less mature stages of development	__________ Suppressing painful memories and thoughts
__________ Attributing unacceptable desires to others	__________ Justifying behaviors by substituting acceptable reasons for real reasons

On Your Own

The lesson discusses a man named Joe who is sexually attracted to males but engages in behaviors such as acting "macho," making gay jokes, and bullying a gay peer. What defense mechanisms do you see in his behaviors?

Stages of Psychosexual Development

Sigmund Freud believed that personality developed through early ______________, where

______________-seeking urges would be focused on a different erogenous zone.

Complete the following table.

Stage	Age (years)	Erogenous Zone	Major Conflict	Adult Fixation Example
______	0–1	Mouth	Weaning off breast or bottle	__________, overeating
Anal	1–3	________	________ __________	Neatness, messiness

Phallic	_______	Genitals	Oedipus/Electra complex	Vanity, _______________
___________	6–12	________	None	None
Genital	_______	Genitals	None	None

Psychology and You

Defense Mechanisms

Provide an example of a time when you observed a defense mechanism (either your own or someone else's).

Lesson Wrap-up

Say It in a Sentence

In one sentence, explain Freud's impact on psychology.

Test Yourself

Choose the correct answer for each of the following questions. Check your work using the Answer Key in the back of the book.

____ 1. According to Freud, ____ of the mind is conscious.

- **A.** 5%
- **B.** 10%
- **C.** 25%
- **D.** 50%

____ 2. According to Freud, _____ of the mind is unconscious.

- **A.** 10%
- **B.** 40%
- **C.** 70%
- **D.** 90%

____ 3. According to Freud, ____ comprises the self.

A. id
B. ego
C. superego

Answer each of the following questions. Check your work using the Answer Key in the back of the book.

4. When Michael's mother yells at him, he kicks his baby brother. Which defense mechanism is he using?

5. When the family dog starts having accidents in the house after the introduction of the new family cat, which defense mechanism is occurring?

6. Several politicians who appear to be adamantly against equal rights for homosexuals are later discovered to have homosexual backgrounds. This situation fits which defense mechanism?

7. James likes Sally, but he tells his friend, Max, "You like Sally!" Which defense mechanism is at work?

Key Terms

Match each key term with its definition.

A. Anal Stage
B. Conscious
C. Defense Mechanism
D. Displacement
E. Ego
F. Genital Stage
G. Id
H. Latency Period
I. Neurosis
J. Oral Stage
K. Phallic Stage
L. Projection
M. Psychosexual Stages of Development
N. Rationalization
O. Reaction Formation
P. Regression
Q. Sublimation
R. Superego
S. Unconscious

____ Psychosexual stage in which sexual feelings are dormant
____ Psychosexual stage in which the focus is on mature sexual interests
____ Ego defense mechanism in which a person confronted with anxiety makes excuses to justify behavior
____ Psychosexual stage in which an infant's pleasure is focused on the mouth
____ Stages of child development in which pleasure-seeking urges are focused at different erogenous zones
____ Psychosexual stage in which children experience pleasure in their bowel and bladder movements
____ Ego defense mechanism in which a person confronted with anxiety swaps unacceptable urges for their opposites
____ Ego defense mechanism in which a person confronted with anxiety returns to a more immature behavioral state

_____ Aspect of personality that serves as the conscience

_____ Mental activity of which we are unaware and unable to access

_____ Mental activity that we can access at any time

_____ Ego defense mechanism in which a person confronted with anxiety disguises their unacceptable urges by attributing them to others

_____ Unconscious protective behaviors designed to reduce ego anxiety

_____ Tendency to experience negative emotions

_____ Aspect of personality that consists of our most primitive urges

_____ Ego defense mechanism in which a person transfers inappropriate urges or behaviors towards a more acceptable or less threatening target

_____ Ego defense mechanism in which unacceptable urges are channeled into more appropriate activities

_____ Aspect of personality that represents the self

_____ Psychosexual stage in which the focus is on the genitals

Lesson 10.3

Neo-Freudians: Adler, Erikson, Jung, and Horney

OBJECTIVES

- ★ Discuss the concept of the inferiority complex.
- ★ Discuss the core difference between Erikson's and Freud's views on personality.
- ★ Discuss Jung's ideas of the collective unconscious and archetypes.
- ★ Discuss the work of Karen Horney, including her revision of Freud's "penis envy."

BIG IDEA

Sigmund Freud's theories of personality were revised by several theorists, who de-emphasized the role of sexual motivation and instead emphasized the role of the social environment.

In this lesson, you will learn about the following:

- Alfred Adler
- Erik Erikson
- Carl Jung
- Karen Horney

Alfred Adler

Alfred Adler started ________________ psychology and theorized that individuals were motivated by a desire to not feel ________________ to others. An inferiority complex refers to a person's feelings that they lack ______________ and do not measure up to the ________________ of others or society.

Complete the following graphic.

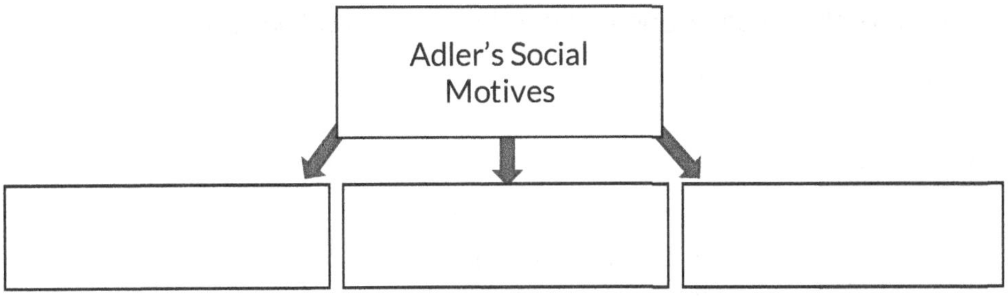

On Your Own

What are your thoughts about the idea that birth order can influence who we are and how we behave? Do you see evidence of this theory in your own life?

Erik Erikson

Complete the following table.

Stage	Age	Erikson Stage of Development
1	Birth to 1 year	
2		Autonomy vs. shame/doubt
3	3 to 6 years	
4	7 to 11 years	
5		Identity vs. confusion
6	19 to 29 years	
7		Generativity vs. stagnation
8		Integrity vs. despair

Carl Jung

Carl Jung started _______________ psychology, which focused on balancing opposing forces of conscious and unconscious thought and experience within one's personality. His focus was on the collective unconscious rather than the personal unconscious. Specifically, he felt that there was a _______________ version of the personal unconscious, holding mental patterns (_______________) which are common to us all.

Complete the following graphic:

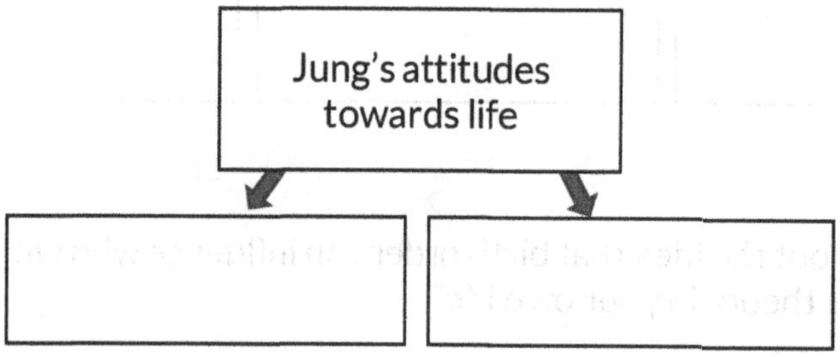

Complete the following table.

Introvert	Extrovert
	Energized by being with others
Avoids attention	
	Speaks quickly and loudly
	Thinks out loud
Stays on one topic	
	Prefers verbal communication
Pays attention easily	
Cautious	

Karen Horney

Karen Horney believed that each individual had the potential for self-__________________, allowing the person to move towards a healthy self. She also disagreed with Freud's idea of "___________ envy" and instead thought that any envious feelings stemmed from the male position in society.

Complete the following graphic.

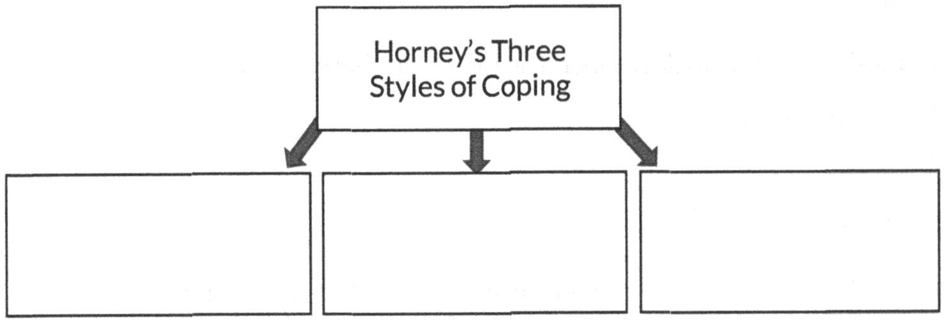

Complete the following table.

Coping Style	Description	Example
	Affiliation and dependence	Child seeking positive attention and affection from parent; adult needing love
Moving against people		Child fighting or bullying other children; adult who is abrasive and verbally hurtful or exploits others

	Detachment and isolation	Child withdrawn from the world and isolated; adult loner

Psychology and You

Introvert vs. Extrovert

Would you consider yourself an extrovert or introvert? Support your answer.

Lesson Wrap-up

Say It in a Sentence

In one sentence, explain the difference between Freud and the Neo-Freudians as a whole.

Test Yourself

Choose the correct answer for each of the following questions. Check your work using the Answer Key in the back of the book.

____ 1. The Neo-Freudian who developed the idea of archetypes was:

- **A.** Karen Horney
- **B.** Carl Jung
- **C.** Alfred Adler
- **D.** Erik Erikson

____ 2. The Neo-Freudian who developed the idea of trust vs. mistrust was:

- **A.** Karen Horney
- **B.** Carl Jung
- **C.** Alfred Adler
- **D.** Erik Erikson

Next to each statement, write **T** for True or **F** for False. Check your work using the Answer Key in the back of the book.

3. ____ Freud believed that we continue to develop across the lifespan, whereas Erikson felt personality development stops in childhood.

4. ____ Adler believed we are motivated by sex and aggression; Freud felt we strive against feeling inferior.

Key Terms

Write a paraphrased definition for each key term.

Analytical Psychology:

Archetype:

Collective Unconscious:

Individual Psychology:

Inferiority Complex:

Lesson 10.4

Learning Approaches

OBJECTIVES

- ★ Describe the behaviorist perspective on personality.
- ★ Describe the cognitive perspective on personality.
- ★ Describe the social cognitive perspective on personality.

BIG IDEA

Learning approaches to personality only focus on observable behavior, not inner cognitive processes.

In this lesson, you will learn about the following:

- The Behavioral Perspective
- The Social-Cognitive Perspective
- Julian Rotter and Locus of Control
- Walter Mischel and the Person-Situation Debate

The Behavioral Perspective

Behaviorists do not see personality traits as ____________. Instead, they see personality as significantly shaped by the reinforcements and __________________ of behavior. Essentially, people increase the behaviors that are rewarded and decrease the behaviors that are __________________.

The Social-Cognitive Perspective

Alfred Bandura felt personality develops through ______________, and he felt thinking and _________________ are also important. The social-cognitive theory emphasizes both learning and _________________ as sources of individual differences in personality.

Complete the following graphic.

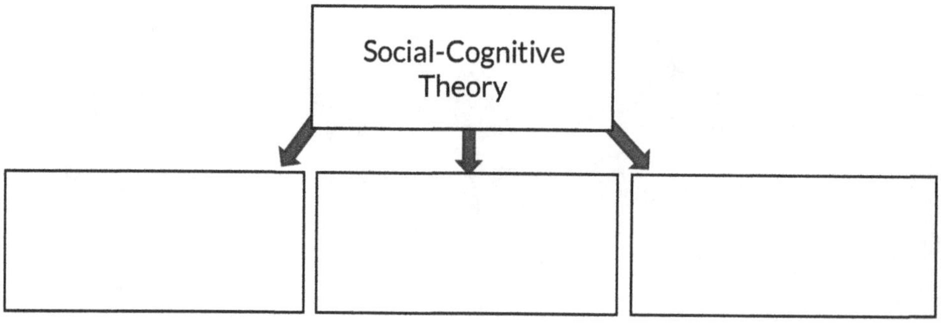

Reciprocal Determinism

Reciprocal determinism posits that ________________ processes, behavior, and ______________ all interact. Cognitive processes refer to all characteristics previously ______________, including beliefs, expectations, and personality characteristics. Behavior refers to anything that we do that may be ________________ or punished. Finally, the ______________ in which the behavior occurs refers to the environment or situation, which includes rewarding/punishing stimuli.

Complete the following graphic.

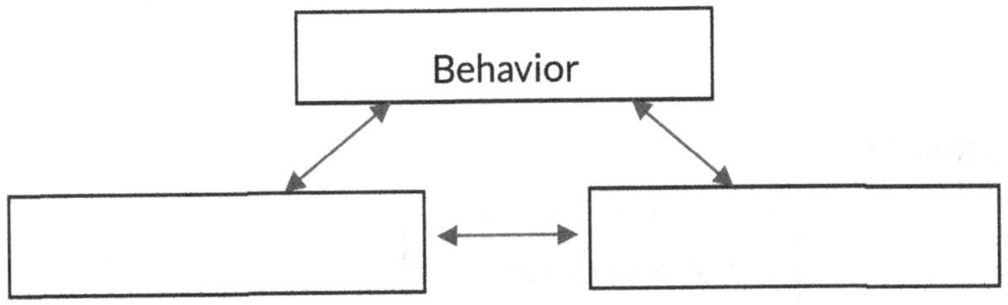

On Your Own

Provide an example that demonstrates the three aspects of reciprocal determinism.

Observational Learning

Individuals often learn by ________________ others and then choosing to imitate the observed behavior. In some cases, if the model is ________________, individuals may opt to refrain from imitation.

Self-Efficacy

Self-efficacy is our level of ________________ in our own abilities, developed through our social ________________.

On Your Own

What are the characteristics of people with high self-efficacy?

1.
2.
3.
4.

What are the characteristics of people with low self-efficacy?

1.

2.

3.

4.

Julian Rotter and Locus of Control

Julian Rotter proposed the concept of locus of control, which is the belief regarding the ____________ one has over his or her own life.

Complete the following graphic.

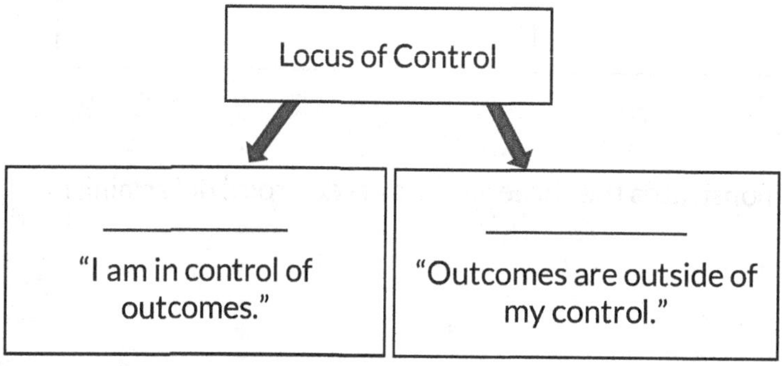

On Your Own

What are the benefits of having an internal locus of control, according to researchers?

1.

2.

3.

4.

5.

6.

Walter Mischel and the Person-Situation Debate

Walter Mischel did not find data to support the idea that personality traits were consistent ____________ situations; however, behavior was consistent ____________ situations.

On Your Own

Would you be able to resist a small reward now to get a larger reward later? Can you think of an example of when you faced this dilemma?

How did the children who were able to resist the marshmallow fare later in life?

1.

2.

3.

4.

5.

Psychology and You

Self-Efficacy

How would you describe your own self-efficacy? When you face a challenge, how do you view it?

Lesson Wrap-up

Say It in a Sentence

In one sentence, explain something the learning approaches to personality all have in common.

Test Yourself

Choose the correct answer for each of the following questions. Check your work using the Answer Key in the back of the book.

____ 1. The idea of observational learning was:

- **A.** Maslow's
- **B.** Bandura's
- **C.** Skinner's
- **D.** Michel's

____ 2. The components of the social-cognitive approach are:

- **A.** Reciprocal determinism, self-regulation, and observational learning
- **B.** Mutual determinism, self-efficacy, and learning
- **C.** Reciprocal determinism, self-efficacy, and observational learning

____ 3. In Mischel's experiment, the children with the best developmental outcomes were:

- **A.** Those who delayed gratification
- **B.** Those who did not delay gratification

Next to each statement, write **T** for True or **F** for False. Check your work using the Answer Key in the back of the book.

4. _____ Learning approaches can be scientifically tested because they involve observable, measurable phenomena.
5. _____ Bandura's key contribution to learning theory was that a great deal of learning is vicarious.
6. _____ Mischel's most notable contribution to personality psychology was the idea of self-presentation.

Key Terms

For each key term, provide an example that exemplifies the meaning of the word.

Locus of Control:

Reciprocal Determinism:

Self-Efficacy:

Social-Cognitive Theory:

Lesson 10.5

Humanistic Approaches

OBJECTIVES

★ Discuss the contributions of Abraham Maslow and Carl Rogers to personality development.

BIG IDEA

The humanistic approaches to personality focus on the ideas of human growth and potential.

In this lesson, you will learn about the following:

- Abraham Maslow
- Carl Rogers

Humanism focuses on how _______________ people develop and can have __________-directed change and transforming personal experiences.

On Your Own

What characteristics did healthy, creative, and productive people have in common, according to Maslow?

1.
2.
3.
4.
5.
6.
7.

Are you in the self-actualization section of Maslow's hierarchy? Why or why not?

Carl Rogers was another humanistic theorist who focused on the idea of __________________: thoughts and feelings of the self.

Complete the following graphic.

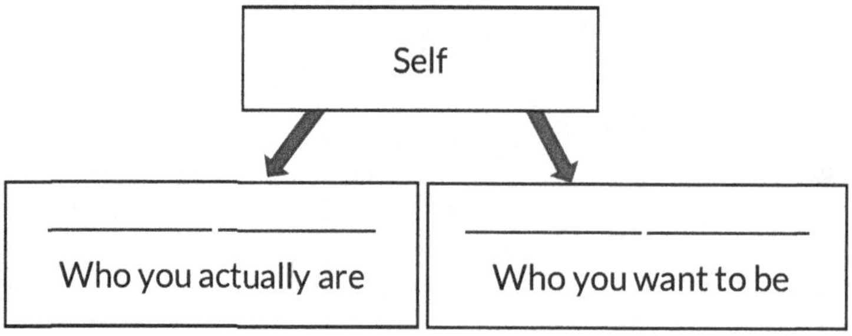

On Your Own

Do you feel that you have congruence or incongruence? Explain.

Psychology and You

Application of Maslow's Hierarchy

If you were Abraham Maslow, who would you study? Name at least three people. Why did you select those people?

Lesson Wrap-up

Say It in a Sentence

In one sentence, explain humanism.

Test Yourself

Choose the correct answer for each of the following questions. Check your work using the Answer Key in the back of the book.

____ 1. People with low congruence would have:

- **A.** Higher likelihood of being maladjusted
- **B.** A greater sense of self-worth

____ 2. People with high congruence would have:

- **A.** Higher likelihood of being maladjusted
- **B.** A greater sense of self-worth

Answer each of the following questions. Check your work using the Answer Key in the back of the book.

3. What is the difference between the real self and ideal self?

4. Which is better for future outcomes: congruence or incongruence?

Key Terms

Use the key terms from the lesson to complete the following crossword puzzle.

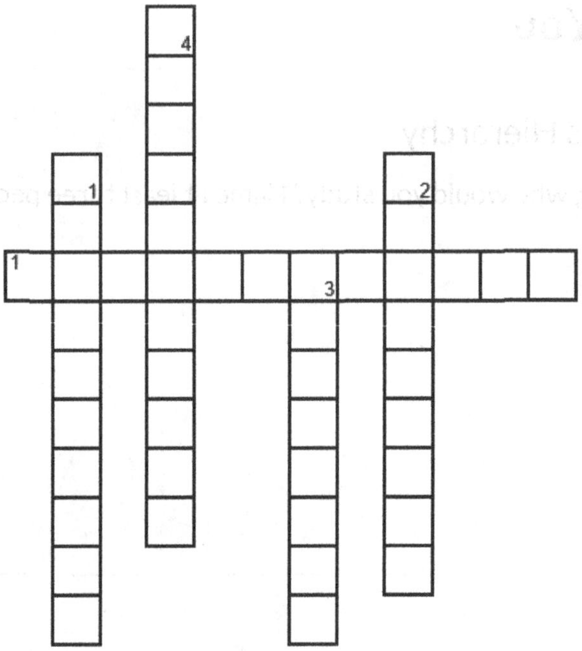

Across

1. State of being in which there is a great discrepancy between our real and ideal selves

Down

1. State of being in which our thoughts about our real and ideal selves are very similar
2. Person we would like to be
3. Person who we actually are
4. Our thoughts and feelings about ourselves

Lesson 10.6

Biological Approaches

OBJECTIVES

★ Discuss the findings of the Minnesota Study of Twins Reared Apart as they relate to personality and genetics.
★ Discuss temperament and describe the three infant temperaments identified by Thomas and Chess.
★ Discuss the evolutionary perspective on personality development.

BIG IDEA

Biological theories of personality posit that the primary drive behind personality differences is biological rather than learned.

In this lesson, you will learn about the following:

- Temperament

The Minnesota Study of Twins Reared Apart was conducted between 1979 and 1999 on ________ pairs of twins (both identical and fraternal). It found that ________________ twins have similar personalities.

________________ refers to the proportion of difference among people that is attributed to genetics.

On Your Own

Which traits had more than a 0.50 heritability ratio?

1.
2.
3.
4.
5.
6.

Temperament

Complete the following graphic.

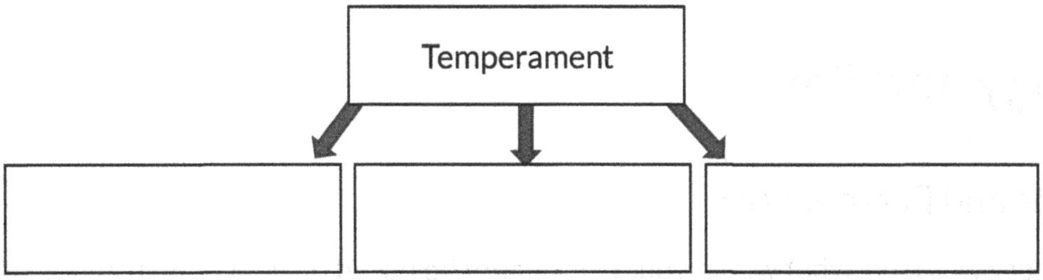

Research suggests there are two dimensions of temperament that are important parts of adult personality: ________________ and self-regulation. ________________ refers to how individuals respond to new or challenging environmental stimuli; self-regulation refers to our ability to ______________ that response.

The constitutional perspective suggests there may be a relationship between body type and temperament.

Complete the following graphic.

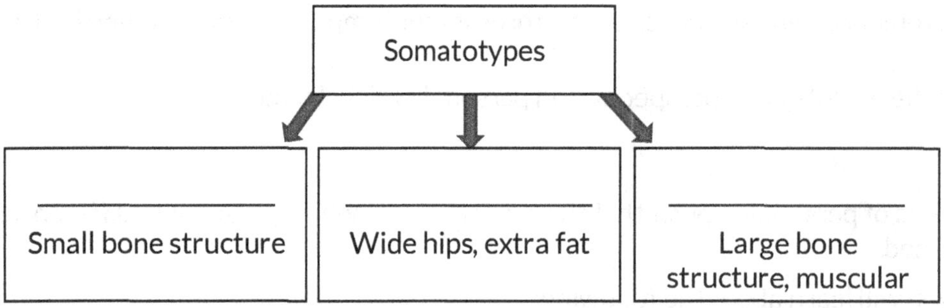

On Your Own

According to Sheldon, what characterizes ectomorphs?

1.
2.
3.
4.
5.
6.

According to Sheldon, what characterizes endomorphs?

1.
2.
3.
4.
5.
6.

According to Sheldon, what characterizes mesomorphs?

1.
2.
3.
4.

What do you think about the idea that body shape could be related to personality? Can you think of other explanations for Sheldon's findings?

Psychology and You

Somatotypes and Personalities

If Sheldon's theory was true, what would your personality be based on your somatotype? How does the theory compare to the reality of your personality?

Lesson Wrap-up

Say It in a Sentence

In one sentence, explain the biological approach to personality.

Test Yourself

Choose the correct answer for each of the following questions. Check your work using the Answer Key in the back of the book.

____ 1. How many pairs of twins were studied in the Minnesota Study of Twins Reared Apart?

- **A.** 100
- **B.** 250
- **C.** 350
- **D.** 450

____ 2. The Minnesota Study of Twins Reared Apart found that ______ twins were closer in personality.

- **A.** identical
- **B.** fraternal

____ 3. Endomorphs tend to be:

- **A.** Assertive
- **B.** Relaxed
- **C.** Self-conscious

Answer each of the following questions. Check your work using the Answer Key in the back of the book.

4. According to Sheldon, which somatotype would tend toward good humor?

5. According to Sheldon, which somatotype would tend toward aggression?

Key Terms

Write a paraphrased definition for each key term.

Heritability:

Temperament:

Lesson 10.7

Trait Theorists

OBJECTIVES

- ★ Discuss early trait theories of Cattell and Eysenck.
- ★ Discuss the Big Five factors and describe someone who is high and low on each of the five traits.

BIG IDEA

Trait theorists believe there are universal traits that help define an individual's personality.

In this lesson, you will learn about the following:

- Early Trait Theories
- Big Five Factors

Traits are characteristic ways of ________________. Gordon Allport found ______________ words that could be used to describe an individual and organized these into cardinal, central, and secondary traits. _______________ traits were traits that dominated an individual personality. ______________ traits were those that made up personality, such as loyalty. Finally, ____________________ traits were not as obvious or consistent, such as a person who liked to sleep on his or her side at night.

On Your Own

What is your opinion about the secondary traits? Does sleeping on your side or disliking being tickled count as a trait?

Raymond Cattell narrowed the list down to 171 traits and used these to identify 16 dimensions of personality.

List the Cattell's 16 dimensions of personality.

1.
2.
3.
4.
5.
6.
7.
8.
9.
10.
11.
12.
13.
14.
15.
16.

On Your Own

What is your opinion of the 16PF? Are there some traits you think are more valid than others? Why?

Label the following figure.

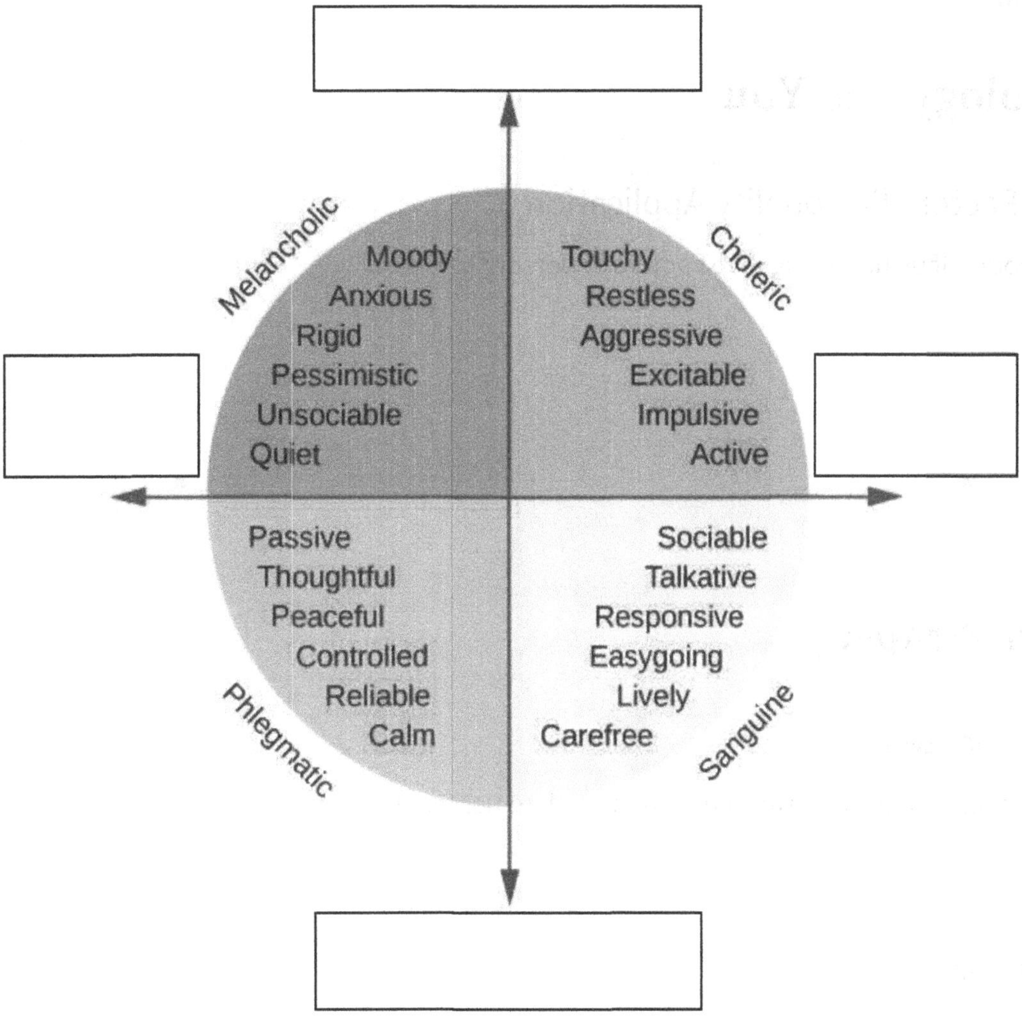

List the traits in the Five Factor Model.

1.
2.
3.
4.
5.

On Your Own

Can you think of a fictional character that fits each of the five factors of personality? Is the character high or low in each of those traits?

Openness:

Conscientiousness:

Extroversion:

Agreeableness:

Neuroticism:

Psychology and You

Big Five Factors Personality Application

Describe yourself using the Big Five Factors of personality.

Lesson Wrap-up

Say It in a Sentence

In one sentence, explain the trait theory approach to personality.

Test Yourself

Choose the correct answer(s) for each of the following questions. Check your work using the Answer Key in the back of the book.

_____ 1. Which of the following trait theories was criticized as being too broad?

- **A.** Cattrell's 16PF
- **B.** Eysenck two factors
- **C.** Big Five Factors

______ 2. Extroversion appears in which theories?

A. Cattrell 16PF
B. Eysenck two factors
C. Big Five Factors

Answer each of the following questions. Check your work using the Answer Key in the back of the book.

3. Research suggests that these Big Five Factor traits increase with age.

4. Research suggests that these Big Five Factor traits decrease with age.

Key Terms

Write a paraphrased definition for each key term.

Five Factor Model:

Traits:

Lesson 10.8

Cultural Understandings of Personality

OBJECTIVES

★ Discuss personality differences of people from collectivist and individualist cultures.
★ Discuss the three approaches to studying personality in a cultural context.

BIG IDEA

Culture is the beliefs, customs, art, and accepted/unaccepted behaviors of a population or society. The study of personality should place strong consideration on cultural differences.

Why is it important for researchers to consider cultural differences in the study of personality?

List the three approaches to studying culture and personality.

1.

2.

3.

In this lesson, you will learn about the following:

- Personality in Individualist and Collectivist Cultures
- Approaches to Studying Personality in a Cultural Context

Personality in Individualist and Collectivist Cultures

________________ can be partially defined by accepted and unaccepted behavior in society. In some cases, culture can influence personality. For example, western nations like the United States tend to place greater value in __________________, whereas Asian nations are more likely to value __________________. In other cases, people may __________________ ______________ to a specific culture because it fits their personal needs.

On Your Own

Think of a time when you, a friend, or a family member moved for personal reasons. Why do you think you or the person in question decided to move?

Approaches to Studying Personality in a Cultural Context

There are three approaches to studying culture and personality. The ________________ approach looks at two or more cultures using personality characteristics defined using western cultures. For example, introversion and extroversion are personality traits that were identified in the United States but can be measured in any culture. The ________________ approach looks at differences in personality that exist within the society or population being studied. The ________________ approach compares cultures using constructs in the United States but also considers indigenous differences within a specific culture.

Identify which approach *best* aligns with the described study.

Study Description	Approach Type
A study assessing anti-social personality traits in the U.S. and China considers differences between what the U.S. and China would consider anti-social behavior.	
A study assesses differences between the U.S. and China in extroversion.	
A study assesses personality constructs related to gender among a targeted civilization in Africa.	
A study aims to assess personality dimensions in a small community in Moscow, Russia.	
A study assesses the differences in risk-taking behavior among Canadian and French populations, considering what is considered risky in each culture.	
A study assesses the differences in neuroticism between the northeastern United States and the southern United States.	

On Your Own

Using the following diagram, write a study description that matches each of the three approaches to studying culture and personality.

Study Description	Approach
	Comparative Approach
	Indigenous Approach

	Combined Approach

Psychology and You

Defining Your Culture

How would you define your culture?

In what ways do you think your culture has impacted your personality? Explain.

In what ways have you migrated to certain cultures that impacted your personal needs? This can be in the form of physically moving, your choice of friends, the places where you choose to spend your leisure time, or other aspects of culture. Explain.

Lesson Wrap-up

Say It in a Sentence

In one sentence, explain why culture is important to consider when studying personality.

Test Yourself

Fill in the blanks. Check your work using the Answer Key in the back of the book.

1. The ________________ __________________ compares a single trait across multiple cultures.
2. The ______________________ _________________ often uses personality constructs that were developed outside of countries in North America and Western Europe.

3. The ________________ ________________ compares across cultures using personality constructs developed inside and outside of countries in North America and Western Europe.
4. In comparison to Western countries, Asian countries have a more ________________ mindset.
5. ________________ ________________ describes how your culture affects your personality.

Key Terms

Answer the following questions about the key terms from this lesson.

What is **culture**, and how does it affect personality?

Propose a research study idea using the comparative approach that considers **individualistic** and **collectivistic cultures**.

Propose a research study idea that uses the **indigenous approach** and considers **selective migration**.

Why is the **combined approach** effective for studying personality and culture?

Lesson 10.9

Personality Assessment

OBJECTIVES

- ★ Discuss the Minnesota Multiphasic Personality Inventory.
- ★ Recognize and describe common projective tests used in personality assessment.

BIG IDEA

Personality tests are techniques to measure one's personality. They are used to aid in diagnosis of psychiatric disorders and screen candidates for college and employment.

What are the two types of personality assessments?

1.

2.

In this lesson, you will learn about the following:

- Self-Report Inventories
- Projective Tests

Self-Report Personality Tests

Self-report personality assessments are usually constructed in a ____________________ format. For example, an assessment may use a ____________ scale, which may ask an examinee to report their level of agreement on a scale of 1 (strongly disagree) to 5 (strongly agree). The ________________

________________ ________________ ________________ (MMPI-2) is one of the most widely used self-report personality assessments.

Identify the strengths and weaknesses of using self-report personality assessments.

Strengths	Weaknesses

On Your Own

Use the first example in the following table to create two more examples of a self-report personality assessment scale.

Scale/Directions	Item
Rate the following item on a scale of 1 (not at all like me) to 5 (very much like me).	I am a very social person.

Projective Tests

Projective tests ask an examinee to interpret a series of ____________________ designs or complete a ________________. The responses are believed to uncover one's defense mechanisms or unconscious processes.

Complete the following table on the popular projective tests.

Test	Description
	Examiner presents examinee with inkblots. For each inkblot, the examiner asks, "What might this be?"
Thematic Apperception Test (TAT)	
	The examinee is asked to complete a series of sentences that start with phrases like *I feel* or *my biggest regret is*
Contemporary Themes Concerning Blacks Test (C-TCB)	
	A projective assessment designed for Hispanic youth

Identify the strengths and weaknesses of using projective tests to assess personality.

Strengths	Weaknesses

On Your Own

Construct your own question on a projective test.

On Your Own

Label the following assessments as *projective* or *self-report*.

Assessment Description	Projective or Self Report?
An assessment that uses a series of multiple-choice questions.	
A test that asks an individual to interpret a series of paintings on cards.	
Rotter Incomplete Sentence Blank	
MMPI-2	

Psychology and You

Personality Assessments

Have you ever taken a personality assessment? If so, what type of assessment was it? If you don't remember, what was the test like?

What assessment type do you prefer, self-report or projective? Explain your reasoning.

Lesson Wrap-up

Say It in a Sentence

In one sentence, describe the two types of personality assessments.

Test Yourself

Next to each statement, write **T** for True or **F** for False. Check your work using the Answer Key in the back of the book.

1. ______ A projective test uses multiple-choice items.
2. ______ The Thematic Apperception Test is an example of a projective test.
3. ______ The Minnesota Multiphasic Personality Inventory is an example of a self-report personality assessment.

Key Terms

For the following key terms, make groupings out of the related terms. Be sure to explain how they are related.

Key Terms: Contemporized-Themes Concerning Blacks Test (C-TCB), Minnesota Multiphasic Personality Inventory (MMPI), projective test, Rorschach Inkblot Test, Rotter Incomplete Sentence Blank (RISB), TEMAS Multicultural Thematic Apperception Test, Thematic Apperception Test (TAT), self-report assessment

Chapter 11
Social Psychology

Lesson 11.1
What Is Social Psychology?

OBJECTIVES

- ★ Define social psychology.
- ★ Describe situational versus dispositional influences on behavior.
- ★ Describe the fundamental attribution error.

BIG IDEA

Social psychologists study how people and social environment influence the thoughts, feelings, and behavior of others.

Define intrapersonal and interpersonal topics and give an example of each.

	Definition	Example
Intrapersonal		
Interpersonal		

In this lesson, you will learn about the following:

- Situational and Dispositional Influences on Behavior
- Is the Fundamental Attribution Error a Universal Phenomenon?
- Actor-Observer Bias
- Self-Serving Bias
- Just-World Hypothesis

Situational and Dispositional Influences on Behavior

____________________ suggests that our behavior is a direct consequence of our environment. In contrast, ____________________ suggests that behavior is determined by internal traits.

On Your Own

Describe the situational and dispositional influences that led to you choosing your favorite restaurant, sport, and academic subject.

Activity	Situational Influence	Dispositional Influence
Favorite restaurant: ______________		
Favorite sport: ______________		
Favorite subject: ______________		

Fundamental Attribution Error

The fundamental attribution error is when you overestimate ______________ influences on the behavior of other people. Imagine you are eating at a restaurant, and the waiter brings out the wrong food. Your gut explanation may be to use personality traits to explain his behavior. However, the waiter's poor service may be due to recently getting dumped by his girlfriend, a death in the family, or staying up late to soothe his young daughter.

On Your Own

Why do you think we overestimate internal influences on the behavior of others?

Is the Fundamental Attribution Error a Universal Phenomenon?

______________ cultures, which focus on achievement and autonomy, are more likely than collectivist cultures to overestimate internal influences on the behavior of others.

On Your Own

What aspects of collectivist and individualist cultures do you think explain their likelihood of committing the fundamental attribution error?

Actor-Observer Bias

On Your Own

Think about a time you performed below your standards in school. Why do you think this happened?

Did you describe situational or internal factors to explain your performance?

Someone you know is unable to find a full-time job two years after graduating college. Why do you think this happened?

Did you use situational or internal factors to explain this situation?

If you used situational factors to describe your grade and internal factors to describe someone else's bad luck on the job market, you may have committed the actor-observer bias. The actor-observer bias is the phenomenon of attributing other people's behavior to ________________ factors while attributing our own behavior to the ________________.

On Your Own

Why do you think we commit the actor-observer bias?

Self-Serving Bias

Self-serving bias is when we use ______________ attributions for ______________ outcomes and ____________________ attributions for _________________ outcomes.

Explain the following outcomes using self-serving bias.

- I lost my job.
  - Explanation:
- I scored high on my exam.
  - Explanation:
- I lost a tennis match.
  - Explanation:

- My team won the football game.
    - Explanation:

Just-World Hypothesis

Just-world hypothesis is the belief that people who do good get ________________ outcomes and people who do bad get ________________ outcomes.

On Your Own

Why do you think we believe the just-world hypothesis?

Psychology and You

Internal and External Attributions for Recent Decisions

What's a decision you've made recently? What aspects of the decision were internal, and what aspects were external?

Describe a time you used self-serving bias to explain an outcome in your life.

Lesson Wrap-up

Say It in a Sentence

In one sentence, describe how internal and external factors can lead to biased perceptions of others.

Test Yourself

Choose the correct answer for each of the following questions. Check your work using the Answer Key in the back of the book.

____ 1. Joe's cashier was rude to him, and he assumed that she was a mean person. Joe's reaction best fits:

- **A.** Just-world hypothesis
- **B.** Self-serving bias
- **C.** Actor-observer bias
- **D.** Fundamental attribution error

____ 2. Tim said he failed his math test because he "has a bad teacher." Tim's belief best demonstrates:

- **A.** Just-world hypothesis
- **B.** Self-serving bias
- **C.** Actor-observer bias
- **D.** Fundamental attribution error

____ 3. Suzie believes that she chose sales as a career because it's a good fit for her personality but that her friend chose it for the money. Suzie's belief best demonstrates:

- **A.** Just-world hypothesis
- **B.** Self-serving bias
- **C.** Actor-observer bias
- **D.** Fundamental attribution error

____ 4. Kim believes that everyone gets what they deserve in life. Kim's belief best demonstrates:

- **A.** Just-world hypothesis
- **B.** Self-serving bias
- **C.** Actor-observer bias
- **D.** Fundamental attribution error

Next to each statement, write **T** for True or **F** for False. Check your work using the Answer Key in the back of the book.

5. ____ The fundamental attribution error is the belief that people get what they deserve.

6. ____ Raj attributing his good grade on a math test to his intelligence is an example of self-serving bias.

7. ____ Attributing internal factors to a decision someone else has made is an example of actor-observer bias.

Key Terms

Write a paraphrased definition for each key term.

Actor-Observer Bias:

Dispositionalism:

Situationalism:

Fundamental Attribution Error:

Just-World Hypothesis:

Lesson 11.2

Self-Presentation

OBJECTIVES

- ★ Describe social roles and how they influence behavior.
- ★ Explain what social norms are and how they influence behavior.
- ★ Define script.
- ★ Describe the findings of Zimbardo's Stanford prison experiment.

BIG IDEA

Humans use their social environments as sources of information, or cues, on how to behave.

In this lesson, you will learn about the following:

- Social Roles
- Social Norms
- Scripts
- Zimbardo's Stanford Prison Experiment

Social Roles

Social roles are ____________________ of how you should behave in a ______________. They are often determined by ____________________. For example, it may be alright for a coach to raise her voice at practice but not when she is teaching a class.

Using the following diagram, list three things you did yesterday. For each activity, identify your social role.

#	Daily Activity	Social Role
1		
2		
3		

Social Norms

A social norm is a group's expectation of how its members should ______________, ___________, and ______________ in a certain situation. Social norms are heavily influenced by ________________. In the United States, it may be acceptable for women to wear shorts or skirts at night, whereas in other countries this type of attire may not be viewed as socially appropriate.

Identify a place or situation where each of the following actions would be acceptable and unacceptable.

Action	Acceptable	Not acceptable
Drinking alcohol		
Wearing shorts and a t-shirt		
Yelling and screaming		

On Your Own

Why do you think social roles and norms are a part of human behavior?

Scripts

A script is a person's _________________ of a ________________ of events that is supposed to happen in a _______________ setting. For example, you know after you eat at a restaurant that the waiter is supposed to bring you a check.

Come up with your own script by completing the following diagram.

If this happens:	
I am supposed to behave in this way:	

Zimbardo's Stanford Prison Experiment

On Your Own

Identify a question you have about the limitations of social roles and scripts and write a hypothesis that answers this question. How would you test this hypothesis?

Psychology and You

Social Roles

Discuss a few of your social roles.

Have you changed your behavior to be more consistent with social norms? How so?

Lesson Wrap-up

Say It in a Sentence

In only one sentence, summarize social roles, norms, and scripts.

Test Yourself

Choose the correct answer for each of the following questions. Check your work using the Answer Key in the back of the book.

____ 1. Group standards for how members should act, think, and feel in certain situations is an example of:

A. Social role
B. Social norm
C. Script

____ 2. Kate knows that as a student, she should pay attention and listen to her teacher during class. This example best fits which of the following terms?

A. Social role
B. Social norm
C. Script

____ 3. Kristy knows that when the teacher starts talking, she must stop talking and begin taking notes. This example best fits which of the following terms?

A. Social role
B. Social norm
C. Script

Next to each statement, write **T** for True or **F** for False. Check your work using the Answer Key in the back of the book.

4. ______ Scripts are understanding the sequence of social behaviors.
5. ______ Social norms are individual rules for behavior.
6. ______ Social roles are how others behave toward you.

Key Terms

Write a paraphrased definition for each key term.

Social Roles:

Social Norms:

Scripts:

Lesson 11.3

Attitudes and Persuasion

OBJECTIVES

- ★ Define attitude.
- ★ Describe how people's attitudes are internally changed through cognitive dissonance.
- ★ Explain how people's attitudes are externally changed through persuasion.
- ★ Describe the peripheral and central routes to persuasion.

BIG IDEA

An attitude is feelings or evaluation of an idea or an object. Complete the following diagram on how to change attitudes.

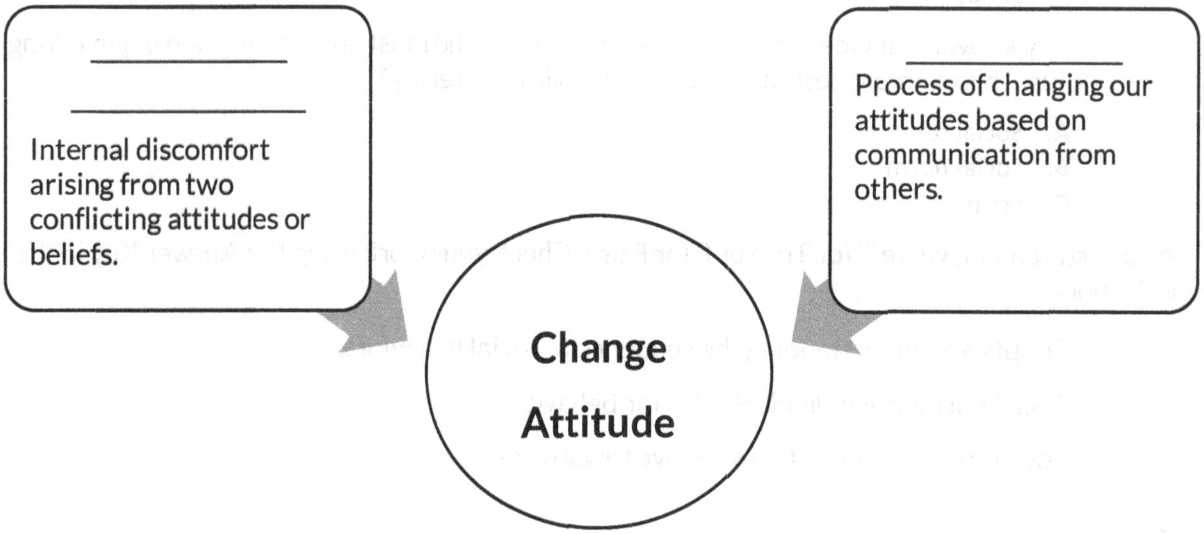

In this lesson, you will learn about the following:

- What Is Cognitive Dissonance?
- Persuasion

What Is Cognitive Dissonance?

Cognitive dissonance is when two conflicting attitudes are present in our consciousness, causing ____________________. The way we handle dissonance is to remove the tension by defending one of them and supporting it with our actions.

On Your Own

Steve loves to eat red meat. He recently watched a documentary that suggests red meat can cause colon cancer. Complete the following diagram to help explain Steve's dissonance and the actions he could take to support each of the conflicting attitudes.

Attitude 1

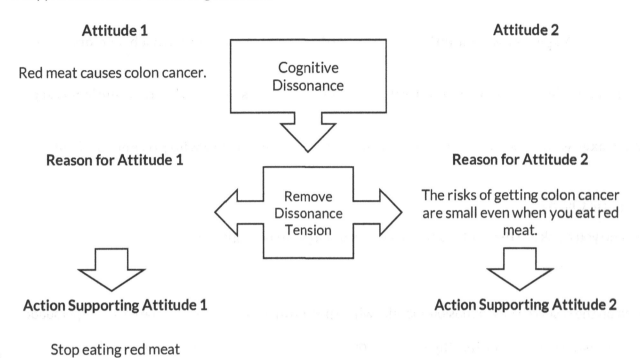

Red meat causes colon cancer.

Attitude 2

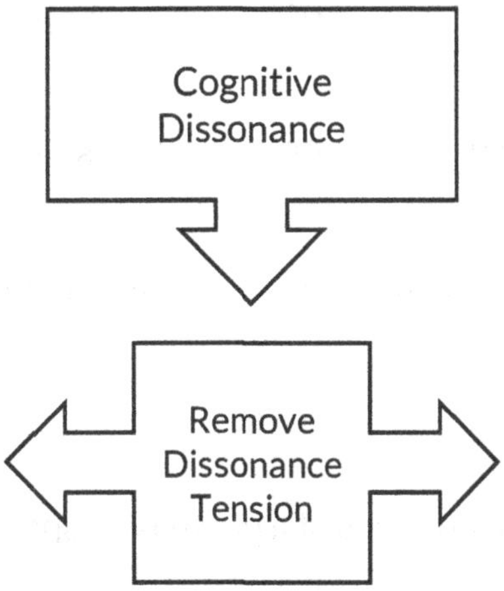

Reason for Attitude 1

Reason for Attitude 2

The risks of getting colon cancer are small even when you eat red meat.

Action Supporting Attitude 1

Stop eating red meat

Action Supporting Attitude 2

The Effect of Initiation

The amount of effort one puts in to belong to a group is defined as ________________. The more effort one puts in to be a part of a group, the ______________ they like the group.

On Your Own

Based on what you know about initiation, answer the following questions about the scenarios.

John and Paul decide to join a fraternity at their college. John joins a fraternity that accepts you into brotherhood immediately, whereas Paul joins a fraternity that requires a rigorous five-month initiation process. Who will give more positive reviews of their fraternity?	
Rebecca takes a psychology course with a teacher who gives a lot of work but does not give any tests. Ben takes the same course with a different teacher who doesn't require much work and gives tests to assess learning. Which student is more likely to like their psychology class?	

Yale Attitude Change Approach

Use the research on persuasion to identify which individual in each pair would be more persuasive.

An attractive athlete	or	An overweight comedian
A speaker with a PhD	or	A speaker with a bachelors' degree
A speaker who is very straight forward	or	A speaker who uses subtle messages
A speaker who presents one side very well	or	A speaker who presents multiple sides

On Your Own

What do you think are the most important qualities of a persuasive speaker?

Based on the research on persuasion, identify which person in the following pairs be easier to persuade.

A listener with low intelligence	or	A listener with high intelligence
A listener with low self-esteem	or	A listener with moderate self-esteem
A 21-year-old listener	or	A 45-year-old listener

Elaboration Likelihood Model

Central route persuasion is to logic as peripheral route persuasion is to emotions. Using the following diagram, report which of the following advertisements would use central or peripheral route persuasion.

Commercial	Route of Persuasion
A football player advertising shampoo	
Save 10% or more on your car insurance by switching to this brand.	
A commercial from a car company comparing price and safety features with its competitors	
A commercial where a man opens a beer on a beach	
An ice cream commercial comparing calories to its competitors	

On Your Own

Which 2–3 examples from the previous table do you think would have the most lasting change on attitude?

Foot-in-the-Door Technique

The foot-in-the-door technique is persuading someone to do something small, only to later request something larger. An example of the foot-in-the-door technique is a car salesman allowing a potential customer to take the prospective car with them for the day.

On Your Own

Why do you think the foot-in-the-door technique works?

Psychology and You

Cognitive Dissonance Reflection

Describe a time when you experienced cognitive dissonance. What were the two attitudes causing dissonance? How did you resolve the dissonance?

Describe a time when someone used the "foot-in-the-door technique" on you. Did it work? Why or why not?

Lesson Wrap-up

Say It in a Sentence

In one sentence, describe how an attitude about something can be changed.

Test Yourself

Choose the correct answer for each of the following questions. Check your work using the Answer Key in the back of the book.

____ 1. Supervisors were asked to rate how much effort employees put into their work on a scale of 1 to 10, with 1 meaning "very little effort" and 10 meaning "a great deal of effort." Based on the research discussed in the lesson, which employee would like their job least?

- **A.** Employee with a rating of 1
- **B.** Employee with a rating of 5
- **C.** Employee with a rating of 8
- **D.** Employee with a rating of 10

____ 2. A commercial that focuses on getting the viewer to feel positive is an example of which of the following techniques of persuasion?

- **A.** Foot-in-the-door technique
- **B.** Central route persuasion
- **C.** Peripheral route persuasion
- **D.** Cognitive dissonance

____ 3. Grocery stores that give free samples of products are using which of the following techniques of persuasion?

- **A.** Foot-in-the-door technique
- **B.** Central route persuasion
- **C.** Peripheral route persuasion
- **D.** Cognitive dissonance

____ 4. Joe is convinced that coffee is giving him acid reflux, but he loves drinking coffee. Joe's situation would most likely subject him to:

- **A.** Foot-in-the-door technique
- **B.** Central route persuasion
- **C.** Peripheral route persuasion
- **D.** Cognitive dissonance

Key Terms

Match each key term with its example.

A. Attitude	_____ A positive or negative belief about something
B. Central Route Persuasion	_____ Most people who quit smoking experience it.
C. Cognitive Dissonance	_____ A clothing company ad with a picture of a beautiful girl wearing their clothing
D. Foot-in-the-Door Technique	

E. Peripheral Route Persuasion

_____ An informercial in which a company that makes a cleaning product is testing their product compared to a competitor

_____ A free trial of software

Lesson 11.4

Conformity, Compliance, and Obedience

OBJECTIVES

★ Define conformity and types of social influence.
★ Describe Stanley Milgram's experiment and its implications.

BIG IDEA

Conformity, social influence, obedience, and group processes demonstrate the power of social situations to change our thoughts, feelings, and behaviors.

In this lesson, you will learn about the following:

- Conformity
- Stanley Milgram's Experiment
- Groupthink
- Group Polarization

Conformity

Conformity is a change in ____________________ to go along with the group. Solomon Asche conducted an influential study on conformity in which he asked participants to compare the lengths of four different lines.

Use the following diagram to describe Asche's study.

Scientific Method	Description
Purpose	
Procedure	
Results	
Conclusion	

List three factors Asche identified that increase one's likelihood to conform to the group.

1.

2.

3.

There are two types of social influences. ________________ social influences involve conforming to the group to fit in or feel good, whereas ____________________ social influence is conforming because people believe they have competent or correct information.

Identify each of the following scenarios as an example of *normative* or *informational* social influence.

- ________________: Bella doesn't really like cheerleading, but she decides to join the team so she can feel accepted by peers.
- ________________: Mike decides to join a political party because he believes the leaders are competent and their policy would do the greatest amount of good for the American people.
- ________________: Hector decides to buy a big truck to fit in with his friends.

Stanley Milgram's Experiment

Stanley Milgram conducted an influential study on ________________, which is an individual complying with the demand of an authority figure. Using the following diagram, explain Milgram's study.

Scientific Method	Description
Purpose	
Procedure	
Results	
Conclusion	

According to the text, what factors contributed to an increase or decrease in the shock in Milgram's series of studies?

Groupthink

Groupthink is members of the group changing their opinions to go along with the group consensus.

What reasons does your textbook provide on why groupthink might occur?

List at least five ways to identify that groupthink is happening.

On Your Own

What are some examples of groupthink in history or popular culture?

What are some ways that groupthink can be avoided?

Group Polarization

Group polarization is the strengthening of a group attitude after a discussion of views within the group. If a group favors a viewpoint, discussion leads to ____________________ group support for that viewpoint. If a group is against a viewpoint, discussion leads to ____________________ opposition to that viewpoint.

On Your Own

Based on what you know about group polarization, what do you think happens when two groups debate on issues they have dissenting opinions on?

Social Facilitation

Social facilitation is when ____________________ increases when being observed by a group.

According to the research on social facilitation, would the following individuals perform better or worse in front of a large crowd?

Situation	Perform Better or Worse?
A rookie quarterback in the NFL who is not familiar with the playbook	
A basketball player who is skilled in shooting free throws	
An experienced musician who is about to play a concert	
A medical resident who is assisting with brain surgery on his own for the first time	

Social Loafing

Social loafing is when group performance ________________ when individual performance is evaluated separately from the group. Social loafing is more likely to happen during easy tasks.

On Your Own

Why do you think group performance declines on easy tasks?

Why do you think social loafing does not occur as frequently on difficult tasks?

Social loafing is more likely to occur within a large group. Why do you think that is the case?

Psychology and You

Groupthink Reflection

Was there a time in your life when you conformed your opinion or behaviors to a group even though you didn't necessarily agree? Explain the forces that led you to change your decision.

Lesson Wrap-up

Say It in a Sentence

In one sentence, explain how social influences can lead you to conform to the group.

Test Yourself

Choose the correct answer for each of the following questions. Check your work using the Answer Key in the back of the book.

____ 1. Bernice is on jury duty. She went into deliberations thinking that the man on trial was guilty. However, after the deliberations, she changes her opinion to innocent. This example best describes which of the following terms or concepts?

- **A.** Social facilitation
- **B.** Obedience
- **C.** Groupthink
- **D.** Social loafing

____ 2. Jake is one of the top high school quarterback recruits in the country. He says that he enjoys playing in front of an opposing team's crowd. This best describes which of the following terms or concepts?

A. Social facilitation
B. Obedience
C. Groupthink
D. Social loafing

____ 3. Stanley Milgram's studies best illustrated which of the following terms or concepts?

A. Social facilitation
B. Obedience
C. Groupthink
D. Social loafing

Fill in the blank. Check your work using the Answer Key in the back of the book.

4. ____________ ____________ ____________ is when you change your behavior or opinion to fit in because it makes you feel good to be a part of the group.

5. ____________ ____________ ____________ is when you change your behavior or opinion to fit in with the group because you think the group has good information.

6. Following the orders of an authority figure is an example of ____________.

7. ____________ ____________ is when you perform poorly because you are exerting less effort as a part of the group.

8. ____________ ____________ is when you perform better because you are being watched by a group.

Key Terms

Match each term with its description.

A. Conformity
B. Difficult
C. Groupthink
D. Informational
E. Larger
F. Normative
G. Polarization
H. Shock
I. Social Loafing

____ The purpose of Solomon Asche's research was to study this.
____ According to Asche, people are more likely to conform in this kind of group.
____ Groups tend to perform better when they are presented this type of task.
____ This type of social influence is changing your behaviors to fit in with the group because of the information presented.
____ Exerting less effort when you are part of a group.
____ This type of social influence is represented by changing your attitudes or behaviors to fit in with the group because it makes you feel good.
____ Milgram asked participants in his study to administer this to a learner when they got the answer wrong.
____ This is the term for changing your opinion to go with the consensus of the group.
____ This occurs when a discussion within a group strengthens the initial opinions within the group prior to the discussion.

Lesson 11.5

Prejudice and Discrimination

OBJECTIVES

★ Define and distinguish among prejudice, stereotypes, and discrimination.
★ Provide examples of prejudice, stereotypes, and discrimination.
★ Explain why prejudice and discrimination exist.

BIG IDEA

When diverse groups interact, conflict often arises due to prejudice, stereotypes, and discrimination. Understanding these underlying biases can help eliminate these conflicts.

In this lesson, you will learn about the following:

- Understanding Prejudice and Discrimination
- Types of Prejudice and Discrimination
- Why Do Prejudice and Discrimination Exist?
- Stereotypes and Self-Fulfilling Prophecy
- In-Groups and Out-Groups

Understanding Prejudice and Discrimination

______________________________ is a negative attitude and feeling toward an individual based solely on that individual's membership in a particular social group. ______________________________ are specific beliefs or assumptions about individuals based solely on their membership in a group, regardless of the individual's actual characteristics. ______________________________ occurs when an individual acts on prejudiced attitudes and engages in a negative action towards another as a result of the person's membership in a particular social group.

On Your Own

What social groups do you belong to? Have you ever experienced prejudice based on your group membership?

What can be done to reduce prejudiced attitudes, according to the lesson?

1.

2.

3.

4.

5.

Complete the following graphic by listing the different social groups.

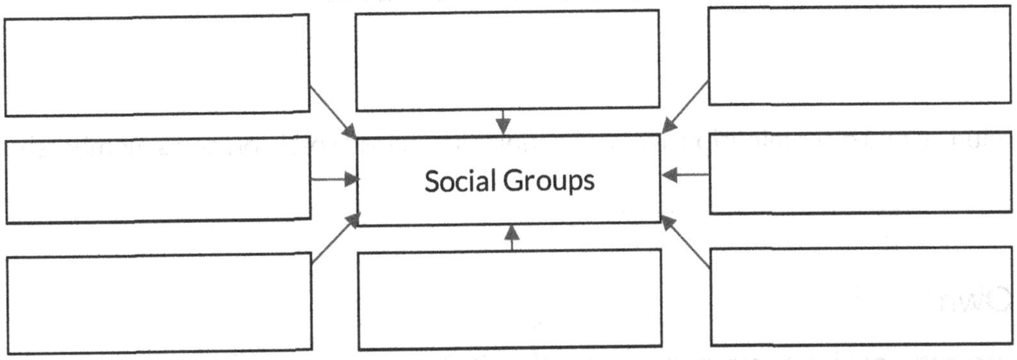

People often have difficulty discussing stereotypes even though they exist for all social groups. List 5 stereotypes about the social groups you are a part of.

Have you ever been the target of a discriminatory action? How did you feel about the situation?

Complete the following table:

Item	Function	Connection
	Cognitive; thoughts about people	Overgeneralized beliefs about others
	Affective; feelings about people	Feelings that may influence treatment of others
	Behavior; treatment of others	Exclusion, avoidance, or biased treatment of others

On Your Own

Stereotypes are not always negative. Can you think of 2 "positive" stereotypes that you have heard?

Types of Prejudice and Discrimination

Racism

Racism is prejudice and discrimination against an individual based solely on one's membership in a specific ______________________ ______________________.

On Your Own

What are 3 stereotypes about your own race or ethnicity?

Describe a situation in which you witnessed racism.

Complete the following table:

Attitude	Conscious?	Controllable?
	Yes	Yes
	No	No

Sexism

Sexism is prejudice and discrimination towards individuals based on their sex. Sexism can include ______________________ role expectations or expectations regarding how someone should ______________________.

On Your Own

Describe a situation in which you witnessed sexism.

Ageism

Ageism is prejudice and discrimination toward individuals based on their ____________________.

On Your Own

Have you ever been the victim of ageism?

Homophobia

Homophobia is prejudice and discrimination of individuals based on ____________________ ______________________________.

On Your Own

What is your reaction to the Adams, Wright, and Lohr (1996) study and its findings?

Why Do Prejudice and Discrimination Exist?

Complete the following graphic.

Why do prejudice and discrimination exist?

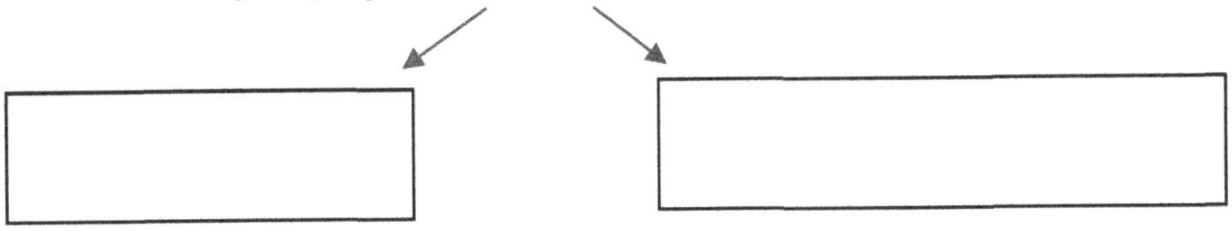

Stereotypes and Self-Fulfilling Prophecy

A self-fulfilling prophecy is an ____________________ held by a person that alters his or her behavior in a way that tends to make it true.

Complete the following cycle of a self-fulfilling prophecy:

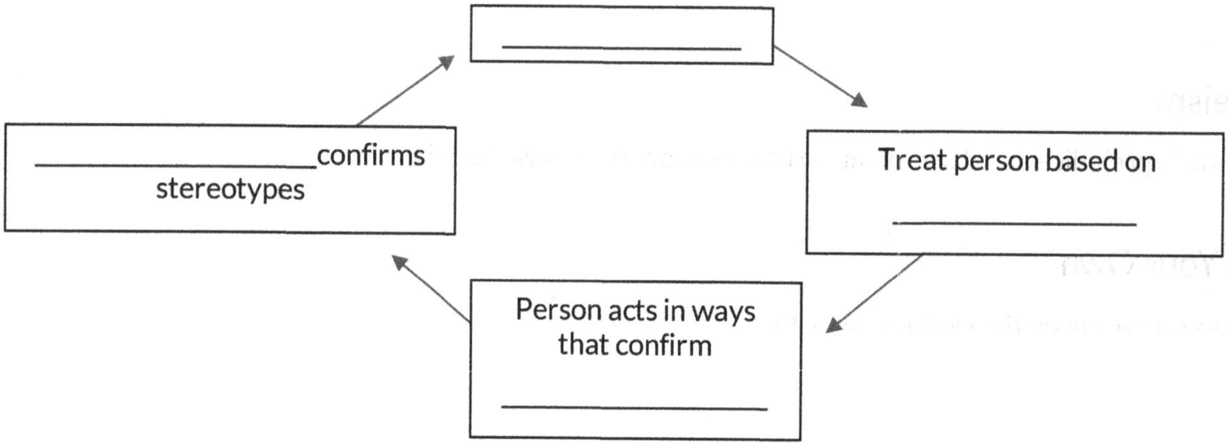

Can you think of a time when you faced a self-fulfilling prophecy? What happened?

In-Groups and Out-Groups

Social groups serve as ____________________, which individuals can identify with or see themselves belonging to. Consequently, anyone not in that in-group are part of the ____________________. Often, individuals develop a favoritism for the in-group known as the ______________ __________. ____________________ is the act of blaming an out-group when the in-group experiences frustration or is blocked from obtaining a goal.

On Your Own

Have you ever engaged in scapegoating? What happened?

Psychology and You

Change the World

Describe how you think individuals could be swayed to engage in less prejudiced behavior.

Lesson Wrap-up

Say It in a Sentence

In one sentence, explain how prejudice and discrimination are socially learned.

Test Yourself

Answer the following questions. Check your work using the Answer Key in the back of the book.

1. Thomas wants to be independent. However, his features make people think he is younger than he actually is, so they prevent him from doing things for himself. Which type of prejudice is this?

2. "Girls are horrible drivers; they shouldn't be issued licenses" is an example of which type of prejudice?

Choose the correct answer for each of the following questions. Check your work using the Answer Key in the back of the book.

____ 3. Sarah is a cheerleader, and she prefers other cheerleaders to anyone else on campus. She is engaging in:

A. Confirmation bias
B. Availability bias
C. In-group bias

____ 4. Walter believes that all blondes are not bright. Though Julie, a blonde, has a degree in neuroscience, Walter discounts this fact. Walter is engaging in:

A. Confirmation bias
B. Availability bias
C. In-group bias

____ 5. Emma honestly does not feel that she is prejudiced against anyone. However, when asked to associate positive adjectives with her own race, she is able to learn that association faster than when she is asked to learn positive adjectives associated with another race. This situation is an example of:

A. Explicit attitudes
B. Implicit attitudes

Key Terms

For the following key terms, make groupings out of the related terms. Be sure to explain how the terms are related.

Key Terms: ageism, confirmation bias, discrimination, homophobia, in-group, in-group bias, out-group, prejudice, racism, scapegoating, self-fulfilling prophecy, sexism, stereotype

Lesson 11.6

Aggression

OBJECTIVES

- ★ Define aggression.
- ★ Define cyberbullying.
- ★ Describe the bystander effect.

BIG IDEA

Aggression, either hostile or instrumental, is the desire to cause harm to others. This harm can come in the form of bullying, either in person or via the internet (cyberbullying).

In this lesson, you will learn about the following:

- Aggression
- The Bystander Effect

Aggression

Complete the following graphic.

____

______________aggression: motivated by feelings of anger	______________________aggression: motivated by achieving a goal

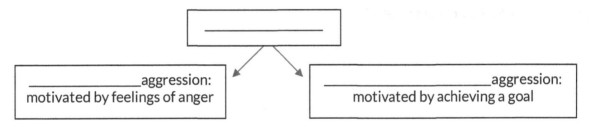

There are a few theories regarding the existence of aggression. First, some researchers suggest that aggression is ____________________________ important, allowing men to protect mates and promote their genes. Another theory is the ______________________ _________________________ theory, in which individuals who are prevented from reaching a goal feel frustration and aggression.

On Your Own

Describe a time when you were prevented from reaching a goal and felt both frustration and aggression.

Bullying

_______________ is repeated negative treatment of another person over time. Bullying can include _______________ harm, humiliation, or _______________ attacks.

On Your Own

Have you ever been the victim or perpetrator of bullying? Describe the situation.

Being a victim of bullying is associated with what negative outcomes?

1.
2.
3.
4.
5.

What are some risk factors of being bullied?

1.

2.

3.

Cyberbullying

_______________ is bullying that occurs via mobile technology and social media. This type of bullying can take many forms, including spreading rumors, defaming the victim, and ignoring, laughing at, insulting, or teasing the victim.

On Your Own

Have you ever been the victim or perpetrator of cyberbullying? Describe the situation.

The Bystander Effect

On Your Own

What is your reaction to the Kitty Genovese situation? Do you feel you would have behaved differently?

The ______________________ effect is a phenomenon in which a witness or bystander does not volunteer to help a victim or person in distress. Depending on the number of people present, bystanders may feel a ______________________ of responsibility such that they are less responsible for helping because there are many individuals present who could help.

On Your Own

Have you ever conquered the bystander effect and helped even though there were others around? Describe the situation.

Psychology and You

Change the World

How can bullying be reduced?

Lesson Wrap-up

Say It in a Sentence

In one sentence, explain the bystander effect.

Test Yourself

Answer each of the following questions. Check your work using the Answer Key in the back of the book.

1. When it comes to bullying, three parties are affected. What are they?

2. If an individual engages in an aggressive action out of anger and with the intent to cause pain, which type of aggression does this describe?

3. If an individual engages in an aggressive action out of frustration with no intention of causing pain, which type of aggression does this describe?

Choose the correct answer for each of the following questions. Check your work using the Answer Key in the back of the book.

____ 4. Women are more likely to engage in ________ forms of aggression.

A. hostile
B. instrumental
C. passive-aggressive

____ 5. When it comes to bullying, boys tend to engage in:

A. Physical attacks
B. Social attacks

____ 6. Who is more likely to be a cyberbully?

A. Boys
B. Girls

Key Terms

For each key term, provide an example that exemplifies the meaning of the word.

Aggression:

Bullying:

Bystander Effect:

Cyberbullying

Diffusion of Responsibility:

Hostile Aggression:

Instrumental Aggression:

Lesson 11.7

Prosocial Behavior

OBJECTIVES

- ★ Describe altruism.
- ★ Describe conditions that influence the formation of relationships.
- ★ Identify what attracts people to each other.
- ★ Describe the triangular theory of love.
- ★ Explain social exchange theory in relationships.

BIG IDEA

Researchers have documented various conditions that influence the development of relationships, both between friends and partners.

In this lesson, you will learn about the following:

- Prosocial Behavior and Altruism
- Forming Relationships
- Attraction
- Sternberg's Triangular Theory of Love
- Social Exchange Theory

Prosocial Behavior and Altruism

Voluntary behavior with the intent to help other people is called ____________________ behavior.

______________________ is people's desire to help others even if the costs outweigh the benefits of helping.

On Your Own

Have you behaved prosocially in the past week? Describe.

Do you believe that altruism requires empathy? Explain.

What are the three theories related to altruism?

1.

2.

3.

Which of the three theories related to altruism do you believe? Why?

Forming Relationships

On Your Own

The lesson indicates that the most important factor in forming relationships is proximity. Do you see evidence of this fact in your own life?

________________________ is the tendency for people to form social networks, including friendships, marriage, business relationships, and many other types of relationships. When ________________________, give-and-take in relationships, is present, individuals are more likely to stay within a relationship.

Attraction

Universally Attractive Features	
Men	Women

Social Traits	
Men	**Women**

On Your Own

What is your reaction to the idea of the matching hypothesis? Can you see evidence of it in your life?

Sternberg's Triangular Theory of Love

Complete the following figure:

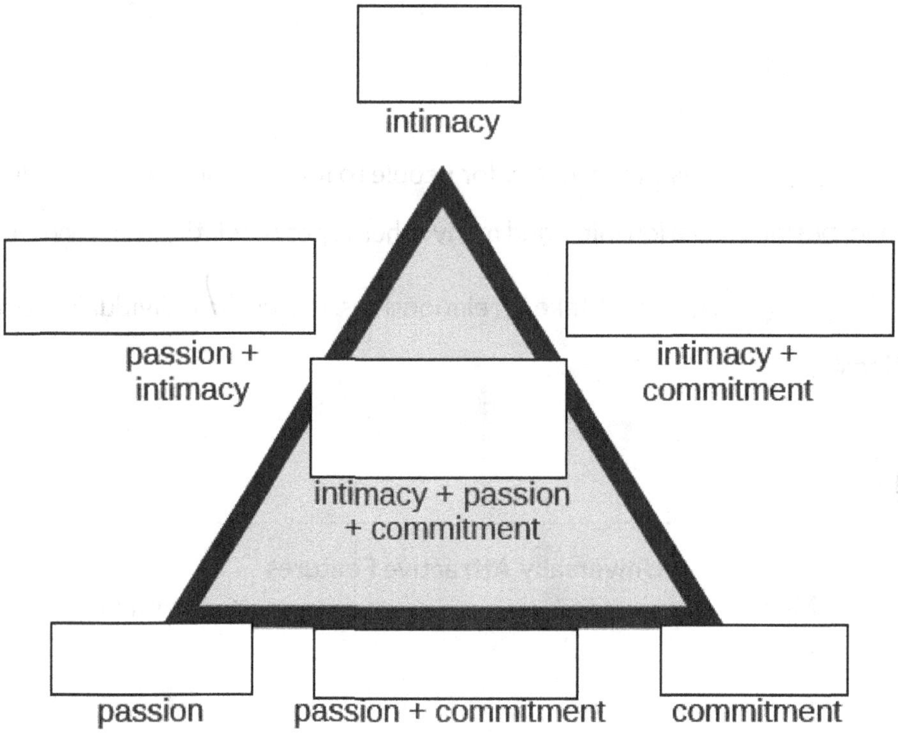

______________________ refers to the sharing of personal details, thoughts, and emotions.

__________________ is physical attraction. ________________________________ is standing by another person through thick or thin.

On Your Own

Have you experienced any of the loves on the Sternberg triangle? Which one(s)?

Social Exchange Theory

Social exchange theory explains why individuals stay in relationships. If the benefits of staying in a relationship ______________________ the costs, an individual is more likely to stay.

Psychology and You

Factors of Friendship

What factors influenced you to be friends with your closest friend? How do these factors compare with what you learned in this lesson?

Lesson Wrap-up

Say It in a Sentence

In one sentence, explain why we form relationships with people.

Test Yourself

Answer each of the following questions. Check your work using the Answer Key in the back of the book.

1. Which components make up consummate love?

2. Which components make up empty love?

3. Which components make up romantic love?

Choose the correct answer for each of the following questions. Check your work using the Answer Key in the back of the book.

____ 4. The most important factor in forming relationships is:

- **A.** Proximity
- **B.** Similarity
- **C.** Attraction

____ 5. The type of love that consists only of commitment is:

- **A.** Romantic love
- **B.** Fatuous love
- **C.** Empty love

____ 6. The type of love that consists of intimacy and commitment is:

- **A.** Consummate love
- **B.** Companionate love
- **C.** Romantic love

Key Terms

For the following key terms, make groupings out of the related terms. Be sure to explain how they are related.

Key Terms: altruism, companionate love, consummate love, empathy, homophily, prosocial behavior, reciprocity, romantic love, self-disclosure, social exchange theory, triangular theory of love

Chapter 12
Industrial-Organizational Psychology

Lesson 12.1
What Is Industrial and Organizational Psychology?

OBJECTIVES

★ Understand the scope of study in the field of industrial and organizational psychology.
★ Describe the history of industrial and organizational psychology.

BIG IDEA

Industrial-organizational psychology focuses on issues related to individuals in the workplace, such as worker selection, worker satisfaction, and the tools used on the job.

In this lesson, you will learn about the following:

- The Historical Development of Industrial and Organizational Psychology
- From WWII to Today

Industrial and organizational psychology is a branch of psychology that studies how human behavior and psychology affect ____________________ and how they are affected by work.

What are the four main contexts of I-O work?

1.
2.
3.
4.

Which branch of I-O psychology fits the description? Complete the following table.

________________ psychology	_____________ _____________-psychology	________________ psychology
Describes job requirements, assesses individuals for ability to meet requirements	Studies how workers interact with the tools of work and how to design those tools to optimize productivity, safety, and health	Focuses on how the relationships among employees affect those employees and the performance of a business

The Historical Development of Industrial and Organizational Psychology

Who are some of the major historical figures in I-O psychology?

-
-
-
-
-
-

The United States' involvement in World War I resulted in a focus on developing screening and ____________________ processes for enlisted men. The Army _______________ and ___________ tests were developed to measure mental abilities.

On Your Own

How else might the field of industrial-organizational psychology be beneficial for the military?

The _________________________ effect describes a phenomenon in which individuals who are noticed, watched, or paid attention to by researchers or supervisors increase their performance.

On Your Own

Why would it be important to control the Hawthorne effect in research efforts?

Kurt ___________________ conducted research on the effects of leadership styles, team structure, and team _________________________. He studied group interactions, cooperation, competition, and communication.

Frederick ____________________ was an engineer who wanted to redesign the workplace to improve worker productivity. He suggested that workers who took __________________ would actually increase in productivity and report less fatigue at the end of the work day.

On Your Own

What is your reaction to the criticism that Frederick Taylor faced?

Lillian ____________________ wanted to reduce the number of motions it took to perform a task. She also focused on employee ____________________ and time management _________________. She is considered the mother of ____________________ ________________________________. This study of how machines and humans fit and interact is known as ergonomics or _______________ _______________ psychology.

On Your Own

Think about objects you interact with on a daily basis. How might they have been improved by human factors researchers?

From WWII to Today

After World War II, concerns about the fairness of employment _________________ arose, and the ethnic and gender biases in various tests were evaluated with mixed results. A great deal of research went into studying job _________________________ and employee _______________________.

Psychology and You

Industrial-Organizational Psychology in Your Workplace

Think of a current or past place of employment. What might an I-O researcher focus on to improve the workplace?

Lesson Wrap-up

Say It in a Sentence

In one sentence, explain the purpose of industrial-organizational psychology.

Test Yourself

Answer each of the following questions. Check your work using the Answer Key in the back of the book.

1. Studying worker satisfaction belongs in which branch of I-O psychology?

2. Focusing on employee training belongs in which branch of I-O psychology?

3. Studying whether standing or sitting when working is more beneficial to worker health and safety belongs in which branch of I-O psychology?

Choose the correct answer for each of the following questions. Check your work using the Answer Key in the back of the book.

____ 4. In 2012, workers in the United States spent ____ hours a week working.

A. 25.4
B. 45.6
C. 56.4

____ 5. Who was among the first psychologists to apply psychology to advertising and management?

A. Cattell
B. Bingham
C. Scott
D. Gilbreth

____ 6. Who coined the term "group dynamics"?

A. Cattell
B. Lewin
C. Scott
D. Gilbreth

Key Terms

Write a paraphrased definition for each key term.

Hawthorne Effect:

Human Factors Psychology:

Industrial and Organizational Psychology:

Industrial Psychology:

Organizational Psychology:

Lesson 12.2

Industrial Psychology: Selecting and Evaluating Employees

OBJECTIVES

- ★ Explain the aspects of employee selection.
- ★ Describe the kinds of job training.
- ★ Describe the approaches to and issues surrounding performance assessment.

BIG IDEA

Industrial psychology studies the attributes of jobs, job applicants, and assessment methods for job performance.

In this lesson, you will learn about the following:

- Selecting Employees
- Evaluating Employees
- Bias and Protections in Hiring
- The U.S. Equal Employment Opportunity Commission (EEOC)
- Americans with Disabilities Act (ADA)

Selecting Employees

What are the two approaches to job analysis?

1. 2.

_____________-oriented job analysis lists, in detail, the tasks that will be performed for the job, whereas

__________________-oriented job analysis describes characteristics required of the worker to

successfully perform the job. This job ___________________________ identifies knowledge, skills, and

abilities (_________________) for the job.

Candidate Analysis and Training

On Your Own

What tests may be used to determine if a candidate is a good fit for a job?

1.
2.
3.
4.
5.

On Your Own

What are your reactions to the case of Robert Jordan and the New London Police department?

Interviews

What are the two types of job interviews?

1.
2.

On Your Own

What are some elements you could address so that you perform better in an interview?

Which of the Big Five personality traits appear to be important in interviews?

-
-
-

Training

On Your Own

In your experience, what has job training consisted of? Did you feel better able to handle the job after training?

What are some benefits of being mentored?

1.
2.
3.

Evaluating Employees

On Your Own

What does a fair evaluation of job performance accomplish?

1.

2.

3.

4.

What are the elements of the face-to-face performance appraisal?

1.

2.

3.

Complete the following image regarding 360-degree feedback:

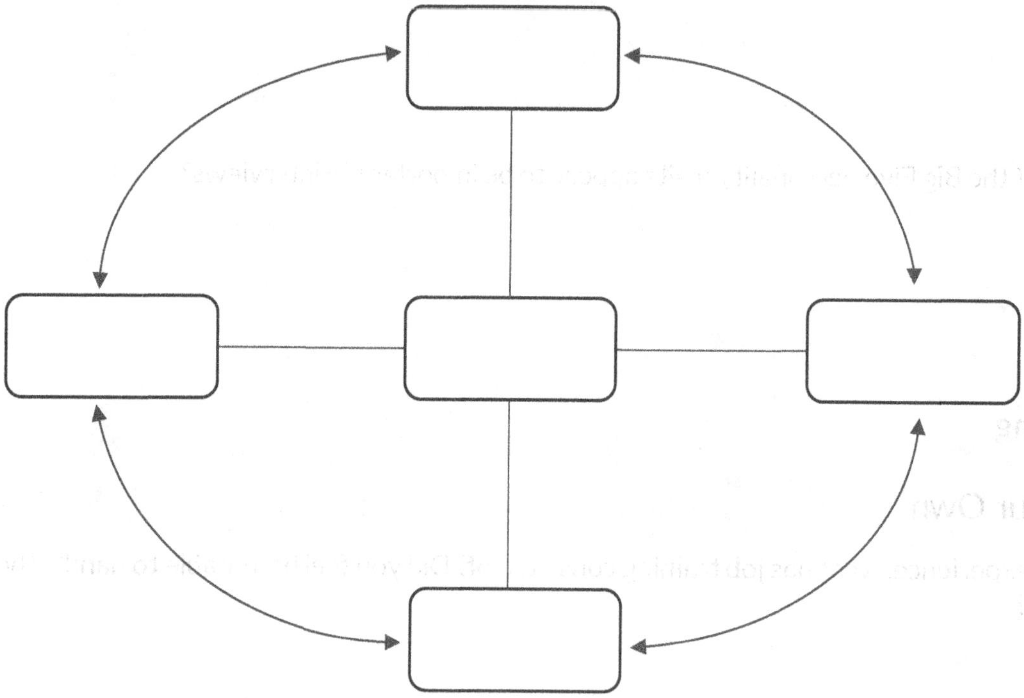

Bias and Protections in Hiring

____________________________ on the job can occur based on a variety of factors, including gender, sexual orientation, race/ethnicity, and physical attractiveness. Unless membership in a group ____________________ affects potential job performance, a decision to hire based on group membership is discriminatory.

On Your Own

If a potential employer asked for your age, what would you say?

The U.S. Equal Employment Opportunity Commission (EEOC)

The U.S. Equal Employment Opportunity Commission is responsible for enforcing federal laws that make it illegal to discriminate against a job applicant or employee because of the person's race, color, religion, sex, national ________________, age, disability, or ________________ information.

Match the following law with what it covers.

Men and women in the same workplace who are performing equal work must be paid equally.	Title VII of the Civil Rights Act
It is illegal to treat individuals unfairly because of their race or the color of their skin.	Pregnancy Discrimination Act of 1978
It is illegal to discriminate based on pregnancy.	Equal Pay Act

Americans with Disabilities Act (ADA)

The Americans with Disabilities Act (ADA) of ______________ states that people cannot be discriminated against due to the nature of their ________________. The Civil Rights Act and the Age Discrimination in Employment Act make provisions for ____________ ______________ occupational qualifications (BFOQs), which are requirements of certain occupations for which denying an individual employment would otherwise violate the law.

On Your Own

What is the three-part test for sex-related BFOQs?

1.

2.

3.

Do you feel that the Hooters case would pass the three-question test for sex-based BFOQs? Explain.

Psychology and You

KSAs on O*Net

Go to O*Net (www.online.onetcenter.org) and look up your dream job. Do you have the KSAs necessary for this job? What will you need to gain to be successful in this field?

Lesson Wrap-up

Say It in a Sentence

In one sentence, explain the purpose of industrial psychology.

Test Yourself

Answer each of the following questions. Check your work using the Answer Key in the back of the book.

1. Dr. Smith is interviewing individuals for a research lab position. For each of the five applicants, he asks a prescribed set of questions and scores each applicant on the answers. Which type of interview is this?

2. Mr. James is interviewing individuals for an assistant position. For each of the three applicants, he asks questions off the cuff, never truly asking the same question of each applicant across the interview process. Which type of interview is this?

Choose the correct answer for each of the following questions. Check your work using the Answer Key in the back of the book.

____ 3. Dierdorff & Wilson found that a job analysis developed by people who held the job themselves was:

A. Most reliable
B. Least reliable

____ 4. Research found that which type of interview was most effective at predicting subsequent job performance?

A. Unstructured
B. Structured

____ 5. Mentoring has been identified as particularly important for the career success of:

A. Men
B. Women

Key Terms

Match each key term with its definition.

A. Americans with Disabilities Act
B. Bona Fide Occupational Qualification
C. Immutable Characteristic
D. Job Analysis
E. Performance Appraisal
F. U.S. Equal Employment Opportunity Commission

_____ Evaluation of an employee's success or lack of success at performing the duties of a job

_____ Employers cannot discriminate against any individual based on a disability

_____ Responsible for enforcing federal laws that make it illegal to discriminate against a job applicant for a person's race, color, religion, sex, national origin, age, disability, or genetic information

_____ Requirement of certain occupations for which denying an individual employment would otherwise violate the law, such as requirements concerning religion or sex

_____ Traits that employers cannot use to discriminate in hiring, benefits, promotions, or termination

_____ Determining and listing tasks associated with a particular job

Lesson 12.3

Organizational Psychology: The Social Dimension of Work

OBJECTIVES

★ Define organizational psychology.
★ Explain the measurement and determinants of job satisfaction.
★ Describe key elements of management and leadership.
★ Explain the significance of organizational culture.

BIG IDEA

Organizational psychology focuses on the interaction between people and their places of employment, including aspects of satisfaction and productivity.

In this lesson, you will learn about the following:

- Job Satisfaction
- Work-Family Balance
- Management and Organizational Structure
- Goals, Teamwork, and Work Teams
- Organizational Culture
- Violence in the Workplace

What do organizational psychologists study?

-
-
-
-
-

Job Satisfaction

Job satisfaction describes the degree to which individuals ________________ their jobs. It is impacted by the work itself, ______________________, and the individual's culture. Job satisfaction is usually measured by ______________________.

On Your Own

Design a Likert-type question to measure job satisfaction.

Complete the following table.

Factor	Description
	Individual responsibility, control over decisions
Work content	Variety, challenge, role ______________
Communication	
	Salary and benefits
Growth and development	Personal growth, ________________, education
	Career advancement opportunity
	Professional relations or adequacy
Supervision and feedback	Support, recognition, ________________
	Time pressure, tedium
Work demands	Extra work requirements, insecurity of ______________________

On Your Own

Do you feel that the questions on the Federal Employee Viewpoint Survey are valid? Would they adequately measure your job satisfaction? Explain.

What are sources of employee stress?

1.
2.
3.
4.
5.
6.
7.
8.
9.
10.

Both ______________________ and mergers can result in job stress related to reduction in number of workers.

Work-Family Balance

___________-_______________ balance refers to the ability to juggle both the demands of work and life adequately without one aspect taking more time and energy. There are many ways to decrease work-family conflict, including emotional and physical support at home, understanding _______________, flextime, leave with pay, and _____________________.

Management and Organizational Structure

What are the two types of management proposed by Douglas McGregor?

1.

2.

Complete the following table that contrasts Theory X and Theory Y:

Theory X	Theory Y
People dislike work and ____________ it.	People enjoy work and find it natural.
People want to be told what to do.	
People avoid __________________.	People are more satisfied when given responsibility.
Goals are achieved through ____________ and __________________.	Goals are achieved through____________ and __________.

Donald ______________ discussed strengths-based management, in which the focus is on the individual's strengths, not weaknesses. Strengths provide the greatest opportunity for __________.

On Your Own

What are some of your strengths that would benefit you on the job?

What four attributes does a transformational leader have?

1.
2.
3.
4.

Goals, Teamwork, and Work Teams

Teams have some negatives, including social ________________, issues due to poor communication, ____________________ effects, and conflict.

What are the four types of teams?

1.
2.
3.
4.

Organizational Culture

________________________ ____________________ encompasses the values, visions, hierarchies, norms, and interactions among its employees. It is made up of ________________ artifacts, espoused _____________, and basic assumptions.

Managing Generational Differences

On Your Own

What are your thoughts about people from different generations working together? Do you feel there are ways to help "bridge the gap"?

According to the U.S. Equal Employment Opportunity Commission, "__________________ sexual advances, requests for sexual favors, and other verbal or physical conduct of a sexual nature constitute sexual harassment when this conduct explicitly or __________________ affects an individual's employment, unreasonably interferes with an individual's work performance, or creates an intimidating, _____________, or offensive work environment."

Violence in the Workplace

_____________________ violence is any act or threat of physical violence, harassment, intimidation, or other threatening disruptive behavior that occurs in the workplace. Warning signs include ______________________ behaviors, threats, _____________________ equipment, or radical behavior changes.

Psychology and You

Leadership Styles

Which leadership style do you think you would flourish under, Theory X or Theory Y? Explain.

Lesson Wrap-up

Say It in a Sentence

In one sentence, explain the purpose of organizational psychology.

Test Yourself

Answer each of the following questions. Check your work using the Answer Key in the back of the book.

1. John, a manager, focuses on supervision and organization of his employees. He uses rewards and punishments to keep employees motivated. Which style of leadership is this?

2. Laura tries to motivate her employees through her charismatic focus on incentives and rewards. Which style of leadership is this?

Choose the correct answer for each of the following questions. Check your work using the Answer Key in the back of the book.

____ 3. There is a ______ correlation between pay level and job satisfaction.

- **A.** strong
- **B.** moderate
- **C.** weak

____ 4. ________ have greater responsibility for family demands, including home care, child care, and caring for aging parents.

- **A.** Men
- **B.** Women

____ 5. Which of the following ways to promote work-life balance seems effective?

A. Telecommuting
B. Support at home
C. Flextime
D. All of the above

____ 6. Murder is the _______ leading cause of death in the workplace.

A. first
B. second
C. third
D. fourth

Key Terms

Match each key term with its definition.

A. Diversity Training
B. Downsizing
C. Job Satisfaction
D. Organizational Culture
E. Procedural Justice
F. Sexual Harassment
G. Scientific Management
H. Telecommuting
I. Theory X
J. Theory Y
K. Transactional Leadership Style
L. Transformational Leadership Style
M. Work-Family Balance
N. Workplace Violence
O. Work Team

_____ Assumes workers are inherently lazy and unproductive
_____ Training employees about cultural differences
_____ Group of people within an organization given a specific task to achieve together
_____ Violence against workers
_____ Assumes workers are people who seek to work hard and productively
_____ Fairness by which means are used to achieve results in an organization
_____ Theory of management that analyzed and synthesized workflows with the main objective of improving economic efficiency, especially labor productivity
_____ Occurs when people juggle the demands of work life with the demands of family life
_____ Degree of pleasure that employees derive from their jobs
_____ Process in which an organization tries to achieve greater overall efficiency by reducing the number of employees
_____ Characteristic of leaders who are charismatic role models, inspirational, intellectually stimulating, and individually considerate
_____ Sexually-based behavior that is knowingly unwanted and has an adverse effect on a person's employment status
_____ Values, visions, hierarchies, norms, and interactions between its employees
_____ Employees' ability to set their own hours, allowing them to work from home at different parts of the day
_____ Characteristic of leaders who focus on supervision and organizational goals achieved through a system of rewards and punishments

Lesson 12.4

Human Factors Psychology and Workplace Design

OBJECTIVES

- ★ Describe the field of human factors psychology.
- ★ Explain the role of human factors psychology in safety, productivity, and job satisfaction.

BIG IDEA

Human factors psychology studies the interface between workers and the machines or tools they use on the job with the goal of providing better support for workers through technology or design improvements.

In this lesson, you will learn about the following:

- Human Factors Psychology

Human factors psychology focuses on the ______________________ of the human-machine interface in the workplace through researching and designing machines that fit human requirements. Possible jobs of a human factors psychologist include design, testing and ______________________, and development of regulations and principles. Workplace safety is a big concern. To minimize accidents, workplaces often use comprehensive ______________________ to ensure that operators go through procedures correctly.

On Your Own

Have you ever worked somewhere that required a checklist? Describe.

Complete the following table on the areas of study in human factors psychology.

Area	Description
	Vigilance and monitoring, recognizing signals in noise, mental resources, divided attention
	Human software interactions in complex automated systems, decision-making processes of workers
	Breaking down the elements of the task
	Breaking down the elements of a cognitive task

Psychology and You

Human Factors Psychology Applied

Think of your workplace or living quarters. What areas would benefit from further investigation by a human factors psychologist?

Lesson Wrap-up

Say It in a Sentence

In one sentence, explain the purpose of human factors psychology.

Test Yourself

Next to each statement, write **T** for True or **F** for False. Check your work using the Answer Key in the back of the book.

1. ______ Lillian Gilbreth was a human factors psychologist.
2. ______ Checklists have been proven ineffective in increasing workplace safety.
3. ______ Safety concerns have led to restrictions on how long an operator can perform a job without a break.

Choose the correct answer for each of the following questions. Check your work using the Answer Key in the back of the book.

____ 4. Which of the following was a human factors psychologist?

A. Cattell
B. Bingham
C. Scott
D. Gilbreth

____ 5. Which of the following was responsible for the design of the control-center workstations?

A. NRC
B. ANSI
C. ADA
D. EOCC

Key Terms

Write a paraphrased definition for the following key term.

Checklist:

Chapter 13
Stress, Lifestyle, and Health

Lesson 13.1
What Is Stress?

OBJECTIVES

★ Differentiate between stimulus-based and response-based definitions of stress.
★ Define stress as a process.
★ Differentiate between good stress and bad stress.
★ Describe the early contributions of Walter Cannon and Hans Selye to the stress research field.
★ Understand the physiological basis of stress and describe the general adaptation syndrome.

BIG IDEA

Stress is a ubiquitous experience that everyone faces. It is based on a physiological process that occurs in the face of either good or bad stress.

In this lesson, you will learn about the following:

- Good Stress?
- The Prevalence of Stress
- Early Contributions to the Study of Stress
- The Physiological Basis of Stress

On Your Own

Researchers have had some difficulty in defining stress. How do you define stress?

If an individual experiences stress based on an event or situation, this situation is referred to as a

____________________-based stress. On the other hand, a ____________________-based definition of stress is related to the physiological experiences of stress rather than what caused it. It is probably best to view stress as a ____________________ whereby an individual perceives and responds to events that are appraised as overwhelming or threatening.

Responses to stress involve two appraisals: ____________________ and secondary. A ____________________ appraisal involves judgement about the degree of potential harm or threat to well-being that a stressor might entail. A ____________________ appraisal involves the judgement of options available to cope with a stressor.

On Your Own

In general, how do you normally react for your secondary appraisal? Are you a negative or positive thinker?

Complete the following figure:

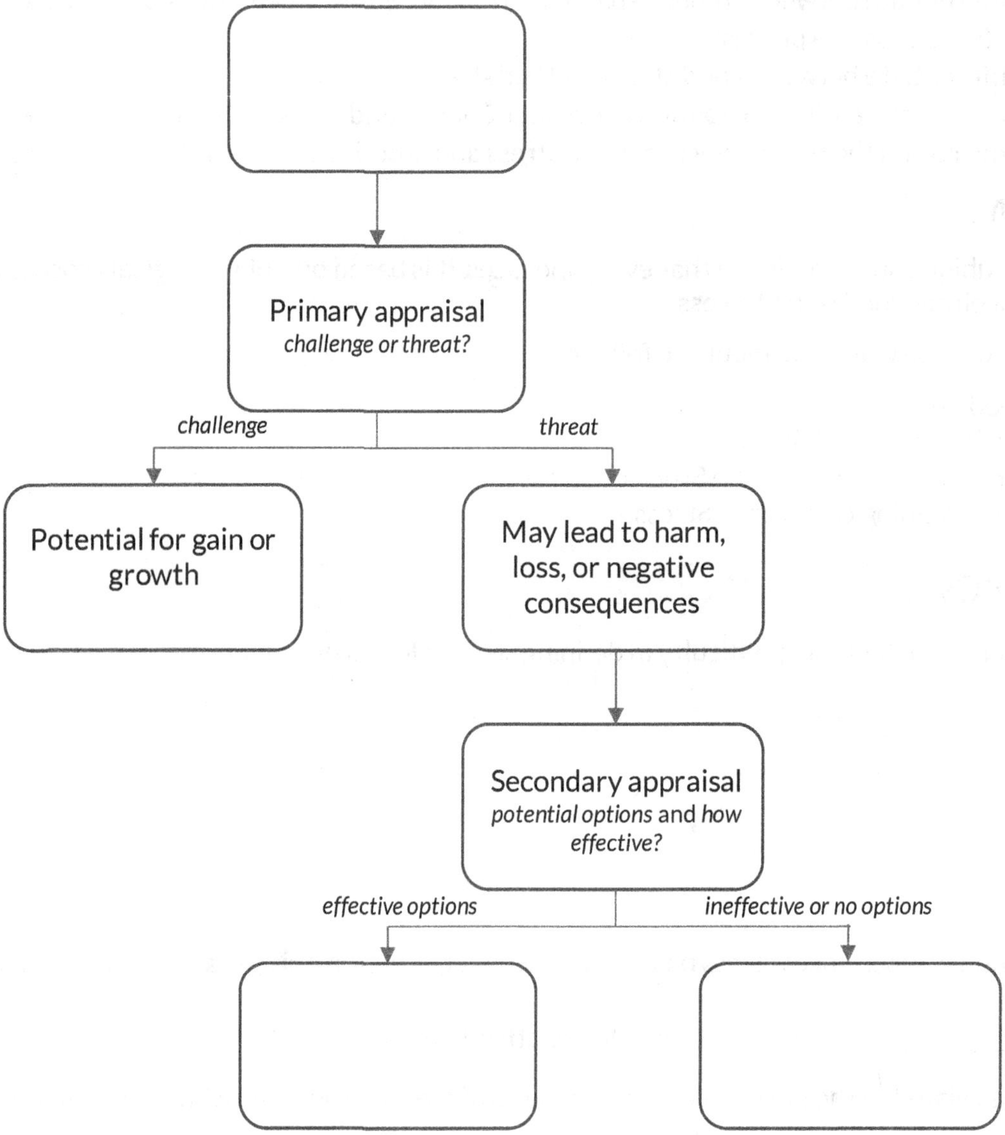

_________________________ events trigger stress reactions by the way they are interpreted and the meanings they are assigned. In short, stress is largely in the eye of the ____________________.

Good Stress?

What are some benefits of stress?

-
-
-

Complete the following figure:

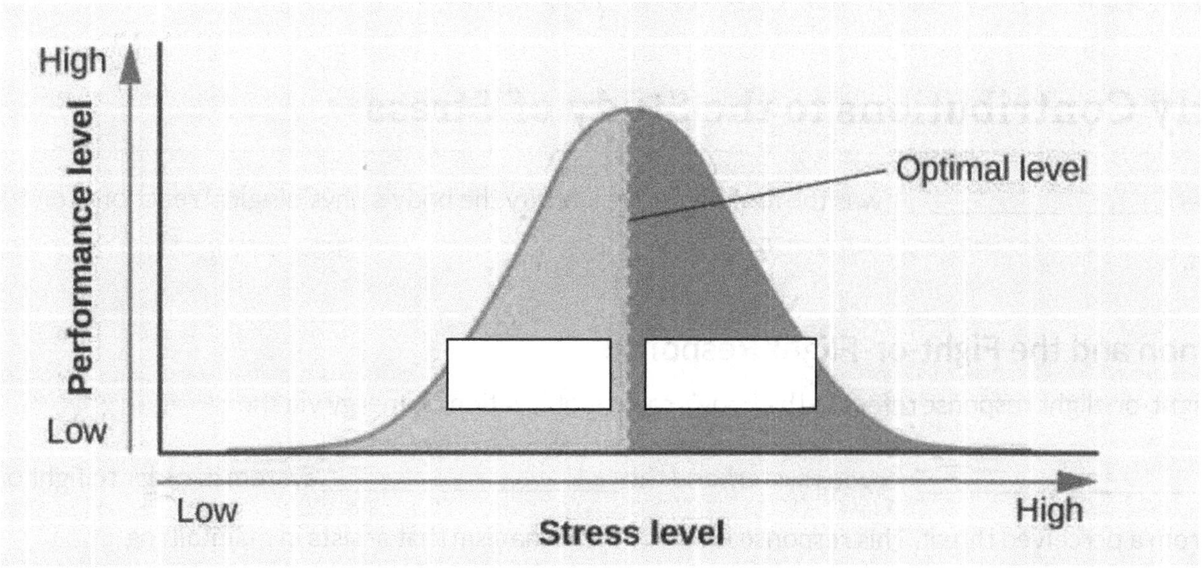

The Prevalence of Stress

On Your Own

According to the lesson, nearly half of U.S. adults reported feeling more stressed over the past 5 years. Why do you suppose this is happening?

What are the responses to stress?

Response Type	Symptoms
	Accelerated heart rate, headaches, GI issues
	Difficulty concentrating or making decisions
	Drinking alcohol, smoking

____________________ psychology is a subfield of psychology devoted to understanding the importance of psychological influences on health, illness, and how people respond when they become ill.

Early Contributions to the Study of Stress

Walter ____________________ was the first person to identify the body's physiological reactions to stress.

Cannon and the Fight-or-Flight Response

The fight-or-flight response refers to the body's rapid mobilization of energy via the ________________________ nervous system and the ____________________ system in order to fight or flee from a perceived threat. This response is a built-in mechanism that assists in maintaining ________________________ (an internal environment in which physiological variables are stabilized at optimal levels).

Selye and the General Adaptation Syndrome

Hans _____________ discovered that animals exposed to prolonged stressors showed signs of _________________ enlargement, thymus and lymph node shrinkage, and stomach ulcers.

What are the three stages of the general adaptation syndrome?

1. 2. 3.

Complete the following figure:

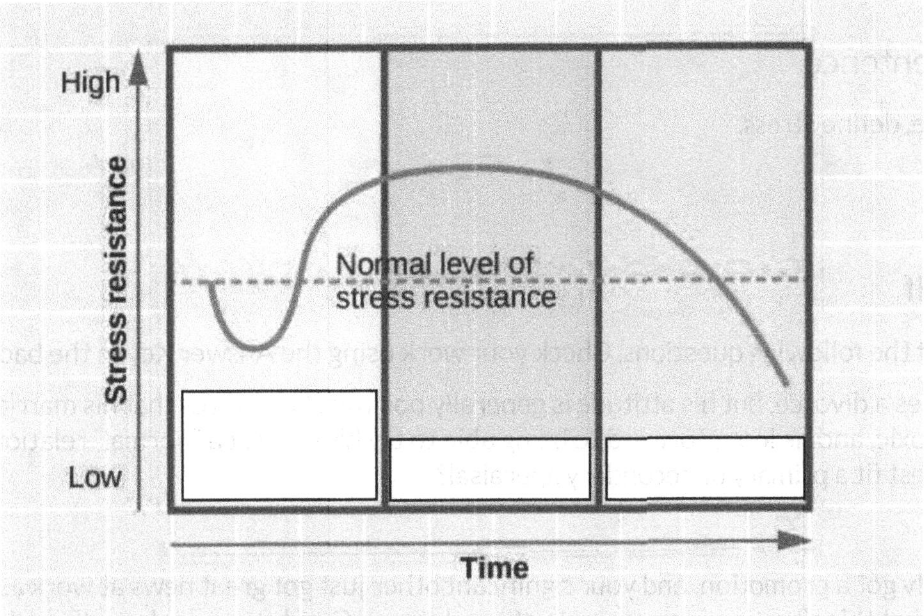

The Physiological Basis of Stress

Complete the following graphic:

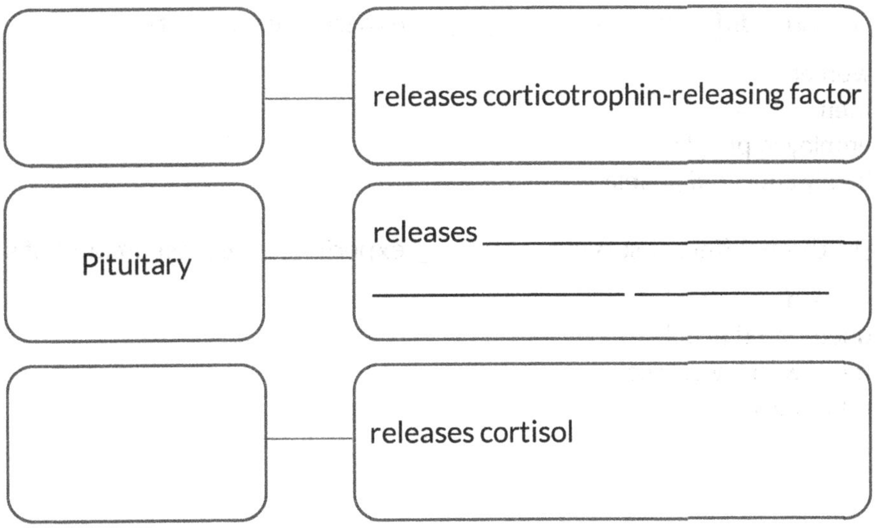

Psychology and You

Stress Effects

Describe a time when your health suffered due to excess stress. How can you explain what happened using information from this lesson?

Lesson Wrap-up

Say It in a Sentence

In one sentence, define stress.

Test Yourself

Answer each of the following questions. Check your work using the Answer Key in the back of the book.

1. Charles faces a divorce, but his attitude is generally positive; he realizes that his marriage has been relatively toxic, and he looks forward to being able to try his hand at a "normal" relationship. Does his response best fit a primary or secondary appraisal?

2. You recently got a promotion, and your significant other just got great news at work as well. Selye would say that this situation is an example of good stress. Good stress is also called what?

Choose the correct answer for each of the following questions. Check your work using the Answer Key in the back of the book.

____ 3. According to three different surveys, ________ experience more stress.

- **A.** women
- **B.** men
- **C.** employed people
- **D.** highly educated people

____ 4. According to three different surveys, ________ experience the least amount of stress.

- **A.** women
- **B.** uneducated people
- **C.** those with lower income
- **D.** retired people

Key Terms

For the following key terms, make groupings out of the related terms. Be sure to explain how they are related.

Key Terms: alarm reaction, cortisol, distress, eustress, fight-or-flight response, general adaptation syndrome, health psychology, hypothalamic-pituitary-adrenal (HPA) axis, primary appraisal, secondary appraisal, stage of exhaustion, stage of resistance, stress, stressors

Lesson 13.2

Stressors

OBJECTIVES

- ★ Describe different types of possible stressors.
- ★ Explain the importance of life changes as potential stressors.
- ★ Describe the Social Readjustment Rating Scale.
- ★ Understand the concepts of job strain and job burnout.

BIG IDEA

Stressors can be short- or long-term and come from a variety of sources, including traumatic events, life changes, and daily hassles.

In this lesson, you will learn about the following:

- Traumatic Events
- Life Changes
- Hassles
- Other Stressors

Traumatic Events

Traumatic events are situations in which a person is exposed to actual or threatened ____________ or serious injury. Some of these situations can result in ________________________ stress disorder, a chronic stress reaction characterized by experiences and behaviors that may include intrusive and painful memories of the stressor event, jumpiness, persistent negative emotional states, _______________ from others, angry outbursts, and avoidance.

Life Changes

On Your Own

What life changes have you experienced in the past 6 months?

Thomas ______________ and Richard ____________ wanted to measure the relationship between stressful life changes and issues with physical health. They developed the ____________ ____________________ Rating Scale (SRRS).

On Your Own

Using the SRRS stressors listed in the lesson, what would your stress score be? Given that the possible total from this section is 436, how do you compare?

If it were possible to demonstrate a causal tie between stress and illness, which would you think came first? Does stress cause illness, or does illness cause stress?

Hassles

__________ ____________ are the minor irritations and annoyances that are part of everyday life.

Researchers have demonstrated that the frequency of daily hassles is actually a __________ predictor of physical and psychological health than life changes.

On Your Own

What daily hassles have you experienced in the past week?

Other Stressors

When individuals experience stress related to work, the issue appears to stem from two components: heavy workload and uncertainty or lack of control over certain aspects of a job.

What are some effects of job strain?

-
-
-
-
-

What are the components of job burnout?

-
-
-

Psychology and You

School Burnout

Have you ever experienced school burnout? Discuss the three components of burnout in relation to how you felt during the school year.

Lesson Wrap-up

Say It in a Sentence

In one sentence, define stressors.

Test Yourself

Answer each of the following questions. Check your work using the Answer Key in the back of the book.

1. Trisha is late for work and, of course, she cannot find her keys anywhere. She has looked in all the logical places, and they are nowhere to be found. Which type of stressor is being described in this situation?

2. John is relocating for a new job. As a result, he needs to find a new place to live, set up his new utilities, and learn a new town. Which type of stressor is being described in this situation?

Choose the correct answer for each of the following questions. Check your work using the Answer Key in the back of the book.

____ 3. Who is more likely to experience a traumatic event?

A. Women
B. White people
C. Upper class individuals
D. Men

____ 4. According to research, which events are more strongly associated with poor outcomes?

- **A.** Positive life changes
- **B.** Negative life changes

____ 5. Who is at biggest risk for job strain?

- **A.** Younger workers
- **B.** Married people
- **C.** Older workers

Key Terms

Match each key term with its definition.

A. Daily Hassles
B. Job Burnout
C. Job Strain
D. Social Readjustment Rating Scale (SRRS)

____ Work situation involving the combination of excessive job demands and workload with little decision-making latitude or job control
____ Popular scale designed to measure stress
____ General sense of emotional exhaustion and cynicism in relation to one's job
____ Minor irritations and annoyances that are part of everyday life

Lesson 13.3

Stress and Illness

OBJECTIVES

★ Explain the nature of psychophysiological disorders.
★ Describe the immune system and how stress impacts its functioning.
★ Describe how stress and emotional factors can lead to the development and exacerbation of cardiovascular disorders, asthma, and tension headaches.

BIG IDEA

Psychophysiological disorders, such as cardiovascular issues, asthma, and tension headaches, are underlying illnesses made worse by stress and other psychological factors.

In this lesson, you will learn about the following:

- Psychophysiological Disorders
- Stress and the Immune System
- Cardiovascular Disorders
- Are You Type A or Type B?
- Depression and the Heart
- Asthma
- Tension Headaches

Psychophysiological Disorders

Physical disorders or diseases whose symptoms are brought about or worsened by ____________ and ______________________ factors are called psychophysiological disorders.

On Your Own

Do you have any of the physical ailments listed in the "Types of Psychophysiological Disorders" (Everyly & Lating, 2002) table? Do you feel they result from stress?

Stress and the Immune System

Immune System Errors

Autoimmune diseases, such as rheumatoid arthritis and lupus, result when the body's immune system attacks __________________ cells.

Immunosuppression refers to the ______________________ effectiveness of the immune system.

When people experience immunosuppression, they become ___________________ to any number of infections, illnesses, and diseases.

Stressors and Immune Function

Psychoneuroimmunology is the field that studies how ______________________ factors, such as stress, influence the immune system and immune functioning. Research has repeatedly demonstrated that many kinds of stressors are associated with poor or weakened __________________ functioning.

On Your Own

Have you noticed a relationship between stress and health in your own life? Explain.

______________________ are segments of DNA that protect the ends of chromosomes. If these telomeres are ______________________, they can block cell division, resulting in more rapid aging. Research has found that stress can shorten telomeres.

On Your Own

Using the idea of telomeres, explain why someone who is athletic and fit may look a great deal younger than his/her age.

Cardiovascular Disorders

What makes up the cardiovascular system?

1.

2.

On Your Own

How do the symptoms of a heart attack differ for men and women?

A major risk factor for heart disease is hypertension—____________ blood pressure—which forces a person's heart to pump harder.

Hypertension can lead to:

-
-
-
-
-

Generate a list of risk factors for cardiovascular diseases. What are your odds of developing it over your lifetime?

1.
2.
3.
4.
5.
6.
7.
8.
9.
10.

Are You Type A or Type B?

__________ _______ individuals are intensely driven workaholics who are preoccupied with deadlines and always seem to be in a rush. ________ _______ individuals, on the other hand, are more relaxed and laid-back. ________ ______ behavior patterns of aggression and hostility have been linked with increased cardiovascular risk.

On Your Own

Are you more of a Type A or Type B personality? Based on your answer, will you be more likely to have cardiac issues?

Diagram the transactional model of hostility for predicting social interactions:

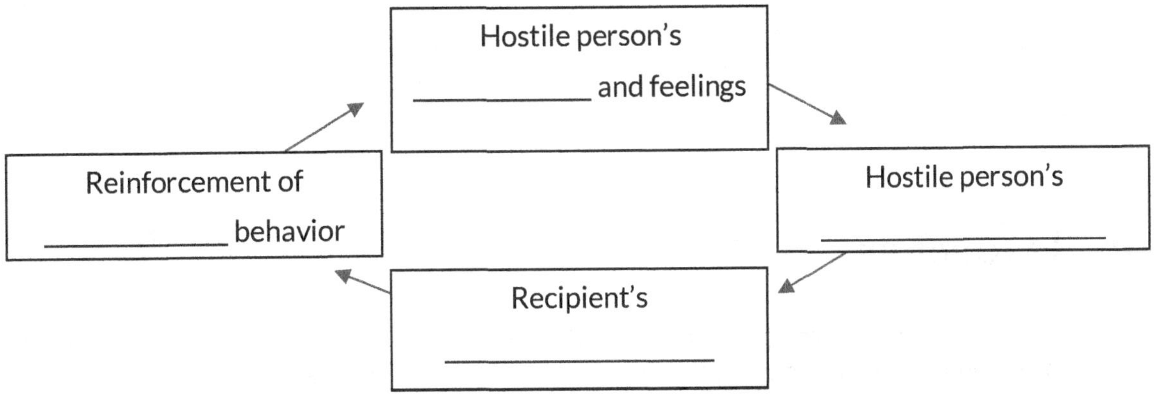

Depression and the Heart

On Your Own

What is your reaction to the idea that depression and heart disease are related?

From the multitude of studies on depression and the heart, which do you find most compelling, and why?

Asthma

Asthma is a disease in which the airways of the respiratory system become inflamed and

________________, leading to great difficulty expelling air from the lungs.

On Your Own

Why do you think people from lower education and income levels are more prone to have asthma?

What may exacerbate asthma?

1.
2.
3.
4.
5.
6.

What is your reaction to the idea that asthma may be related to higher levels of negative emotions, such as anxiety?

Tension Headaches

Migraines are characterized by severe pain on one or both sides of the head, an upset stomach, and visual disturbances. Tension headaches are triggered by tightening of facial and neck muscles.

What contributes to tension headaches?

-
-
-
-
-
-

Psychology and You

Lifestyle Changes

Using the information from the lesson, what changes can you make in your lifestyle that will prevent later health issues?

Lesson Wrap-up

Say It in a Sentence

In one sentence, explain how stress impacts health.

Test Yourself

Next to each statement, write **T** for True or **F** for False. Check your work using the Answer Key in the back of the book.

1. ______ Men are more likely to experience migraines.
2. ______ Parenting difficulties in the first year of life increased the chances that a child developed asthma by 207%.
3. ______ Experiencing a natural disaster could result in cardiovascular problems.

Choose the correct answer for each of the following questions. Check your work using the Answer Key in the back of the book.

____ 4. Research has shown that ________ is a risk factor for all major disease-related causes of death.

- **A.** posttraumatic stress
- **B.** smoking
- **C.** depression

____ 5. Which personality trait (of the Big Five) has been identified as a risk factor for chronic health problems and mortality?

- **A.** Extroversion
- **B.** Openness
- **C.** Conscientiousness
- **D.** Neuroticism
- **E.** Agreeableness

____ 6. Heart disease causes ____ of deaths in the United States.

- **A.** 50%
- **B.** 33%
- **C.** 15%

Key Terms

Write a paraphrased definition for each key term.

Asthma:

Cardiovascular Disease:

Heart Disease:

Hypertension:

Immune System:

Immunosuppression:

Lymphocytes:

Negative Affectivity:

Psychoneuroimmunology:

Psychophysiological Disorders:

Type A:

Type B:

Lesson 13.4

Regulation of Stress

OBJECTIVES

- ★ Define coping and differentiate between problem-focused and emotion-focused coping.
- ★ Describe the importance of perceived control in our reactions to stress.
- ★ Explain how social support is vital in health and longevity.

BIG IDEA

People must determine how best to cope with stress-inducing stimuli, and there are a multitude of factors that can influence how well individuals cope.

In this lesson, you will learn about the following:

- Coping Styles
- Control and Stress
- Social Support
- Stress Reduction Techniques

Coping Styles

________________________ refers to mental and behavioral efforts that we use to deal with problems related to stress.

What are the two coping mechanisms as defined by Lazarus and Folkman (1984)?

1. __________________-focused
2. _____________________-focused

On Your Own

What are the steps of problem-centered coping?

1.

2.

3.

4.

What are the components of emotion-centered coping?

1.

2.

3.

When it comes to coping strategy, which do you tend to use, and why?

Control and Stress

Perceived ______________ is the belief about the personal capacity to exert influence over and shape outcomes.

Perceptions of personal control have been associated with:

1.
2.
3.
4.

Learned Helplessness

Martin ______________ conducted a series of classic experiments whereby dogs were placed in a chamber in which they received electrical shock but were unable to ______________. Later, the dogs were allowed to escape by jumping across a ______________, but many of the dogs failed to even try.

On Your Own

What is your reaction to the Seligman and Maier (1967) study? Do you see any modern-day applications of their findings?

Learned helplessness is an ______________ belief that individuals are ______________ to do anything to change their situations. This idea has direct implications for human______________.

Negative attributions can lead to the idea that the individual is unable to control the situation, ultimately leading to learned helplessness.

What are the three kinds of attributions?

1. ______________ vs. ______________
2. ______________ vs. ______________
3. ______________ vs. ______________

People who report __________________ levels of perceived control view their health as controllable and are, therefore, more likely to engage in __________________ health behaviors. This link may explain why more __________________ individuals experience better health, as these individuals have the resources to control health outcomes.

Social Support

On Your Own

What are the forms that social support can take?

1.
2.
3.
4.
5.
6.

What is your reaction to the idea that social support can reduce mortality? Which study in the lesson did you find most compelling?

If you were unable to have physical social support, would online support be a sufficient replacement? Explain.

Coping with Prejudice and Discrimination

Being the target of racism has been linked with:

-
-
-
-

On Your Own

What are three coping strategies to handle racism-related stress?

1.

2.

3.

Stress Reduction Techniques

One of the ways that individuals can help reduce their stress levels is through ________________.

Both long (______________) and short (__________________) exercise is beneficial to both physical and mental health. Physically fit individuals are more ___________________ to the adverse effects of stress and recover more quickly from stress than less fit individuals.

On Your Own

What are the steps in the relaxation response training?

1.

2.

3.

4.

________________________ is another technique used to combat stress, in which electronic equipment is used to accurately measure a person's neuromuscular and autonomic activity.

Psychology and You

Impacts of Stress

Using the information from the lesson, what changes can you make in your lifestyle that would help you better combat the impacts of stress?

Lesson Wrap-up

Say It in a Sentence

In one sentence, explain coping with stress.

Test Yourself

Choose the correct answer for each of the following questions. Check your work using the Answer Key in the back of the book.

____ 1. When a problem seems within our control, we are more likely to use:

A. Emotion-focused coping
B. Problem-focused coping

____ 2. People who make global attributions to negative events are _______ likely to experience symptoms of depression.

A. less
B. more

Answer each of the following questions. Check your work using the Answer Key in the back of the book.

3. When it comes to attributions in coping styles, which would be more likely to result in negative outcomes when faced with a negative event—stable or unstable attributions?

4. When it comes to attributions in coping styles, which would be more likely to result in positive outcomes when faced with a negative event—internal or external attributions?

5. When it comes to attributions in coping styles, which would be more likely to result in negative outcomes when faced with a negative event—global or specific attributions?

Key Terms

Write the definition for each of the following terms.

Biofeedback:

Coping:

Perceived Control:

Relaxation Response Technique:

Social Support:

Lesson 13.5

The Pursuit of Happiness

OBJECTIVES

- ★ Define and discuss happiness, including its determinants.
- ★ Describe the field of positive psychology and identify the kinds of problems it addresses.
- ★ Explain the meaning of positive affect and discuss its importance in health outcomes.
- ★ Describe the concept of flow and its relationship to happiness and fulfillment.

BIG IDEA

Researchers have studied factors that contribute to happiness and have discovered a variety of impacts on individual levels of contentment and joy.

In this lesson, you will learn about the following:

- Happiness
- Positive Psychology
- Flow

Happiness

On Your Own

How would you define happiness?

What are three components that people may say comprise happiness?

-
-
-

Elements of Happiness

Complete the following figure:

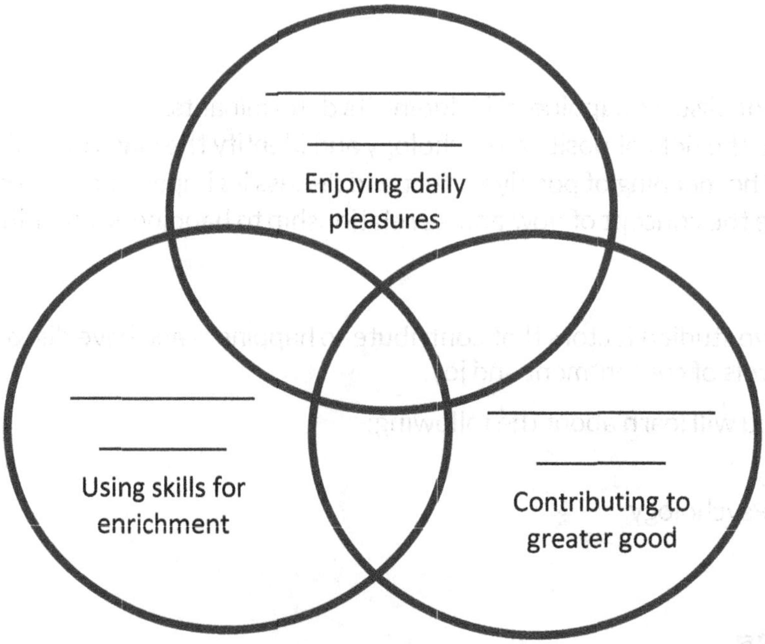

On Your Own

Do you believe that happiness is a long-term or transient state? Explain.

Why do you think happiness levels in the United States are declining?

Factors Connected to Happiness

On Your Own

Based on the lesson, which components linked with increased happiness do you currently have in your life?

What do you think about the finding that money makes a difference in happiness up until about $75,000?

Life Events and Happiness

__________________ forecasting refers to the degree to which people can predict the intensity and duration of future emotions.

On Your Own

Describe a situation that you thought would make you happy, but ultimately, you "reset" back to a normal level of happiness afterwards.

Explain how affective forecasting can impact emotions after winning the lottery.

Increasing Happiness

Average happiness scores strongly relate to these key variables:

-
-
-
-
-
-

Positive Psychology

Martin __________________ started the modern movement of positive psychology, a branch of psychology that studies how to identify and promote those qualities that lead to greatest fulfillment.

On Your Own

What do positive psychologists study?

1.
2.
3.
4.
5.
6.
7.

Positive Affect and Optimism

Qualities that help promote ____________________ well-being are linked with a range of favorable health outcomes, mainly through their relationships with biological functions and health behaviors.

Positive affect, pleasurable engagement with the environment, has been linked to:

-
-
-
-
-
-

On Your Own

Explain the difference between positive affect and optimism.

What positive impacts does optimism have?

1.
2.
3.
4.
5.
6.

Flow

Flow is described as an experience that is so ____________________ and engrossing that it becomes worth doing for its own sake.

On Your Own

When do you experience flow?

Psychology and You

Happiness

Are you happy? What elements discussed in the lesson do you have in your life?

Lesson Wrap-up

Say It in a Sentence

In one sentence, explain the goals of positive psychology.

Test Yourself

Choose the correct answer for each of the following questions. Check your work using the Answer Key in the back of the book.

____ 1. According to research, the happiest country is:

- **A.** United States
- **B.** Norway
- **C.** Denmark
- **D.** Switzerland

____ 2. Which of the following has *not* been shown to increase levels of happiness?

- **A.** Older age
- **B.** Good living conditions
- **C.** Parenthood

____ 3. Research has shown that people have difficulty readjusting happiness levels after:

- **A.** Marriage
- **B.** A new job
- **C.** Unemployment

Next to each statement, write **T** for True or **F** for False. Check your work using the Answer Key in the back of the book.

4. ______ Optimism is considered a general emotional state.

5. ______ Living a meaningful life means using our unique abilities to enrich our own lives.

6. ______ The lowest reported happiness levels were for sub-Saharan Africa.

7. _____ Recent studies have shown that the happiness of recent college graduates has declined.

Key Terms

Match each key term with its definition.

A. Flow
B. Happiness
C. Optimism
D. Positive Affect
E. Positive Psychology

_____ Scientific area of study seeking to identify and promote those qualities that lead to a happy, fulfilled, and contented life

_____ Tendency toward a positive outlook and positive expectations

_____ State involving intense engagement in an activity

_____ Enduring state of mind consisting of joy, contentment, and other positive emotions

_____ State or a trait that involves pleasurable engagement with the environment, the dimensions of which include happiness, joy, enthusiasm, alertness, and excitement

Chapter 14
Psychological Disorders

Lesson 14.1
What Are Psychological Disorders?

OBJECTIVES

- ★ Understand the problems inherent in defining the concept of psychological disorder.
- ★ Describe what is meant by harmful dysfunction.
- ★ Identify the formal criteria that thoughts, feelings, and behaviors must meet to be considered abnormal and, thus, symptomatic of a psychological disorder.

BIG IDEA

Psychological disorders are quite complex but can primarily be distinguished from more typical and accepted experiences through varying thoughts, feelings, and behaviors. Cultural expectations and the effects of such thoughts, feelings, and behaviors help us classify disorders. In addition, the American Psychiatric Association (APA) has formally defined the concept of psychological disorder.

Complete the following diagram by identifying the three components that are often considered when identifying psychological disorders.

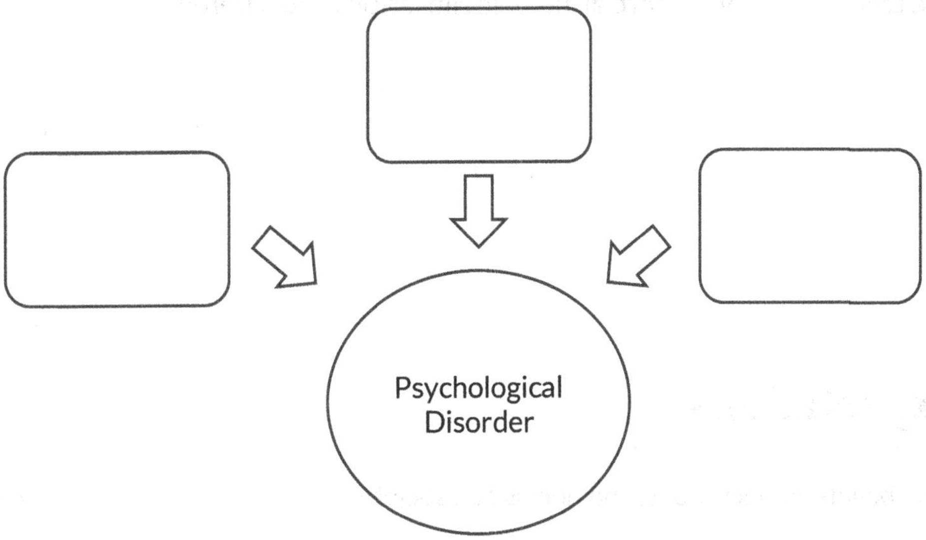

In this lesson, you will learn about the following:

- Definition of a Psychological Disorder
- Cultural Expectations
- Harmful Dysfunction
- The American Psychiatric Association (APA) Definition

Definition of a Psychological Disorder

Part of defining a psychological disorder requires distinguishing between the more common, or

_____________ thoughts, feelings, and behaviors in our population and those that are relatively

__________________, or uncommon and unexpected.

Categorize each of the following as typical or atypical:

- Having a high IQ:
- Having two cats:
- Sleeping only three hours each night:

On Your Own

Being atypical does not necessarily indicate abnormality or psychological disorder. Identify each of the following that would qualify as both atypical *and* potentially harmful/abnormal:

- ☐ Calling one's doctor at least 2 times a day
- ☐ Avoiding a hallway at school to avoid bullying
- ☐ Frequently waking up from bad dreams
- ☐ Consuming three or more hard alcoholic drinks each night

Ask at least three friends, coworkers, or family members what they think of when they hear the words "psychological disorder." Based on their experiences, ask them to define a disorder; then, compare their definitions with the text description. Record all notable similarities and differences.

Cultural Expectations

Culture includes the beliefs, expectations, and norms of a society. ____________________ varies from

one _________________ to another; therefore, accepted and common behaviors in one

________________ may not be viewed the same way in other locations or during varying generations. In order to more fully understand psychological disorders, we must also appreciate these cultural differences.

On Your Own

List three social norms or accepted practices/behaviors within your current culture that may be viewed differently in other cultures (for example, putting your phone on silent in a public or professional setting):

1.

2.

3.

Visit with a friend, reach out to someone from another culture, or speak with someone who has traveled to another country/culture. Identify one practice from that culture that varies from your current culture. For example, many people in India use water instead of toilet paper; people from other cultures find this practice surprising.

Complete the following diagram by including the components of one's culture:

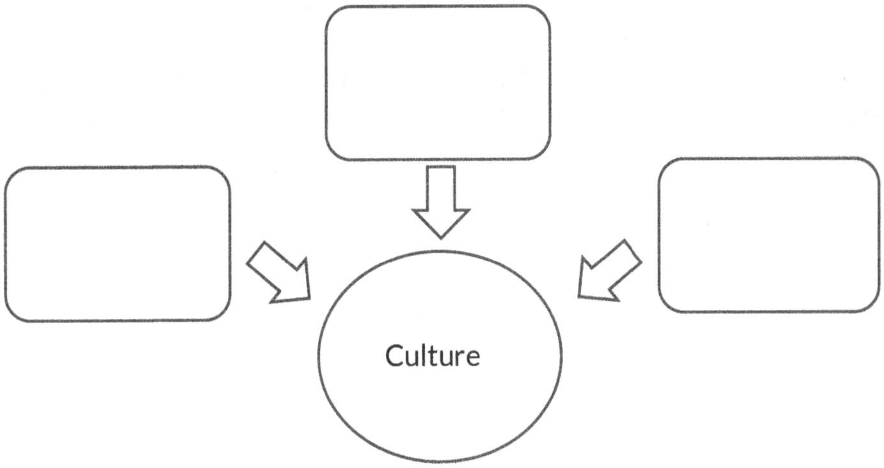

On Your Own

Sometimes, we are unaware of social norms and cultural expectations until they are violated. If someone violates a social norm, how might others react? For example, if someone sneezes without covering their nose and mouth, how might others respond? (Try to identify thoughts, feelings, and behaviors that others might have/exhibit in response to this scenario.)

Thought(s):

Feelings(s):

Behavior(s):

Harmful Dysfunction

There is no single definition of *psychological disorder* that exists today and applies to all scenarios. However, one prominent and common component (identified originally by Wakefield) is known as ____________ ________________. According to the model, psychological disorders are characterized by a dysfunction of ____________ ________________(such as learning or perception). The presence of a dysfunction by itself, much like abnormality, does not determine a disorder. The dysfunction must also be ________________ in that it leads to ____________ consequences for the individual or for others (within that culture). The harm may include perceptions of distress (e.g., intense sadness) and/or impaired functioning in some domain (e.g., financial problems).

On Your Own

Psychological disorders can cause many forms of distress and/or impairment. List two examples of distress and two examples of impairment that may be observed in relation to varying psychological disorders:

Distress:

Distress:

Impairment:

Impairment:

The concept of "harmful dysfunction" can be broken down into two components: (1) dysfunction of an internal mechanism and/or (2) harm. Dysfunction of an internal mechanism can involve cognitions, perceptions, and learning. Harm may include impairment and/or distress. To visually organize this information, fill in the empty boxes using the following terms:

Distress | Harm

Cognition | Learning

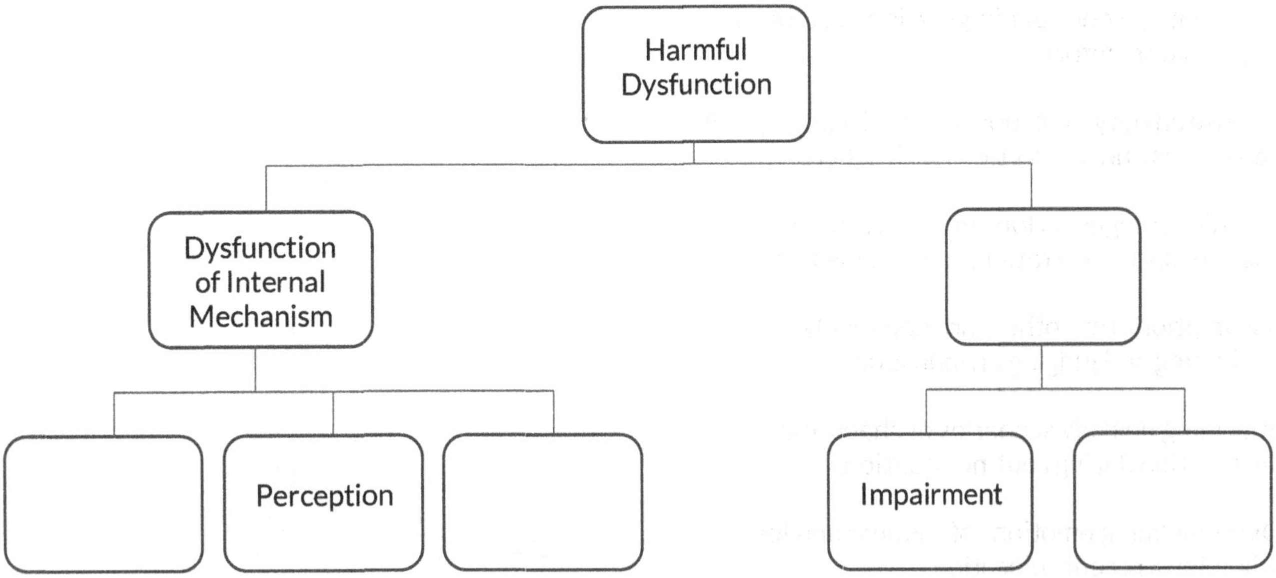

On Your Own

Think of a time when you experienced a dysfunction of an internal mechanism (for example, a time when your learning, cognition, or perception was impaired). Reflect on that experience and identify any short-term or long-term effects.

The American Psychiatric Association (APA) Definition

To more completely understand the concept of a psychological disorder, it is important to recognize the components of the American Psychiatric Association's (APA's) definition. As indicated by the APA (2013), a psychological disorder consists of the following:

- Disturbances in ________________, ________________, and ____________________
- These disturbances involve some form of __________________, ________________________, or ______________________________ dysfunction.

- The disturbances cause considerable ________________ or ____________________ in one's life.
- The disturbances are not accepted within one's ________________.

Categorize the following list of disturbances as one of the following: *thought*, *feeling*, or *behavior*.

Frequent episodes of binge eating, resulting in physical discomfort	
Intense anxiety in response to anticipated public gatherings and interactions with others	
Avoiding bridges on long drives, including vacations, due to irrational and vague fears	
Assumptions that others are negatively evaluating and judging an individual	
Imagining unlikely scenarios of chaos and destruction during routine situations	
Overwhelming emotions of sadness and loss following a recent relocation	

Fill in the boxes using the following terms: *biological*, *psychological*, or *developmental*.

High levels of stress hormones	Confusion or disorientation regarding time or day	Failure to meet language-learning milestones

On Your Own

Most people experience feelings of sadness and anxiety from time to time and have unwanted thoughts now and again. Give a few examples of common, short-term symptoms that would *not* be classified as a psychological disorder.

1.
2.
3.

List three behaviors or symptoms that might indicate a psychological disorder and provide the APA criteria associated with each.

Behavior	APA Criteria

Psychology and You

Mental Health

If a friend or family member was struggling with a psychological disorder, how would you know? Based on the information in this section, provide some concrete examples of observable signs (for example, atypical behaviors, signs of distress or impairment, socially unaccepted responses, etc.) that could indicate the presence of a psychological disorder.

Lesson Wrap-up

Say It in a Sentence

In one sentence, summarize the key elements of a psychological disorder.

Test Yourself

Next to each statement, write **T** for True or **F** for False. Check your work using the Answer Key in the back of the book.

1. _____ Behavior is always disordered if it is considered atypical.
2. _____ To be considered a disorder, a dysfunction must be harmful in that it leads to negative consequences for an individual or for others, as judged by the standards of the individual's culture.
3. _____ No single approach to defining a psychological disorder is adequate by itself.

Key Terms

Match each key term with its definition.

A. Atypical	_____	The customs, beliefs, and social norms within a group of people
B. Culture	_____	Causes of a psychological disorder
C. Dysfunction	_____	Harmful and leading to negative consequences
D. Etiology	_____	The study of psychological disorders
E. Inner States	_____	Thoughts and/or feelings
F. Psychopathology	_____	To deviate from the norm

Lesson 14.2

Diagnosing and Classifying Psychological Disorders

OBJECTIVES

★ Explain why classification systems are necessary in the study of psychopathology.
★ Describe the basic features of *The Diagnostic and Statistical Manual of Mental Disorders*, Fifth Edition (DSM-5).
★ Discuss changes in the DSM over time, including criticisms of the current edition.
★ Identify which disorders are generally the most common.

BIG IDEA

In order to accurately and consistently study and understand psychological disorders, the primary signs and symptoms must be identified. This allows for accurate diagnosis, which helps professionals and patients communicate effectively and contributes to treatment planning and prevention.

In this lesson, you will learn about the following:

- *The Diagnostic and Statistical Manual of Mental Disorders* (DSM)
- The *International Classification of Diseases*
- The Compassionate View of Psychological Disorders

The Diagnostic and Statistical Manual of Mental Disorders (DSM)

The primary diagnostic manual of psychological disorders used today, the ________, has been updated and revised many times over the years. The most recent edition, published in ________, is the DSM-5. This text includes many categories of disorders, such as ____________ disorders, ________________ disorders, and ________________ disorders. Each disorder is carefully described with an ______________, specific ________________ used for diagnosis (also known as ________________ ________________), ________________ data (the frequency of when the disorder occurs in our population), and __________ ________________ (predictors).

Complete the following diagram using terms from the lesson summary. What components are included in *The Diagnostic and Statistical Manual of Mental Disorders* (DSM)?

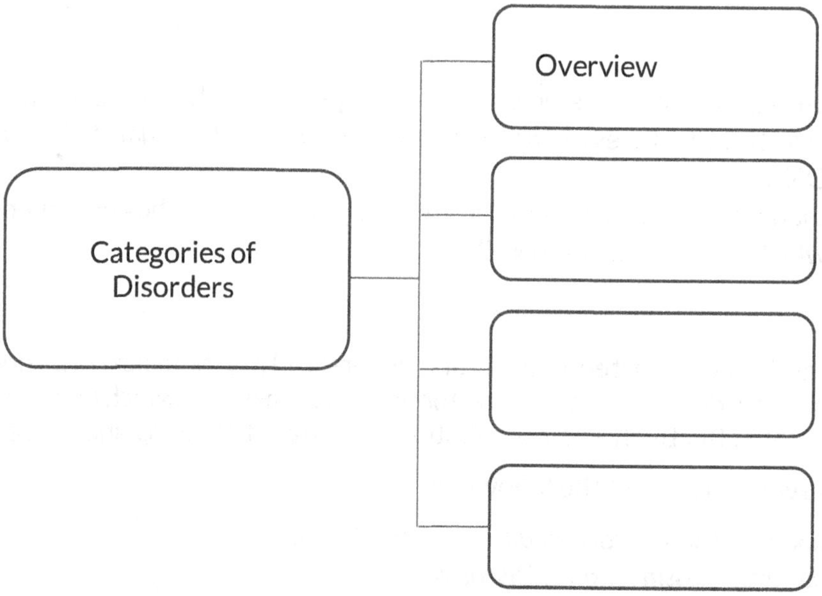

The DSM has been modified and adjusted many times over the years. Some changes have included the ______________ of diagnoses (for example, the removal of ______________________ in 1973), changes in the descriptions, and the ______________ of diagnoses (for example, Binge Eating Disorder). Over time, the total number of diagnosable conditions has ____________. DSM-I included ________ diagnoses, while the DSM-5 includes ________ disorders. The latest edition, DSM-5, includes revisions and reorganization and emphasizes careful consideration of both ____________ and ____________ ____________________ in the expression of various symptoms.

On Your Own

Why do you think the DSM has been revised so many times? What are the benefits of revisions and changing the diagnostics system over time? List three reasons:

1.

2.

3.

Many are concerned that adding new diagnoses may ______________________ our population by labeling and diagnosing normal/typical human problems. This issue is emphasized by a striking statistic: roughly ___________ of all Americans will meet the criteria for a DSM disorder at some point in their life. Some have also criticized the DSM-5 for changes in diagnostic criteria that allow for an increase in diagnosis. One example is ____________ ____________________ __________________, where the criteria are no longer as strict or rigid.

On Your Own

List a few symptoms or behaviors/responses that you feel might be overpathologized or could be misinterpreted as a psychological disorder:

1.

2.

3.

What do you think might be common risk factors (biological and environmental) for various psychological disorders? When writing your response, consider life stressors (job loss, work, etc.) that might be particularly taxing or difficult to cope with.

The *International Classification of Diseases*

A second classification system, the International Classification of Diseases (ICD), is also widely recognized. Published by the World Health Organization (WHO), the ICD was developed in ________________ and, like the DSM, has been revised several times. The categories of psychological disorders in both the DSM and ICD are similar, as are the criteria for specific disorders; however, some differences exist. Although the ICD is used for clinical purposes, it is also used to examine the ________________ ______________ of populations and to monitor the prevalence of ______________ and other health problems internationally (WHO, 2013).

On Your Own

Restate the primary differences between the ICD and the DSM in your own words.

Research has shown that the ICD is more frequently used worldwide for ______ ______, whereas the DSM is more valued for ______. Further, most research findings concerning the ______ and ______ of psychological disorders are based on criteria described in the ______. The DSM also includes more explicit disorder ______, along with thorough explanations. The DSM is the classification system of choice among U.S. ______ ______ professionals.

On Your Own

Using the internet (or a hard copy of the DSM-5), find and list the criteria for one current disorder.

The Compassionate View of Psychological Disorders

Note that psychological disorders represent extremes of ______ ______ and ______. Do not be concerned if you personally relate to any of the symptoms or disorders discussed; we all experience episodes of ______, ______, and preoccupation with certain ______. Most episodes are not problematic and will not become extreme, nor will they typically cause impairment.

A psychological disorder is not what a person ______; it is something that a person ______. Those with psychological disorders deserve to be viewed and treated with compassion, ______, and dignity.

On Your Own

List a television show, novel, or movie that includes a portrayal of a person with a psychological disorder. (For example, the movie *A Beautiful Mind* loosely portrays the life of mathematician John Forbes Nash Jr., who was diagnosed with schizophrenia.) What impression of the disorder does this work give you?

Consult a few of your friends, classmates, or family members. List some common biases or assumptions in our culture regarding mental illness and psychological disorders.

Psychology and You

Would You Rather

If you or a loved one struggled with symptoms of a disorder, would you rather it be diagnosed as a psychological disorder or a medical condition? Why? How do others respond to people with physical illnesses, and how do they respond to people with psychological disorders?

Lesson Wrap-up

Say It in a Sentence

In one sentence, summarize the key elements/ideas of each perspective in diagnosis and classification.

Test Yourself

Write out the full name for each acronym used in this lesson. Check your work using the Answer Key in the back of the book.

1. APA:
2. APA:
3. DSM:
4. ICD:
5. WHO:

Key Terms

Write a paraphrased definition for each key term.

Diagnosis:

Comorbidity:

Lesson 14.3

Perspectives on Psychological Disorders

OBJECTIVES

- ★ Discuss supernatural perspectives on the origin of psychological disorders in their historical context.
- ★ Describe modern biological and psychological perspectives on the origin of psychological disorders.
- ★ Identify which disorders generally show the highest degree of heritability.
- ★ Describe the diathesis-stress model and its importance to the study of psychopathology.

BIG IDEA

Many psychological theories have been developed over the years, each attempting to describe and explain the development of psychological disorders. This diversity in the field provides options for understanding and thinking about psychological disorders.

In this lesson, you will learn about the following:

- Supernatural Perspectives of Psychological Disorders
- Biological Perspectives of Psychological Disorders
- The Diathesis-Stress Model of Psychological Disorders

Supernatural Perspectives of Psychological Disorders

For centuries, psychological disorders were viewed from a ______________________ perspective; they were attributed to a force beyond scientific understanding. Those with psychological disorders were often assumed to be possessed by evil _______________ or practicing dark _______________. As a result, many were treated harshly and punished, imprisoned, or tortured. Some societies and cultures maintain these beliefs today.

On Your Own

Provide a few examples of supernatural treatments used in the past (for example, exorcism). Use the internet if needed.

1.

2.

3.

You've read about the phenomenon of "dancing mania." Do an internet search of historical examples of mania and describe the most interesting account.

Biological Perspectives of Psychological Disorders

The biological perspective views psychological disorders as linked to biological variables, such as

_______________ factors, ____________________ imbalances, and __________________ abnormalities.

Much evidence suggests that most psychological disorders have a ____________________ component.

The biological perspective is currently ______________________ in the study of psychological disorders.

Complete the following diagram by listing the variables often emphasized by the biological perspective:

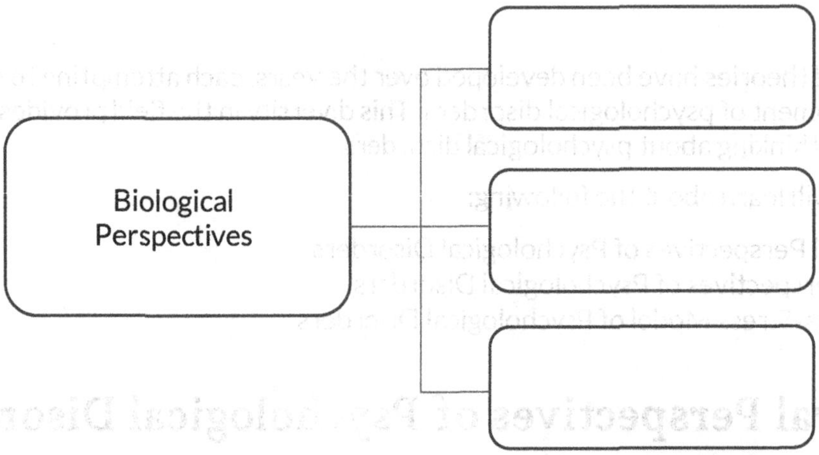

On Your Own

Perform a quick internet search of brain changes associated with Alzheimer's Disease. List three brain changes/abnormalities that have been linked to this disorder.

1.

2.

3.

Diathesis-Stress Model of Psychological Disorders

The **diathesis-stress model** acknowledges both ____________________ and _________________________

factors that contribute to psychological disorders. This theory suggests that people with an underlying predisposition for a disorder (____________________) are more likely than others to develop a disorder when they experience an adverse environmental, social, or psychological event (________________). A diathesis may also include psychological variables or personality characteristics.

List two examples of adverse events or stressors that may contribute to the development of psychological disorders:

1.

2.

Complete the diagram to include the factors emphasized by this model:

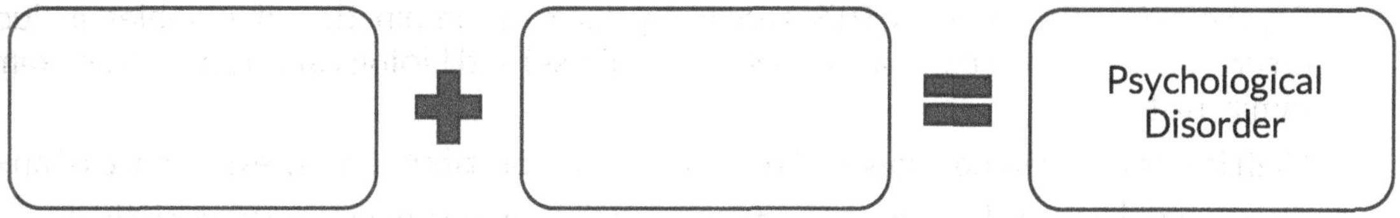

On Your Own

Apply the diathesis-stress model to alcohol use disorder by brainstorming a few diatheses and stressors that might contribute to it.

Psychology and You

Understanding Psychological Disorders

You have just learned about three approaches to understanding psychological disorders. Why is it important to identify the causes of psychological disorders? Which perspective do you most agree with, and why?

Lesson Wrap-up

Say It in a Sentence

In one sentence, summarize the diathesis-stress model.

Test Yourself

Next to each statement, write the applicable theory: **S** for *supernatural*, **B** for *biological*, or **DS** for *diathesis-stress*. Check your work using the Answer Key in the back of the book.

1. _____ Depression is often linked to low levels of the neurotransmitter serotonin.
2. _____ The devil is responsible for hallucinations (seeing or hearing things that are not there) and delusions (false beliefs).
3. _____ Psychological disorders like PTSD are likely due to a combination of variables, including environmental stressors (for example, child abuse) and biological variables (for example, family history).
4. _____ High levels of stress hormones, like cortisol, may contribute to the experience of anxiety.
5. _____ Those with high intelligence and sufficient social support may have lower risk of developing psychological disorders.
6. _____ The best way to treat psychological disorders is through religious practices like praying or exorcism.

Key Terms

Write a related word for each of the following key terms.

Diathesis:

Stress:

Supernatural:

Heritability:

Lesson 14.4

Anxiety Disorders

OBJECTIVES

★ Distinguish normal anxiety from pathological anxiety.
★ List and describe the major anxiety disorders, including their main features and prevalence.
★ Describe basic psychological and biological factors that are suspected to be important in the etiology of anxiety disorder.

BIG IDEA

Anxiety and fear are distinct reactions that most people experience from time to time.

In this lesson, you will learn about the following:

- Specific Phobia
- Acquisition of Phobias Through Learning
- Social Anxiety Disorder
- Panic Disorder
- Generalized Anxiety Disorder

While anxiety is typically viewed as unpleasant and distressing, it can be adaptive. Anxiety often ______________ us to complete tasks and/or to avoid negative consequences. For example, anxiety may prompt a student to write a paper or motivate an individual to avoid a dangerous act, such as hang-gliding.

On Your Own

How has anxiety served you? List a few behaviors or decisions that benefited you or others and that you engaged in or did not engage in as a result of anxiety.

1.

2.

3.

Most people experience anxiety that is consistent with the level of the stressor. Some people, however, experience anxiety that is ______________, ________________, and greatly

______ ______ ____________________ to the actual threat.

On Your Own

Anxiety is clearly a subjective experience, yet we often make judgments regarding levels of anxiety when diagnosing. On a scale of 0–10 (0 = no anxiety, 10 = extreme anxiety), how much anxiety do you believe the following scenarios would typically trigger?

Scenario	Anxiety Level
Moving to a new city	
Getting married	
Speaking in class	
Owing a friend money	
Losing your wallet	
Having a disagreement with a coworker	

________________ ____________________ are characterized by excessive and persistent fear and anxiety and related disturbances in __________________. Although they are quite common (approximately 25%–30% of the U.S. population meets the criteria for at least one anxiety disorder during their lifetime), these disorders cause considerable ________________. They occur more commonly in _____________ than in ___________.

Anxiety disorders are the most common category of diagnosis in the U.S. population.

Specific Phobia

_______________ is Greek for *fear*. A person diagnosed with a _________________ **phobia** experiences excessive, distressing, and persistent fear or anxiety about a specific object or situation. Many kinds of phobias have been identified over the years.

List three objects or situations that may be the target of a specific phobia.

1.

2.

3.

Although many phobic reactions are __________________, they are typically impairing. Those with phobias will often go to great lengths to ____________ the feared stimuli.

How might the following phobias lead to impairment or dysfunction?

Fear of bridges:

Fear of spiders:

Fear of electricity:

____________________ leads to intense fear, anxiety, and ____________________ of situations in which it might be difficult to escape or receive help if one experiences symptoms of a ____________ ____________ (a state of extreme anxiety that we will discuss shortly). About ________ of Americans experience agoraphobia during their lifetime.

List 3 settings, locations, or situations someone with agoraphobia might avoid:

1.

2.

3.

Complete the following graphic to highlight the symptoms of a specific phobia:

Acquisition of Phobias Through Learning

Many theories suggest that phobias develop through three methods of ______________. The first pathway is through ________________ conditioning.

Fill in the missing terms to display the role of conditioning in the establishment of a phobia.

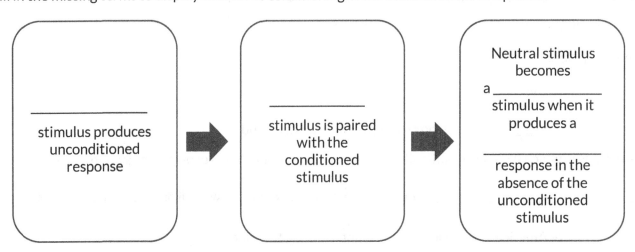

______ stimulus produces unconditioned response	→	______ stimulus is paired with the conditioned stimulus	→	Neutral stimulus becomes a ______ stimulus when it produces a ______ response in the absence of the unconditioned stimulus

Identify the UCS, UCR, NS, CS, and CR in the following scenario:

> Brittany received a painful bee sting while she was eating corn on the cob at a summer fair. She had an allergic reaction and was very uncomfortable. As a result of the association she formed, she now dislikes corn on the cob.

UCS:

UCR:

NS:

CS:

CR:

The second pathway of phobia acquisition is through ______ learning, also known as ______.

On Your Own

List three potential fears (objects and/or situations) that may be learned through observation.

1.

2.

3.

The third pathway is through ______ transmission of information.

Complete the following graphic by identifying the modes of learning that contribute to phobias.

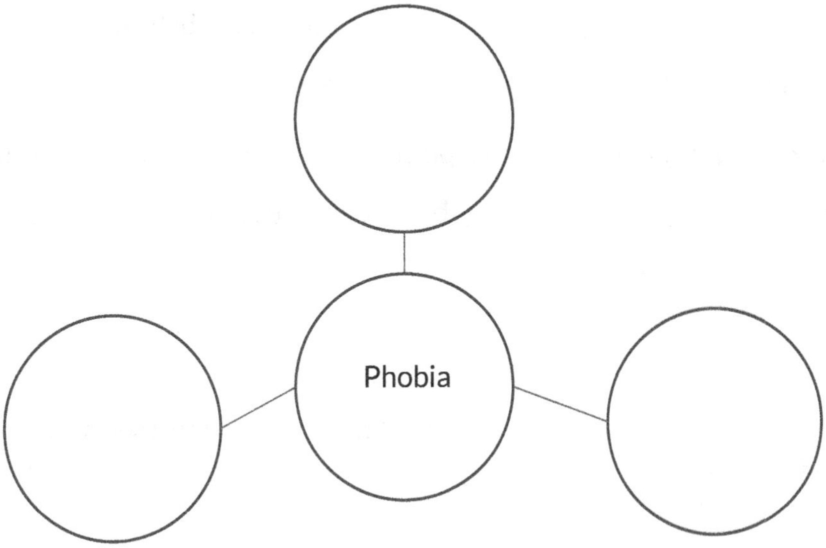

On Your Own

Provide your own example of a classically conditioned phobia. Be sure to identify the UCS, UCR, NS, CS, and CR.

Social Anxiety Disorder

____________ ________________ **disorder** is characterized by extreme and persistent fear or anxiety and avoidance of social situations in which the person could potentially be negatively __________________ by others.

On Your Own

List a few social situations (for example, speaking in class) and a corresponding consequence of avoiding that situation (for example, failing the course).

Social Situation	Consequence

When people with social anxiety disorder are unable to avoid situations that provoke anxiety, they typically perform ______________ ____________________: mental or behavioral acts that reduce anxiety in social situations by reducing the chance of negative social outcomes.

Unfortunately, engaging in safety behaviors often perpetuates the false beliefs, as the individual is unable to disconfirm any ____________________ beliefs, often eliciting ______________________ and other negative reactions from others.

On Your Own

What is one form of self-medication that someone might use to cope with a social anxiety disorder? What negative consequences might this have?

Complete the graphic to identify the two primary factors that contribute to the development of social anxiety disorder.

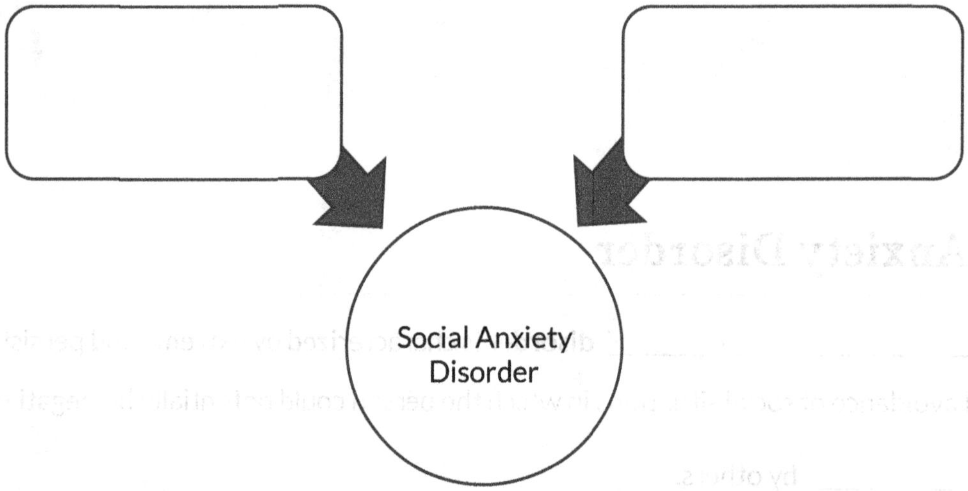

On Your Own

List a situation that may cause anxiety or fear of negative evaluations for most people. List a situation that would *not* typically cause fear or anxiety for most people but might for those with social anxiety disorder. What signs/behaviors might indicate their discomfort in these situations?

	Situation	**Signs/behaviors that indicate discomfort**
May cause anxiety or fear of negative evaluations in most people		
May cause anxiety or fear of negative evaluations in people with social anxiety disorder		

Panic Disorder

People with ____________ **disorder** experience recurrent (multiple) and unexpected

__________ ____________, along with at least one month of persistent concern about additional panic attacks, worry over the consequences of the attacks, or self-defeating changes in behavior related to the attacks. A **panic attack** is defined as a period of extreme __________ or

______________ that develops abruptly and reaches a peak within ______ minutes.

On Your Own

What are two common locations or situations that could trigger panic?

1.

2.

List three symptoms of a panic attack that may look or feel like a medical problem.

1.

2.

3.

Insert the appropriate statistics to complete the graphic:

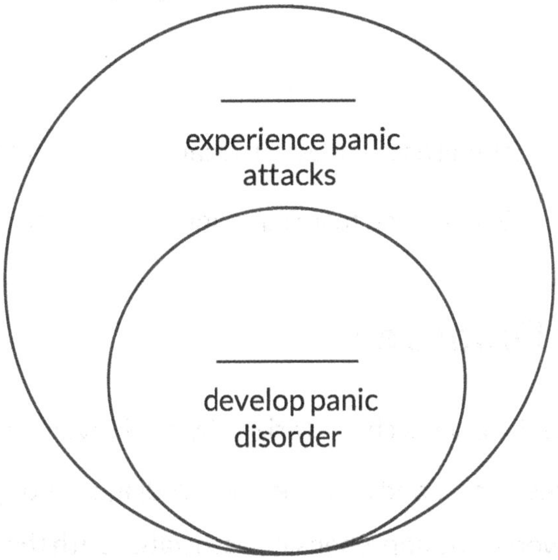

______________ theories of panic disorder suggest that a region of the brain called the __________ ____________ may play a role in this disorder. This structure is the brain's

primary source of norepinephrine, a ______________________ that triggers the body's fight-or-flight response. Activation of the locus coeruleus is associated with anxiety and fear.

Conditioning theories of panic disorder propose that panic attacks are ________________

________________ responses to subtle bodily sensations resembling those normally occurring when one is anxious or frightened.

________________ theories argue that those with panic disorder are prone to misinterpret ordinary body sensations catastrophically, and these fearful ________________ set the stage for panic attacks.

On Your Own

Identify two daily activities/experiences that could trigger a bodily sensation or symptom. Next, identify a potential misinterpretation of that symptom. (For example, a cluster of headaches may be irrationally assumed to be indicative of a brain tumor.)

Daily Activity/Experience	**Potential Misinterpretation**

Correctly label the columns to represent the influences contributing to panic disorder.

Genetic influence	Stimuli associated with fear	Catastrophic thoughts
Locus coeruleus	Generalized fear reactions	Misinterpreting body sensations

Generalized Anxiety Disorder

________________ anxiety disorder is characterized by a relatively continuous state of excessive, uncontrollable, and pointless worry and apprehension. A diagnosis of generalized anxiety disorder requires that the constant worry and apprehension associated with this disorder are not part of another disorder, occurs more days than not for at least ________ months, and are accompanied by any ____________ of the following symptoms: restlessness, difficulty concentrating, being easily fatigued, muscle tension, irritability, and sleep difficulties.

On Your Own

Everyone experiences episodes of worry or apprehension from time to time. List a few situations or events that trigger anxiety for you.

Why do you think generalized anxiety disorder is more prevalent among women? What factors may influence this trend?

It can be difficult to distinguish between generalized anxiety disorder and typical, expected levels of apprehension or worry. Using the material from this lesson, how might you make the distinction? In other words, how would you know if a friend or family member was experiencing excessive or unnecessary worry/fear?

Psychology and You

What Does Anxiety Look Like to You?

Anxiety is a universal experience, yet for many people it can be difficult to identify and/or describe. Draw a picture of anxiety (what it may look like, feel like, etc.) to represent the general concept. Choose a specific anxiety disorder if you like.

Lesson Wrap-up

Say It in a Sentence

In one sentence, describe anxiety disorders as they were presented in this lesson.

Test Yourself

Choose all correct answers for the following questions. Check your work using the Answer Key in the back of the book.

_____________ 1. Which of the following are safety behaviors?

- **A.** Sitting in the back of class to minimize participation
- **B.** Walking one's dog in secluded areas to avoid bumping into neighbors
- **C.** Wearing bright clothing to a football game
- **D.** Staying in the kitchen during a dinner party to avoid socializing with guests
- **E.** Avoiding eye contact

_____________ 2. Which of the following are symptoms of a panic attack?

- **A.** Hot flashes or chills
- **B.** Sleepiness
- **C.** Sweating and trembling
- **D.** Slowed heart rate
- **E.** Racing heart
- **F.** Low blood pressure
- **G.** Fear of dying or losing control
- **H.** Choking sensations
- **I.** Loss of hearing
- **J.** Lightheadedness

Key Terms

The following key terms have been scrambled. Use the definition to unscramble the letters and determine the correct term.

pogoraiahba		Anxiety disorder characterized by intense fear, anxiety, and avoidance of situations in which it might be difficult to escape if one experiences symptoms of a panic attack
nyieatx eodrsrid		Characterized by excessive and persistent fear and anxiety, and by related disturbances in behavior
erdnaegliez itnyaxe soirderd		Characterized by a continuous state of excessive, uncontrollable, and pointless worry and apprehension

cluso ecsuloeru		Area of the brainstem that contains norepinephrine, a neurotransmitter that triggers the body's fight-or-flight response; has been implicated in panic disorder
canip ktacta		Period of extreme fear or discomfort that develops abruptly; symptoms are both physiological and psychological
cnpia resoirdd		Anxiety disorder characterized by unexpected panic attacks, along with at least one month of worry about panic attacks or self-defeating behavior related to the attacks
etfsya heiobvra		Mental and behavior acts designed to reduce anxiety in social situations by reducing the chance of negative social outcomes; common in social anxiety disorder
cisalo antyxie rdiseodr		Characterized by extreme and persistent fear or anxiety and avoidance of social situations in which one could potentially be evaluated negatively by others
cificeps aibohp		Anxiety disorder characterized by excessive, distressing, and persistent fear or anxiety about a specific object or situation

Lesson 14.5

Obsessive-Compulsive and Related Disorders

OBJECTIVES

- ★ Describe the main features and prevalence of obsessive-compulsive disorder, body dysmorphic disorder, and hoarding disorder.
- ★ Understand some of the factors in the development of obsessive-compulsive disorder.

BIG IDEA

While we all experience intrusive thoughts and behaviors, some people experience them in extreme ways that limit their functioning and interfere with their lives.

In this lesson, you will learn about the following:

- Obsessive-Compulsive Disorder
- Body Dysmorphic Disorder
- Hoarding Disorder
- Causes of OCD

Obsessive-Compulsive Disorder

Obsessive-compulsive disorder (OCD) is characterized by intrusive thoughts and urges

(______________________) and/or the impulse to engage in repetitive behaviors or mental acts

(______________________).

Fill in the missing components (primary symptoms) of OCD.

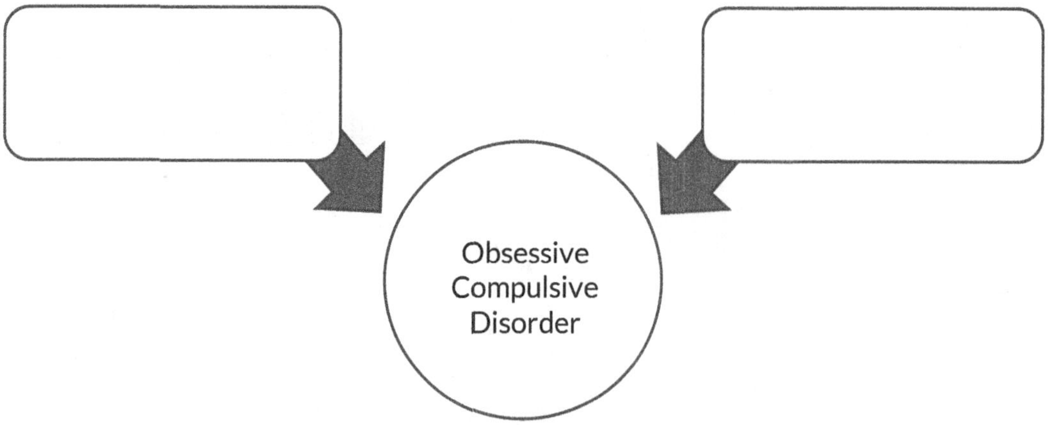

Obsessions are characterized as ______________________, unintentional, and ________________ thoughts

and urges that are highly intrusive, unpleasant, and ______________________.

________________________ are repetitive and ritualistic acts that are typically carried out primarily as a means to ____________________ the distress that obsessions trigger or to reduce the likelihood of a feared event.

Label each of the following as an obsession or compulsion.

- Needing to count to ten each time they enter a new room:
- Constant fear of contracting a deadly virus:
- The perceived need to check all outlets in the home:
- Excessive fear of house or electrical fires:

On Your Own

Many of us perform rituals, have preferences, and/or entertain superstitions. Perform an informal survey by asking friends and family members to share any quirks, eccentricities, or particularities they have. List any that apply.

Body Dysmorphic Disorder

An individual with ____________ ______________________ disorder is preoccupied with a perceived flaw in his or her physical appearance that is either nonexistent or barely noticeable to other people.

On Your Own

Check the box next to all the acts that are likely to be performed by an individual with body dysmorphic disorder.

- ☐ Hiding flaws with makeup or hats
- ☐ Using large words to sound intelligent
- ☐ Cosmetic surgery
- ☐ Excessive exercise
- ☐ Using Skype or FaceTime in place of texting
- ☐ Frequently checking mirrors
- ☐ Changing clothes frequently

Most people have some mild to moderate body image concerns or sensitivities. How and why do you think these concerns develop?

Hoarding Disorder

People with ________________ disorder cannot bear to part with personal possessions, regardless of how valueless or useless these possessions are. As a result, these individuals accumulate ________________ amounts of usually ________________ items that clutter their living areas.

On Your Own

Name two objects or items that you keep due to sentimental attachment:

1.

2.

Have you ever started a collection of items or objects? If so, did you have difficulty parting with the items? Did the collection impact your living or functioning in any way?

Causes of OCD

Although much of the research is based on small sample sizes and has been correlational in nature, results from family and twin studies suggest that OCD has a ________________ genetic component. The genes believed to be associated with this disorder regulate the function of three neurotransmitters: ________________, ________________, and ________________.

List one function or behavior that is influenced by each of the neurotransmitters implicated in OCD. Consult Lesson 2.2 or conduct a quick internet search for reference.

Neurotransmitter	Function/Behavior
Serotonin	
Dopamine	
Glutamate	

A brain region believed to play a key role in OCD is the ______________ ______________, an area of the frontal lobe involved in learning and decision-making. This structure is part of a series of brain regions that, collectively, is called the __________ ______________, consisting of several interconnected regions that influence the perceived emotional value of stimuli and the selection of both

______________ and ______________ responses. People with OCD show a substantially higher degree of ______________ of the orbitofrontal cortex and other regions of the OCD circuit than do those without OCD.

On Your Own

Perform an internet search on the OCD circuit and recommended treatments. Discuss one recommended technique.

In addition to biological influences, ______________ and conditioning have also been identified as key factors in the development of OCD.

On Your Own

Choose the correct option at each stage of learning.

1. Stage 1: __________ stimulus associated with UCS.
   - ☐ Learned
   - ☐ Neutral
2. Stage 2: Anxiety and obsessive thoughts become a __________.
   - ☐ CR
   - ☐ CS
3. Stage 3: __________ is performed.
   - ☐ Ritual
   - ☐ Math
4. Stage 4: Anxiety is ______________.
   - ☐ increased
   - ☐ reduced
5. Stage 5: Response is ______________.
   - ☐ weakened
   - ☐ strengthened

On Your Own

Briefly describe an obsession that might develop due to classical conditioning (for example, anxiety associated with a school assignment may be linked to the classroom or building). Next, identify a compulsion that may follow due to operant conditioning (for example, the student may begin biting nails to distract themselves and reduce the anxiety felt when entering the school/classroom).

Psychology and You

Consequences of Obsessive-Compulsive and Related Disorders

Consider the diagnoses discussed in this lesson: OCD, body dysmorphic disorder, and hoarding disorder. Each of these disorders disrupts functioning and daily living. In what ways might these disorders impact a person's functioning, and how might it decrease their satisfaction in life? Provide at least three examples.

1.

2.

3.

Lesson Wrap-up

Say It in a Sentence

In one sentence, summarize the obsessive-compulsive disorders.

Test Yourself

Identify the disorder for each of the following scenarios. Check your work using the Answer Key in the back of the book.

____ 1. Jonathan has extreme difficulty parting with his possessions. His home has become cluttered, and it is impacting his ability to live a healthy lifestyle and function normally.

  A. Hoarding disorder
  B. Obsessive-compulsive disorder
  C. Body dysmorphic disorder

____ 2. Cam is convinced that he looks disgusting to other people although no one sees him that way. He wears big, baggy clothing and avoids social events in order to hide himself and is considering cosmetic surgery.

A. Hoarding disorder
B. Obsessive-compulsive disorder
C. Body dysmorphic disorder

____ 3. Sarah stops to check that her door is locked exactly 14 times when she leaves the house each day. She counts each one and is distressed if she doesn't follow this ritual. When others are waiting for her, she feels anxious about this behavior but has difficulty getting herself to stop.

A. Hoarding disorder
B. Obsessive-compulsive disorder
C. Body dysmorphic disorder

Key Terms

Imagine that you must describe each of the following terms to a young child; how would you summarize or describe each concept?

Body Dysmorphic Disorder:

Hoarding Disorder:

Obsessive-Compulsive Disorder:

Orbitofrontal Cortex:

Lesson 14.6

Posttraumatic Stress Disorder

OBJECTIVES

- ★ Describe the nature and symptoms of posttraumatic stress disorder.
- ★ Identify the risk factors associated with this disorder.
- ★ Understand the role of learning and cognitive factors in its development.

BIG IDEA

When a person experiences a ____________________ or __________________________ event, they are at risk of developing posttraumatic stress disorder, also known as ______________. Posttraumatic stress disorder can happen to __________________ with a history of psychological trauma.

In this lesson, you will learn about the following:

- A Broader Definition of PTSD
- Risk Factors for PTSD
- Support for Sufferers of PTSD
- Learning and the Development of PTSD

A Broader Definition of PTSD

PTSD was previously categorized as an ______________ ________________ in earlier editions of the DSM. However, in the DSM-5, it is now included in a new category: _______________-________-

_____________-________________ __________________. To warrant a diagnosis of PTSD, one must be

_____________ _______, _____________, or ______________________ the details of a traumatic experience. The traumatic experience must also involve "actual or threatened _______________, serious

_____________, or ________________ violence." These experiences can include such events as

_________________, threatened or actual _______________ attack, sexual assault, natural disasters, terrorist attacks, and ___________________ accidents. PTSD is the only disorder in the DSM to list a cause (extreme trauma) of the psychological disorder.

On Your Own

Which of the following experiences would you categorize as "trauma?" Choose all that apply.

- ☐ Not being accepted to graduate school
- ☐ Witnessing a power outage
- ☐ Being physically abused by a parent
- ☐ Losing a loved one suddenly and unexpectedly
- ☐ Surviving a devastating earthquake
- ☐ Being the first person on the scene at a serious car accident

PTSD often includes ____________________ and ______________________ memories of the event, called **flashbacks**.

On Your Own

In your own words, describe a few of the symptoms of PTSD; then, give an example of each:

Symptom	Example

Roughly ______ of adults in the United States experience PTSD in their lifetime. Even higher rates occur among people exposed to ________________ trauma and people whose jobs involve ____________-related trauma exposure.

On Your Own

List a few professions that may be associated with mass trauma or work-related trauma exposure:

Most people experience troubling, upsetting, or even stressful events, but many never meet the criteria for PTSD. Why do you think some individuals develop PTSD symptoms and others do not, even when they have experienced the same or similar traumas?

Risk Factors for PTSD

The development of PTSD symptoms is complex and often involves multiple variables. Fill in the table by listing examples of risk factors for each category:

Risk Factor	Example
Trauma/Stressor	
Biological Risk	
Personal Trait	

On Your Own

Choose one risk factor mentioned in the previous section. Knowing that this is a risk factor for PTSD, what measures can or could be taken to address or prevent this issue? You may suggest or discuss small- or large-scale interventions.

Support for Sufferers of PTSD

Much evidence suggests that __________ ________________ may reduce the risk of developing PTSD. Social support can help people cope following traumatic or stressful events by allowing them to __________ ____________ and experiences and by helping them to feel ___________ and ________________.

On Your Own

List an example of social support that could be offered by someone in each of the following social roles:

- Teacher:
- Neighbor:
- Co-worker:
- Friend:
- Relative:

Discuss a time when you have either received or provided social support. What were the emotional and/or psychological effects of this support? What are some signs that someone may need support?

Learning and the Development of PTSD

Much evidence suggests that symptoms of PTSD are established and maintained through

________________ conditioning. The initial traumatic event or stressor may act as an

____________________ stimulus that elicits an ______________________ response of anxiety and fear.

Cognitive, emotional, physiological, and environmental cues associated with the event can become

___________________ stimuli. Later, these cues may elicit ____________________ responses of anxiety and fear.

On Your Own

To illustrate this process, consider the following scenario:

> A person has been mugged and associated the smell of the cologne worn by the mugger with the event and the experience of fear/anxiety. In the future, the smell of that cologne (worn by a different person) triggered an anxiety response.

Based on the scenario, identify the following:

- Unconditioned Stimulus:
- Unconditioned Response:
- Conditioned Stimulus:
- Conditioned Response:

Stimuli (both pleasant and unpleasant) that we associate with various settings or events can be easily learned. List one stimulus that you associate with each of the following environments (this could be a smell, a sound, etc.):

- School:
- Home:
- Work:

Cognitive factors are important elements in the development and maintenance of PTSD.

Complete the diagram by identifying the missing cognitive components that contribute to PTSD symptoms.

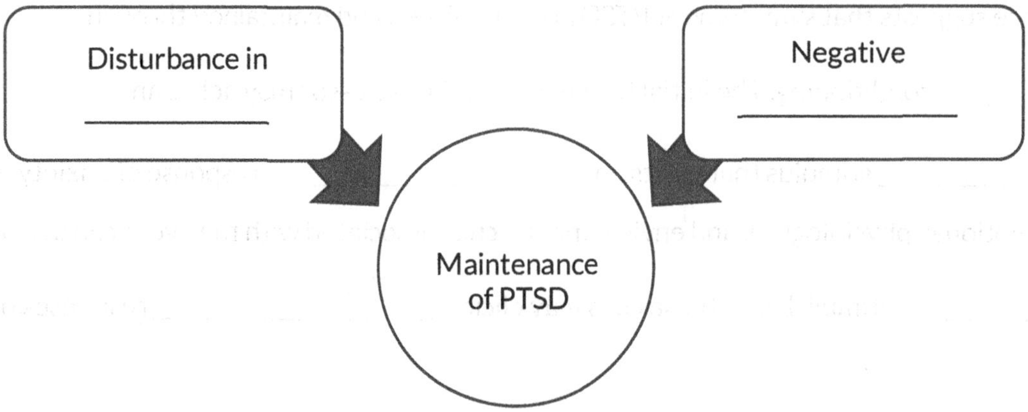

On Your Own

List a memory and the accompanying thoughts that you have associated with an event (positive or negative) that demonstrates the connection illustrated by the previous graphic.

Psychology and You

PTSD Made Personal

Briefly describe a stressful (or traumatic) event that you (or someone you know) have experienced. How did you (or they) cope with this experience? Was it helpful? Why or why not?

Lesson Wrap-up

Say It in a Sentence

In one sentence, summarize what can be done to support people experiencing PTSD.

Test Yourself

Choose the correct answer for each of the following questions. Check your work using the Answer Key in the back of the book.

____ 1. Symptoms of PTSD include all of the following *except*:

- **A.** Intrusive thoughts or memories of a traumatic event
- **B.** Avoidance of things that remind one of a traumatic event
- **C.** Jumpiness
- **D.** Physical complaints that cannot be explained medically

____ 2. Which of the following elevates the risk for developing PTSD?

- **A.** Severity of the trauma
- **B.** Frequency of the trauma
- **C.** High levels of intelligence
- **D.** Social support

Key Terms

For each key term, provide an example that exemplifies the meaning of the word.

Sexual Trauma:

Flashback:

Somatization:

Social Support:

Lesson 14.7

Mood Disorders

OBJECTIVES

- ★ Distinguish normal states of sadness and euphoria from states of depression and mania.
- ★ Describe the symptoms of major depressive disorder and bipolar disorder.
- ★ Understand the differences between major depressive disorder and persistent depressive disorder, and identify two subtypes of depression.
- ★ Define the criteria for a manic episode.
- ★ Understand genetic, biological, and psychological explanations of major depressive disorder.
- ★ Discuss the relationship between mood disorders and suicidal ideation, as well as factors associated with suicide.

BIG IDEA

Mood disorders, including major depressive disorder and bipolar disorder, involve extreme disturbances in mood and emotion.

In this lesson, you will learn about the following:

- Major Depressive Disorder
- Subtypes of Depression
- Bipolar Disorder
- The Biological Basis of Mood Disorders
- Suicide
- Risk Factors for Suicide

Mood disorders are characterized by severe disturbances in mood and ____________________, such as depression, mania, and elation. People with mood disorders experience mood ____________________ that are extreme, distort their outlook on life, and impair their ability to ________________.

What are the two main categories of mood disorders according to the DSM-5?

1. ____________________ ____________________: intense and persistent sadness

2. ________________ and related disorders: states of extreme elation and agitation

Major Depressive Disorder

What are the two defining symptoms of major depressive disorder?

1.

2.

In addition to the two defining symptoms of major depressive disorder described previously, what are the other symptoms of depression?

- Significant weight loss or ____________
- Difficulty ____________________
- Suicidal _______________
- Feelings of worthlessness or ____________
- Difficulty _____________ _____________ or sleeping too much
- Psychomotor agitation or ____________________ __________________
- Fatigue or loss of ______________

Results of Major Depressive Disorder

A person living with major depressive disorder lives a profoundly miserable life that often impacts his or her ability to __________ or attend school, resulting in abandonment of _____________ and lost wages.

Risk Factors for Major Depressive Disorder

Major depressive disorder affects more _______________ than men, and lifetime rates appear to be highest for ____________ and South America, _______________, and Australia. Major depressive disorder is also more common among the ________________.

What are the greatest risk factors for major depressive disorder?

-
-
-
-

Subtypes of Depression

Subtypes, or ________________, of depression are not specific to the disorder but are labels used to indicate specific patterns of symptoms or to specify ____________ ________ __________ in which the symptoms may be present.

What are the three subtypes of depression listed in the lesson?

1.
2.
3.

On Your Own

Have you ever experienced the winter blues? How did you feel?

Bipolar Disorder

A person with bipolar disorder often experiences mood states that vacillate between depression and

_____________. _______________ is the defining attribute of bipolar disorder.

What might be experienced during a manic episode?

1.
2.
3.
4.
5.
6.
7.
8.
9.
10.

Risk Factors for Bipolar Disorder

Rates of bipolar disorder are higher in __________ than women, and most cases have age of onset earlier than ________ years of age.

The Biological Basis of Mood Disorders

Mood disorders have been shown to have a strong ______________ and biological basis. Relatives of those with major depressive disorder have ____________ the risk of developing major depressive disorder, whereas relatives of patients with bipolar disorder have over _________ times the risk.

What two neurotransmitters are often imbalanced in mood disorders?

1.

2.

On Your Own

How do the treatments for major depressive disorder and bipolar disorder differ?

Complete the following figure:

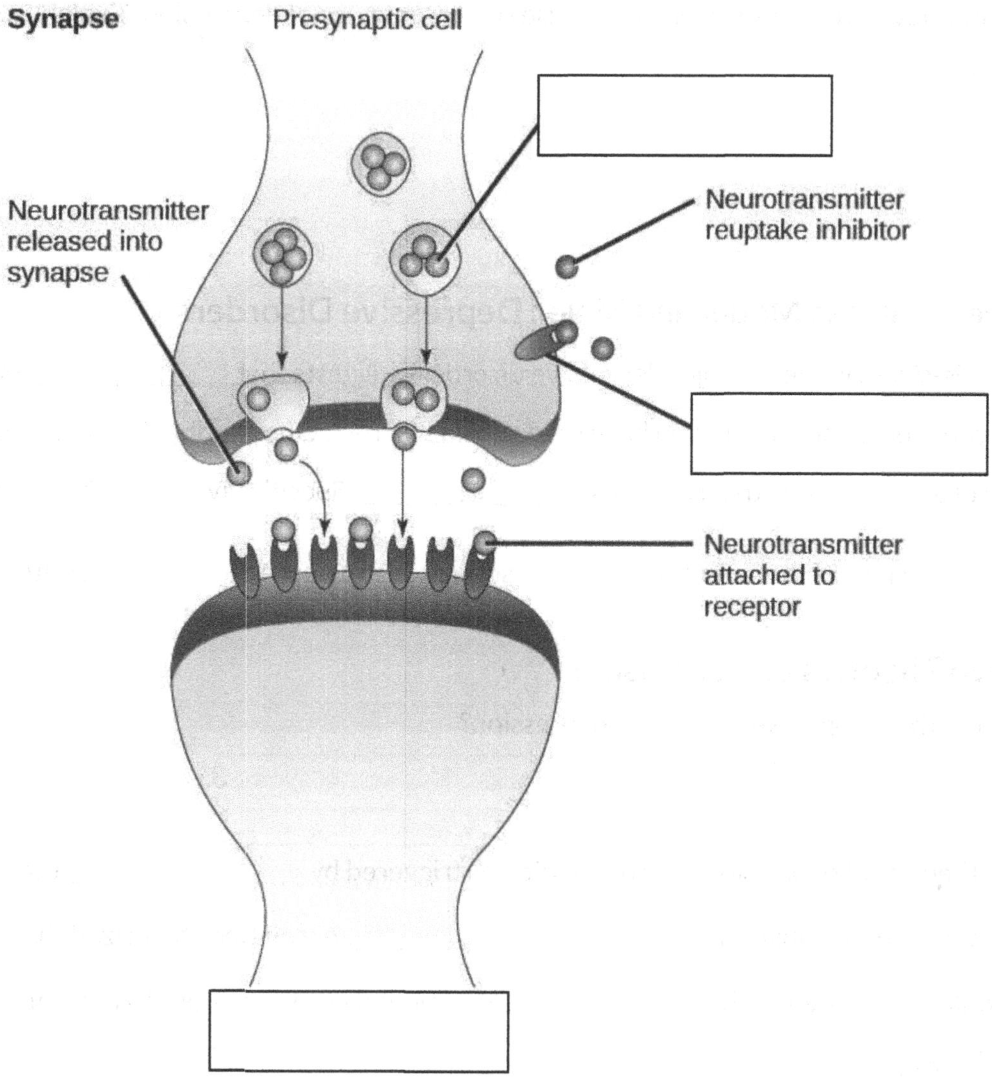

Depression is linked to abnormal activity in several regions of the brain, such as the

__________________ (responsible for assessing emotional importance of stimuli and experiencing emotions) and the _________________ cortex (responsible for regulating and controlling emotions).

Indicate if there would be more or less activation of each brain area.

- ___________ prefrontal cortex activation
- ___________ amygdala activation
- ___________ negative mood states

On Your Own

Do you think elevated cortisol levels are a cause or consequence of depression? Explain your answer.

A Diathesis-Stress Model and Major Depressive Disorders

The diathesis-stress model of major depressive disorders suggests that ______________ events can trigger depression in individuals who have predisposing factors. One possible factor may be the alteration of a specific gene that regulates _______________. Specifically, if individuals carry one or two __________ versions of the gene, they are more susceptible to depression after stressful events.

Cognitive Theories of Depression

What are the three cognitive theories of depression?

1.
2.
3.

Cognitive theories of depression view depression as triggered by ________________ thoughts, interpretations, self-evaluations, and ____________________. Aaron Beck theorized that depression-prone people possess depressive ________________ (mental predispositions to think about most things in a negative way).

Depressive schemas contain which themes?

-
-
-
-
-

On Your Own

Do you have any depressive schemas? How do you manage them?

The ______________________ theory of depression postulates that a particular style of negative thinking leads to a sense of hopelessness, which then leads to depression. ____________________ is an expectation that negative outcomes will occur, and there is nothing that can be done to prevent this occurrence.

A final cognitive theory of depression suggests that __________________, repetitive and passive focus on the fact that one is depressed and dwelling on the depressed symptoms, can increase symptoms of depression.

Suicide

Suicide is a death that results from _________-_______________ behavior with the intent to die. The individual must be biologically or psychologically ____________________, have the means to perform the suicide, and lack the necessary _________________ factors to prevent the suicide.

On Your Own

Of the facts regarding suicide that were presented in the lesson, which is the most impactful for you, and why?

Risk Factors for Suicide

On Your Own

List some risk factors for suicide.

What is your reaction to the idea that suicide can be "contagious?"

Psychology and You

Reaction to Someone Contemplating Suicide

What would you say to a person who is contemplating suicide? What should you do?

Lesson Wrap-up

Say It in a Sentence

In one sentence, describe the two predominant mood disorders.

Test Yourself

Choose the correct answer for each of the following questions. Check your work using the Answer Key in the back of the book.

____ 1. Individuals who have had three depressive episodes are ______ more likely to have a fourth episode.

- **A.** 50%
- **B.** 60%
- **C.** 80%
- **D.** 90%

____ 2. Research has shown that nearly ______ of women have thoughts of wanting to hurt themselves after giving birth.

- **A.** 5%
- **B.** 10%
- **C.** 20%
- **D.** 25%

____ 3. Approximately ______ of individuals with bipolar disorder attempt suicide at least once in their lifetime.

- **A.** 5%
- **B.** 15%
- **C.** 25%
- **D.** 35%

Next to each statement, write **T** for True or **F** for False. Check your work using the Answer Key in the back of the book.

4. _____ Depression is considered episodic.
5. _____ Approximately 10% of the U.S. population experiences major depressive disorder each year.
6. _____ Depression rates are lowest in Asian countries.
7. _____ Between 15 to 19% of people with bipolar disorder commit suicide.

Key Terms

For the following key terms, make groupings out of the related terms. Be sure to explain how they are related.

Key Terms: bipolar and related disorders, bipolar disorder, depressive disorder, flight of ideas, hopelessness theory, major depressive disorder, mania, manic episode, mood disorder, peripartum onset, persistent depressive disorder, rumination, seasonal pattern, suicidal ideation, suicide

Lesson 14.8

Schizophrenia

OBJECTIVES

- ★ Recognize the essential nature of schizophrenia, avoiding the misconception that it involves a split personality.
- ★ Categorize and describe the major symptoms of schizophrenia.
- ★ Understand the interplay between genetic, biological, and environmental factors that are associated with the development of schizophrenia.
- ★ Discuss the importance of research examining prodromal symptoms of schizophrenia.

BIG IDEA

Schizophrenia is a severe psychotic disorder that results in a separation from reality, often experienced through hallucinations, delusions, and unregulated emotions.

In this lesson, you will learn about the following:

- Symptoms of Schizophrenia
- Causes of Schizophrenia
- Schizophrenia: Early Warning Signs

Schizophrenia is characterized by major disturbances in:

-
-
-
-

On Your Own

What is schizophrenia? Explain it, clearly demonstrating that you understand it is not a split personality.

Symptoms of Schizophrenia

What are the main symptoms of schizophrenia?

-
-
-
-
-

A hallucination is a perceptual experience that occurs in the absence of stimulation.

_______________ hallucinations occur in roughly two-thirds of patients. Delusions are beliefs that are contrary to reality and firmly held, even in the face of contradictory _________________.

On Your Own

Provide an example for each of the following:

Type of Delusion	Example
Paranoid delusion	
Grandiose delusion	
Somatic delusion	

Categorize each of the following examples as disorganized thinking, disorganized motor behavior, or negative symptom.

- Displaying odd facial expressions:
- Avolition (lack of motivation):
- Tangentiality (responding to others with barely related remarks):
- Alogia (reduced speech):
- Loose associations:
- Exhibiting silly, child-like behaviors:
- Anhedonia (inability to experience pleasure):
- Rambling:

Causes of Schizophrenia

Genes

On Your Own

Of the genetic studies that were discussed in the lesson, which one do you feel more strongly demonstrates a genetic link for schizophrenia? Why?

Neurotransmitters

Drugs that increase ____________________ levels can produce schizophrenia-like symptoms, and medications that _____________ dopamine activity reduce the symptoms. This dopamine ____________________ indicates that dopamine overabundance or too many dopamine receptors are responsible for the onset and maintenance of schizophrenia.

On Your Own

Explain the relationship of dopamine to both hallucinations and delusions as well as negative symptoms of schizophrenia.

Brain Anatomy

On Your Own

What are the implications of having enlarged ventricles?

Events during Pregnancy

High rates of ______________ complications in the births of children who later developed schizophrenia have been reported. In addition, individuals are at a greater risk for developing schizophrenia if their mothers contracted the flu during the ________ trimester of pregnancy. In addition, a mother's

_________________ ____________ during pregnancy has been linked to increased risk.

Marijuana

On Your Own

What is your reaction to the idea that marijuana use has been linked to the later development of schizophrenia?

Schizophrenia: Early Warning Signs

________________ symptoms include minor symptoms of psychosis, such as unusual thought content, paranoia, odd _____________________, delusions, problems at school or work, and a decline in social

___________________.

Identify the factors that predict a greater likelihood that individuals will develop a psychotic disorder.

-
-
-
-
-
-

Psychology and You

Symptoms of Schizophrenia

Of the symptoms of schizophrenia, which do you feel would be the worst for you, and why?

Lesson Wrap-up

Say It in a Sentence

In one sentence, describe schizophrenia.

Test Yourself

Choose the correct answer for each of the following questions. Check your work using the Answer Key in the back of the book.

____ 1. Roughly ___ of the population experiences schizophrenia.

A. 1%
B. 3%
C. 5%
D. 10%

____ 2. The risk of developing schizophrenia is ___ times greater if one has a parent with schizophrenia.

A. 2
B. 3
C. 5
D. 6

____ 3. Research has demonstrated that individuals who have used marijuana 50 or more times were ___ times as likely to develop schizophrenia.

A. 2
B. 3
C. 5
D. 6

Answer each of the following questions. Check your work using the Answer Key in the back of the book.

4. Harry is convinced that a secret government agency is watching him. To protect himself, he sits in his darkened apartment with boarded windows and doors. Which type of schizophrenic delusion does this situation demonstrate?

5. Jarrod knows that he is truly Elvis. The singer did not die; instead, he is Jarrod and currently living in Boise, Idaho. Which type of schizophrenic delusion does this situation demonstrate?

6. "Doctor, I'm telling you it's true. There is something worming its way through my brain; I can feel it moving." Which type of schizophrenic delusion does this situation demonstrate?

Key Terms

Complete the following crossword puzzle using key terms from this lesson.

Across

1. Highly unusual behaviors and movements

Down

1. Decreased reactivity to the environment
2. Belief that is contrary to reality and is firmly held, despite contradictory evidence
3. Disjointed and incoherent thought processes
4. Theory of schizophrenia that proposes that an overabundance of dopamine or dopamine receptors is responsible for the onset and maintenance of schizophrenia
5. Characterized by beliefs that one holds special power, unique knowledge, or is extremely important
6. Perceptual experience that occurs in the absence of external stimulation
7. Characterized by decreases and absences in certain normal behaviors, emotions, or drives
8. Characterized by beliefs that others are out to harm them
9. One of the early minor symptoms of psychosis
10. Severe disorder characterized by major disturbances in thought, perception, emotion, and behavior
11. Belief that something highly unusual is happening to one's body or internal organs
12. One of the fluid-filled cavities within the brain

Lesson 14.9

Dissociative Disorders

OBJECTIVES

- ★ Describe the essential nature of dissociative disorders.
- ★ Identify and differentiate the symptoms of dissociative amnesia, depersonalization/derealization disorder, and dissociative identity disorder.
- ★ Discuss the potential role of both social and psychological factors in dissociative identity disorder.

BIG IDEA

Dissociative disorders—including dissociative amnesia, depersonalization disorder, derealization disorder, and dissociative identity disorder—involve an individual becoming removed from his or her sense of self.

In this lesson, you will learn about the following:

- Dissociative Amnesia
- Depersonalization/Derealization Disorder
- Dissociative Identity Disorder

Dissociative disorders are characterized by an individual becoming split off from his or her sense of self. Memory and identity become disturbed.

The DSM-5 includes these dissociative disorders:

-
-
-

Dissociative Amnesia

Dissociative amnesia results in the inability to recall important personal information, typically triggered by an extremely ________________ or traumatic experience. Some individuals experience dissociative ______________, a situation in which the person suddenly wanders away from home, experiences confusion about his or her identity, and may even adopt a new identity.

On Your Own

How would you react if you suddenly did not recall who you were or anything about your life?

Do you feel that dissociative amnesia is valid? Why or why not?

Depersonalization/Derealization Disorder

Depersonalization describes feeling detachment from ___________. In this case, a person may feel his or her ________________ are not his/her own. In derealization, a person feels detached from the ______________. Someone might feel as if the world is a dream.

On Your Own

Imagine what it would feel like to have derealization disorder. How might your life be different?

Dissociative Identity Disorder

Dissociative identity disorder involves exhibiting two or more distinct personalities or identities. In this case, each personality is well-defined, and the individual experiences memory gaps when the other personality is in charge.

Psychology and You

Real or Fake?

If one of your friends claimed that dissociative identity disorder was entirely fake, what evidence would you provide to the contrary?

Lesson Wrap-up

Say It in a Sentence

In one sentence, describe what it means to be disassociated.

Test Yourself

Choose the correct answer for each of the following questions. Check your work using the Answer Key in the back of the book.

____ 1. Sally has wandered away from her home and no longer remembers who she is or where she is from. She is suffering from:

- **A.** Dissociative amnesia
- **B.** Depersonalization
- **C.** Derealization
- **D.** Dissociative identity disorder

____ 2. Adam Duritz, lead singer of the Counting Crows, often feels that he is detached from himself and his thoughts are not his own. He suffers from:

- **A.** Dissociative amnesia
- **B.** Depersonalization
- **C.** Derealization
- **D.** Dissociative identity disorder

____ 3. In *The United States of Tara*, the star has multiple, distinct personalities. She suffers from:

- **A.** Dissociative amnesia
- **B.** Depersonalization
- **C.** Derealization
- **D.** Dissociative identity disorder

Answer each of the following questions. Check your work using the Answer Key in the back of the book.

4. What is the predominant theory regarding why an individual may suffer from dissociative identity disorder?

5. What did dissociative disorder used to be known as?

6. What is the difference between depersonalization and derealization?

Key Terms

Match each key term with its definition.

A. Depersonalization/Derealization Disorder
B. Dissociative Amnesia
C. Dissociative Disorders
D. Dissociative Fugue
E. Dissociative Identity Disorder

_____ A person exhibits two or more distinct, well-defined personalities or identities

_____ Group of DSM-5 disorders in which the primary feature is that a person becomes disassociated from his or her core sense of self

_____ People feel detached from the self and the world feels artificial

_____ Inability to recall important personal information, usually following a stressful or traumatic experience

_____ Symptom in which a person suddenly wanders away from one's home and experiences confusion about his or her identity

Lesson 14.10

Personality Disorders

OBJECTIVES

- ★ Describe the nature of personality disorders and how they differ from other disorders.
- ★ List and distinguish between the three clusters of personality disorders.
- ★ Identify the basic features of borderline personality disorder and antisocial personality disorder and the factors that are important in the etiology of both.

BIG IDEA

Personality disorders are inflexible and cause distress and impairment. Ten different personality disorders have been identified, and each presents its own unique symptoms and challenges.

In this lesson, you will learn about the following:

- Borderline Personality Disorder
- Antisocial Personality Disorder

The term ______________________ refers loosely to one's stable, consistent, and distinctive way of thinking about, feeling, acting, and relating to the world. A personality disorder, on the other hand, refers to a style of personality that differs from societal __________________________, is pervasive and _____________________, and causes distress or impairment.

Complete the following table of personality disorders recognized by the DSM-5.

Cluster A	Cluster B	Cluster C

Borderline Personality Disorder

Borderline personality disorder is characterized chiefly by ______________________ in interpersonal relationships, self-image, and mood, as well as marked impulsivity. They cannot manage the thought of being alone and will make frantic efforts to avoid _________________________.

_________________________ are intense and unstable. They have an _______________________ view of self, displaying shifts in personal attitudes, interests, career plans, and choices of friends.

On Your Own

The lesson indicates that borderline personality disorder is "especially problematic." Which element(s) do you find the most problematic for this disorder, and why?

Biological Basis for Borderline Personality Disorders

On Your Own

Based on the lesson, explain to someone how borderline personality disorder appears to be a product of genetics and environment.

Antisocial Personality Disorder

What are the common characteristics of someone with antisocial personality disorder?

-
-
-
-
-
-

Label each description with the concept is describes (*disinhibition*, *boldness*, or *meanness*).

Major Concept	Description
	Impulse control problems, lack of planning and forethought, insistence on immediate gratification, inability to restrain behavior
	Tendency to remain calm in threatening situations, high self-assurance, a sense of dominance, tendency toward thrill-seeking
	Lack of empathy, disdain for and lack of close relationships with others, tendency to accomplish goals through cruelty

Risk Factors for Antisocial Personality Disorder

Complete the following table that contrasts gender differences in antisocial personality disorder.

Men are more likely to:	Women are more likely to:

Psychology and You

Problematic Personality Disorders

Which personality disorder would you find more personally problematic than the others? Why?

Lesson Wrap-up

Say It in a Sentence

In one sentence, describe personality disorders.

Test Yourself

Choose the correct answer for each of the following questions. Check your work using the Answer Key in the back of the book.

____ 1. Schizoid personality disorder belongs in which DSM-5 cluster?

- **A.** Cluster A
- **B.** Cluster B
- **C.** Cluster C

____ 2. Dependent personality disorder belongs in which DSM-5 cluster?

- **A.** Cluster A
- **B.** Cluster B
- **C.** Cluster C

____ 3. Avoidant personality disorder belongs in which DSM-5 cluster?

- **A.** Cluster A
- **B.** Cluster B
- **C.** Cluster C

Answer each of the following questions. Check your work using the Answer Key in the back of the book.

4. Which cluster of personality disorders describes individuals who are nervous and fearful?

5. Which cluster of personality disorders describes individuals who are impulsive, overly dramatic, highly emotional, and erratic?

6. Which two personality disorders are the most common?

7. Which personality and temperament dimensions are related to antisocial personality disorder?

Key Terms

Match each key term with its definition.

A. Antisocial Personality Disorder
B. Borderline Personality Disorder
C. Personality Disorder

_____ Characterized by a lack of regard for others' rights, impulsivity, deceitfulness, irresponsibility, and lack of remorse over misdeeds

_____ Group of DSM-5 disorders characterized by an inflexible and pervasive personality style that differs markedly from expectations of one's culture and causes distress and impairment

_____ Instability in interpersonal relationships, self-image, and mood; impulsivity

Lesson 14.11

Disorders in Childhood

OBJECTIVES

★ Describe the nature and symptoms of attention deficit/hyperactivity disorder and autism spectrum disorder.
★ Discuss the prevalence and factors that contribute to the development of these disorders.

BIG IDEA

During childhood, some children are affected by neurodevelopmental disorders, such as attention deficit hyperactivity disorder and autism spectrum disorder. These disorders can impact personal, academic, social, and intellectual realms.

In this lesson, you will learn about the following:

- Attention Deficit/Hyperactivity Disorder
- Autism Spectrum Disorder

Neurodevelopmental disorders involve ________________________ problems in personal, social, academic, and intellectual functioning.

Attention Deficit/Hyperactivity Disorder

A child with attention deficit/hyperactivity disorder shows a ___________________ pattern of inattention and/or hyperactive behavior that interferes with normal _______________________.

On Your Own

What are the signs of inattention in ADHD?

1.
2.
3.
4.
5.
6.

What are the signs of hyperactivity in ADHD?

1.
2.
3.
4.
5.
6.

Life Problems from ADHD

What are the possible consequences for a child with ADHD?

-
-
-
-
-
-
-

The Klein et al. (2012) study demonstrated the following regarding children with ADHD who were interviewed as adults:

-
-
-
-
-
-
-
-
-

Causes of ADHD

Genetics, specifically two genes that play a role in the regulation of ____________________, play a significant role in the development of ADHD. Ritalin and Adderall both elevate ______________________ activity. Individuals with ADHD show abnormalities in their _______________ lobes with less volume and activation in this area.

On Your Own

What would you say to a mom that tells you she restricts her son's intake of red dyes in food to help prevent symptoms of ADHD?

Recent studies have indicated that the prevalence rate of ADHD is __________________, with more parents self-reporting that their children are affected. It is possible that the increase results from ____________-diagnosis, greater __________________ of the disorder, increased use of

________________ devices that impact attention spans, or a ________________ in diagnostic criteria.

Autism Spectrum Disorder

When Leo Kanner first defined early infantile amnesia, it was characterized by these key traits:

-
-
-
-

Complete the following table with the types of disturbances that children with autism display.

Social Interaction	Communication	Repetitive behaviors

Life Problems from Autism Spectrum Disorder

On Your Own

What is your reaction to the prevalence rates of autism in the United States?

What are the possible reasons for the increased numbers of reported autism cases?

-
-
-
-

Causes of Autism Spectrum Disorder

On Your Own

What is your reaction to the belief that autism is caused by an individual's mother?

What are some possible (valid) causes of autism?

-
-
-
-

Psychology and You

Autism and Vaccinations

Your friend exclaims that she will never vaccinate her child because she fears that the child will develop autism from the vaccine. Using what you learned in this lesson, refute her claim.

Lesson Wrap-up

Say It in a Sentence

In one sentence, describe autism spectrum disorder.

Test Yourself

Choose the correct answer for each of the following questions. Check your work using the Answer Key in the back of the book.

____ 1. Approximately _____ of adults who were diagnosed with ADHD when younger still showed symptoms in adulthood.

A. 15%
B. 25%
C. 30%
D. 35%

____ 2. Concordance rates of ADHD in identical twins was ___, whereas it was ____ for fraternal twins.

A. .20; .66
B. .25; .75
C. .66; .20
D. .75; .25

Next to each statement, write **T** for True or **F** for False. Check your work using the Answer Key in the back of the book.

3. _____ Young adults with ADHD receive more traffic tickets than young adults without ADHD.

4. _____ Boys are three times more likely to have ADHD than girls.

5. _____ Between 1987 and 1998, California saw an increase of 173% in reported autism cases.

6. _____ Researchers now know an exact cause of autism.

Key Terms

Match each key term with its definition.

A. Attention Deficit/Hyperactivity Disorder
B. Autism Spectrum Disorder
C. Neurodevelopmental Disorder

_____ One of the disorders that is first diagnosed in childhood and involve developmental problems in academic, intellectual, and social functioning

_____ Childhood disorder characterized by inattentiveness and/or hyperactive, impulsive behavior

_____ Childhood disorder characterized by deficits in social interaction and communication and repetitive patterns of behavior or interests

Chapter 15
Therapy and Treatment

Lesson 15.1
Mental Health Treatment: Past and Present

OBJECTIVES

★ Explain how people with psychological disorders have been treated throughout the ages.
★ Discuss deinstitutionalization.
★ Discuss the ways in which mental health services are delivered today.
★ Distinguish between voluntary and involuntary treatment.

BIG IDEA

Treatment of mental health issues has evolved from the original belief that mental disturbance resulted from demonic possession to an understanding that individuals are suffering from differences in the way the brain operates.

In this lesson, you will learn about the following:

- Treatment in the Past
- Mental Health Treatment Today

According to the Substance Abuse and Mental Health Services Administration, ______________ of adults received treatment for a mental health issue in 2008. Approximately __________ of the children with mental disorders received treatment, specifically focused on children with ____________ or __________________ disorder, as compared to children with anxiety.

On Your Own

Why do you think treatment for children with ADHD and conduct disorder occurs more frequently than for children with anxiety?

Treatment in the Past

Initially, it was believed that mental illness was caused by a variety of supernatural sources, such as possession, witchcraft, or angry gods.

What were common treatments for mental illness in the past?

1.
2.
3.
4.
5.

By the 18th century, people were placed in ________________, which were the first institutions used for housing people with mental disorders. In the 19th century, ________________ ________ led reform efforts for mental health care in the United States. She investigated how the mentally ill and poor were cared for, and she discovered an underfunded and unregulated system that perpetuated

____________.

On Your Own

What is your reaction to the treatment of patients at the Willard Psychiatric Center in upstate New York?

The Mental Retardation Facilities and Community Mental Health Centers Construction Act provided

________________ support and funding for ________________ mental health centers. This act started the process of ________________________, the closing of large asylums, by providing other treatment options.

Mental Health Treatment Today

On Your Own

What improvements do we still need to make to treatment of the mentally ill?

According to a 2006 special report by the Bureau of Justice Statistics, approximately 705,600 mentally ill adults were incarcerated in the ______________ prison system, another 78,800 were incarcerated in ________________ prison, and another 479,000 were in _____________ jails.

On Your Own

Do you feel that some individuals should have involuntary, mandated therapy? In what cases?

Identify the places where psychological treatment can occur.

-
-
-
-

Psychology and You

Community Health Centers

Imagine you were planning to open a community health center. What challenges in the mental health system would you attempt to solve with your center?

Lesson Wrap-up

Say It in a Sentence

In one sentence, compare the treatment of mental illness today versus the past.

Test Yourself

Choose the correct answer for each of the following questions. Check your work using the Answer Key in the back of the book.

____ 1. In 2012, what percentage of U. S. adults experienced mental illness?

A. 8%
B. 14%
C. 19%
D. 24%

____ 2. Worldwide, it is estimated that __________ of mentally ill people were killed after being accused of being witches or under the influence of witchcraft.

- **A.** hundreds
- **B.** thousands
- **C.** tens of thousands
- **D.** hundreds of thousands

____ 3. Approximately _____ of people with mental illness receive no care at all.

- **A.** 1/3
- **B.** 1/2
- **C.** 2/3

Next to each statement, write **T** for True or **F** for False. Check your work using the Answer Key in the back of the book.

4. _____ Philippe Pinel argued for more humane treatment of the mentally ill.

5. _____ Dorothea Dix's reform efforts led to the creation of the first mental asylums in the United States.

6. _____ In 1943, doctors at Willard Psychiatric Center administered 1,443 shock treatments.

7. _____ Today, approximately 46% of homeless adults living in the U. S. experience mental illness.

Key Terms

Match each key term with its definition.

A. Asylum
B. Deinstitutionalization
C. Involuntary Treatment
D. Voluntary Treatment

_____ Process of closing large asylums and integrating people back into the community where they can be treated locally

_____ Therapy that is mandated by the courts or other systems

_____ Institution created for the specific purpose of housing people with psychological disorders

_____ Therapy that a person chooses to attend in order to obtain relief from her symptoms

Lesson 15.2

Types of Treatment

OBJECTIVES

★ Distinguish between psychotherapy and biomedical therapy.
★ Recognize various orientations to psychotherapy.
★ Discuss psychotropic medications and recognize which medications are used to treat specific psychological disorders.

BIG IDEA

There are a variety of different therapies, from psychoanalysis to humanistic therapy, that focus on different means of helping individuals, depending on a specific diagnosis.

In this lesson, you will learn about the following:

- Psychotherapy Techniques: Psychoanalysis
- Psychotherapy: Play Therapy
- Psychotherapy: Behavior Therapy
- Psychotherapy: Cognitive Therapy
- Psychotherapy: Cognitive-Behavioral Therapy
- Psychotherapy: Humanistic Therapy
- Evaluating Various Forms of Psychotherapy
- Biomedical Therapies

The goal of therapy is to help individuals stop repeating and reenacting ____________________ patterns and start looking for better solutions to difficult situations.

The two main types of therapy are:

1. 2.

On Your Own

Compare psychotherapy with biomedical therapy.

In the following table, categorize each description with the psychotherapy type.

Type	Description
	Talk therapy based on the unconscious and childhood conflicts
	Interaction with toys is used instead of talk

	Principles of learning are applied to change undesirable behaviors
	Awareness of cognitive process helps patients eliminate thought patterns that lead to distress
	Work to change cognitive distortions and self-defeating behaviors
	Increase self-awareness and acceptance through focus on conscious thoughts

Psychotherapy Techniques: Psychoanalysis

On Your Own

What is your view regarding Freud's belief that most of our psychological problems stem from repressed impulses and trauma in childhood?

What were two of Freud's primary techniques in therapy?

1. ____________ ____________________: patient relaxes and says whatever comes to mind at the moment

2. ______________ __________________: studying the underlying meaning of dreams

Psychotherapy: Play Therapy

Play therapy, used with children, involves the use of ____________________ with toys to help a therapist make a diagnosis. Play can be either __________________, in which the therapist provides instruction and guidance, or ____________________, in which the child can play as he or she sees fit.

Psychotherapy: Behavior Therapy

In behavior therapy, a therapist employs principles of learning to help clients change undesirable behaviors.

Behavioral therapists may use either of these types of conditioning:

-
-

Aversion therapy, a counterconditioning technique, has been used for a variety of behaviors, such as alcoholism, cigarette smoking, and thumb sucking. Essentially, individuals are exposed to an

______________________ stimulus when engaging in an undesirable behavior, such as a drug that makes one feel nauseated when drinking alcohol.

On Your Own

Provide a unique example of exposure therapy.

Describe a token economy that has been used in your own life.

Psychotherapy: Cognitive Therapy

Cognitive therapy is a form of psychotherapy that focuses on how a person's ________________ lead to feelings of ________________. Through questioning, a cognitive therapist can help a client recognize

________________________ ideas, challenge catastrophizing thoughts about themselves and their situations, and find a more positive way to view events.

Psychotherapy: Cognitive-Behavioral Therapy

Cognitive-behavioral therapy (CBT) helps clients change cognitive ____________________ and self-defeating behaviors.

On Your Own

How is CBT similar to cognitive therapy? Behavior therapy?

What are three types of cognitive distortions that CBT therapy tries to change?

1. _______-_____-_____________ ______________: everything is black or white

2. ___________________________: taking a small situation and making it bigger

3. ________________ ________ ___________________: assuming that people are thinking negatively about you

Psychotherapy: Humanistic Therapy

Humanistic psychology focuses on helping people achieve their ____________________. As such, the goal of humanistic therapy is to help people become more aware and accepting of _______________________.

On Your Own

Compare humanistic therapy with psychoanalysis.

In client-centered therapy, therapists should demonstrate:

-
-
-

Evaluating Various Forms of Psychotherapy

According to the American Psychological Association (APA), there are three factors that work together to produce successful treatment:

1. The client's ___________________________
2. _______________________ treatment
3. _____________ _______________ of therapist

On Your Own

Your friend asks you if cognitive-behavioral therapy is effective. Using the information in the lesson, what do you tell your friend?

Biomedical Therapies

Biomedical therapy involves the use of ______________________ medications or other

______________________ based treatments.

Complete the following table of commonly prescribed psychotropic medications and what they treat.

Type	Treatment Use
Antipsychotics	
Atypical antipsychotics	
	Depression/Anxiety
	Anxiety/OCD/PTSD
Mood stabilizers	
Stimulants	

On Your Own

Would you undergo ECT? Why or why not?

Psychology and You

Exposure Therapy

If you were to undergo exposure therapy, what would your fear be? Make a hierarchical list of the least fearful situations to the most fearful.

Lesson Wrap-up

Say It in a Sentence

In one sentence, describe psychotherapy.

Test Yourself

Choose the correct answer for each of the following questions. Check your work using the Answer Key in the back of the book.

____ 1. In psychoanalysis, the patient sometimes begins to develop strong (either positive or negative) feelings towards the therapist. This experience is called:

- **A.** Free association
- **B.** Repression
- **C.** Projection
- **D.** Transference

____ 2. Systematic desensitization is a type of:

- **A.** Operant conditioning
- **B.** Exposure therapy
- **C.** Cognitive therapy

____ 3. Applied Behavior Analysis (ABA) is which type of conditioning?

- **A.** Operant conditioning
- **B.** Classical conditioning

____ 4. Who started client-centered therapy?

- **A.** Beck
- **B.** Ellis
- **C.** Rogers

Answer each of the following questions. Check your work using the Answer Key in the back of the book.

5. In order to stop Jessie's problematic thumb sucking, which other children bully her for, the therapist suggests painting a disgusting substance on Jessie's nails so that she will taste it and stop sucking. This method demonstrates which conditioning technique(s)?

6. Two counterconditioning techniques are:

7. One of the first types of cognitive-behavioral therapy was:

8. What is the ABC model of CBT?

Key Terms

For the following key terms, make groupings out of the related terms. Be sure to explain how they are related.

Key Terms: aversive conditioning, behavior therapy, cognitive-behavioral therapy, cognitive therapy, counterconditioning, dream analysis, electroconvulsive therapy (ECT), exposure therapy, free association, humanistic therapy, nondirective therapy, play therapy, psychoanalysis, psychotherapy, rational emotive therapy (RET), Rogerian (client-centered) therapy, systematic desensitization, token economy, transference, unconditional positive regard, virtual reality exposure therapy

Lesson 15.3

Treatment Modalities

OBJECTIVES

- ★ Distinguish between the various modalities of treatment.
- ★ Discuss benefits of group therapy.

BIG IDEA

Modalities of treatment are the specific parameters under which therapy occur, such as individually or within a group setting.

In this lesson, you will learn about the following:

- Individual Therapy
- Group Therapy
- Couples Therapy
- Family Therapy

An initial intake assesses a client's needs, such as:

-
-
-

____________________________ means that the therapist cannot disclose confidential communications to any third party unless mandated or permitted by law to do so. Therapists help clients develop a _____________________ plan with specific measurable objectives.

On Your Own

What might be a specific measurable objective for someone with a severe phobia?

Individual Therapy

In individual therapy, the client and therapist meet ______________________ weekly or every other week. The therapist helps the client explore his/her feelings, work through life ____________________, and set goals.

Group Therapy

In group therapy, a clinician meets together with several ____________ with ____________ problems.

What are the benefits of group therapy?

-
-
-
-
-
-
-

What are the drawbacks of group therapy?

-
-
-

Couples Therapy

Couples therapy involves two people in an ________________ relationship who are having difficulties and are trying to resolve them. The couple may be dating, partnered, ____________________, or married. Some couples seek therapy to work out their problems, whereas others attend therapy to determine whether ________________ __________________ is the best solution.

Family Therapy

Family therapy is a special form of group therapy that consists of one or more families.
What are the two different types of family therapy?

1. ________________ family therapy: discussion of the boundaries and structure of the family
2. _______________ family therapy: addressing specific problems within the family

Psychology and You

Therapy Choices

Imagine that a family member is considering therapy. Help him/her decide between individual or group therapy.

Lesson Wrap-up

Say It in a Sentence

In one sentence, compare individual and family therapy.

Test Yourself

Choose the correct answer for each of the following questions. Check your work using the Answer Key in the back of the book.

____ 1. Group therapy sessions with a strong educational component are called:

- **A.** Psycho-educational groups
- **B.** Educational groups
- **C.** Group-educational sessions

____ 2. The primary theoretical orientation for family therapy is:

- **A.** Educational
- **B.** Systems approach
- **C.** Cognitive-behavioral

Next to each statement, write **T** for True or **F** for False. Check your work using the Answer Key in the back of the book.

3. _____ Group therapy can only be organized with a central theme.
4. _____ The primary therapeutic orientation used in couples is cognitive-behavioral therapy.
5. _____ Couples who attend therapy inevitably work out their problems and stay together.
6. _____ In many cases of family therapy, there is one person who is detrimentally affecting the rest of the family.

Key Terms

Match each key term with its definition.

A. Confidentiality
B. Couples Therapy
C. Family Therapy
D. Group Therapy
E. Individual Therapy
F. Intake
G. Strategic Family Therapy
H. Structural Family Therapy

_____ Therapist guides the therapy sessions and develops treatment plans for each family member for specific problems that can be addressed in a short amount of time

_____ Special form of group therapy consisting of one or more families

_____ Therapist cannot disclose communications to any third party

_____ Treatment modality in which 5 to 10 people with the same issue or concern meet together with a trained clinician

_____ Two people in an intimate relationship who are having difficulties and are trying to resolve them with therapy

_____ Therapist examines and discusses with the family the boundaries and structure of the family

_____ Therapist's first meeting with the client in which the therapist gathers specific information to address the client's immediate needs

_____ Treatment modality in which the client and clinician meet one-on-one

Lesson 15.4

Substance-Related and Addictive Disorders: A Special Case

OBJECTIVES

- ★ Recognize the goal of substance-related and addictive disorders treatment.
- ★ Discuss what makes for effective treatment.
- ★ Describe how comorbid disorders are related.

BIG IDEA

Addiction rewires the brain. The goal of addiction treatment is to help the addict stop compulsive drug-seeking behaviors.

In this lesson, you will learn about the following:

- What Makes Treatment Effective?
- Comorbid Disorders

Addiction is often viewed as a ______________ disease. The choice to use a substance is initially ____________________, but drug use can permanently alter the ______________ structure in the ________________ cortex, resulting in the individual becoming driven to use the substance in question.

On Your Own

Why do you think so many individuals tend to blame chronic drug users for their drug use when, in fact, the brain becomes rewired to seek the drug of choice?

The goal of substance abuse treatment is to help an addicted person stop ________________ drug-seeking behaviors, which means that treatment needs to occur ___________-term.

On Your Own

What is your reaction to the statement that substance-related treatment is considered more cost-effective than incarceration or not treating those with addiction?

What Makes Treatment Effective?

List the factors that make treatment effective.

1.

2.

3.

When treatment is holistic, it addresses multiple needs. What needs may it affect?

1.
2.
3.
4.
5.
6.

Comorbid Disorders

Frequently, a person who is addicted to drugs and/or alcohol has an additional psychological ____________. Saying a person has a comorbid disorder means that the individual has _______ or more diagnoses. In this case, a person may fit the category of mentally ill and chemically addicted (__________).

Psychology and You

Refute the Argument

Refute this argument: "I have no sympathy for a drug user. He should be able to stop at any time!"

Lesson Wrap-up

Say It in a Sentence

In one sentence, discuss the benefits of group therapy for individuals in need of substance-related therapy.

Test Yourself

Choose the correct answer for each of the following questions. Check your work using the Answer Key in the back of the book.

____ 1. What is the rate of relapse?

- **A.** 10%
- **B.** 20%
- **C.** 30%
- **D.** 40%

____ 2. What is the most common drug used by 18–25 year olds?

- **A.** Illicit drugs
- **B.** Marijuana
- **C.** Hallucinogens
- **D.** Cocaine

____ 3. What treatment modality is most common in substance-related therapy?

- **A.** Individual
- **B.** Couple
- **C.** Group

Answer each of the following questions. Check your work using the Answer Key in the back of the book.

4. What is the area of the brain that gets rewired during repeated drug use, resulting in greater need to seek the drug of choice?

5. With drug addicted teenagers, the most common treatment modality is:

6. Compared with the overall population, substance abusers are how many more times likely to have a mood or anxiety disorder?

Key Terms

Write a paraphrased definition for each key term.

Comorbid Disorder:

Relapse:

Lesson 15.5

The Sociocultural Model and Therapy Utilization

OBJECTIVES

- ★ Explain how the sociocultural model is used in therapy.
- ★ Discuss barriers to mental health services among ethnic minorities.

BIG IDEA

The sociocultural perspective investigates mental illness and treatment in the context of an individual's culture and background.

In this lesson, you will learn about the following:

- Barriers to Treatment

The ________________________ perspective considers the person and the person's symptoms in the context of individual culture and background.

On Your Own

What aspects of your own race, culture, or ethnicity could impact the way you receive therapy?

________________ ________________________ refers to the idea that therapists must understand and address issues of race, culture, and ethnicity in treatment.

Multicultural counseling and therapy aims to do what?

-
-
-

Barriers to Treatment

On Your Own

What is your reaction to the claim that ethnic minorities utilize mental health services less frequently? What can be done to increase treatment rates?

Why do you think fewer African American and Hispanic women seek out treatment for bulimia?

What are the common reasons that individuals do not seek treatment?

1.
2.
3.
4.

Psychology and You

Refute the Argument

"Therapists can all have the exact same training and do not differ in how they work with different people." Refute this claim.

Lesson Wrap-up

Say It in a Sentence

In one sentence, explain the importance of the sociocultural model of therapy.

Test Yourself

Choose the correct answer for each of the following questions. Check your work using the Answer Key in the back of the book.

____ 1. In a recent study, ____ of Korean Americans indicated they thought depression was a sign of personal weakness.

A. 93%
B. 71%
C. 55%
D. 43%

____ 2. In a recent study, _____ of Korean Americans reported that having a mentally ill family member would bring shame to the family.

- **A.** 5%
- **B.** 10%
- **C.** 14%
- **D.** 18%

Next to each statement, write **T** for True or **F** for False. Check your work using the Answer Key in the back of the book.

3. ______ The rates of anorexia are different across races.
4. ______ According to one study, many African American individuals prefer spiritual practices over therapy.
5. ______ Only 20% of high school seniors who need therapy will receive professional help.

Key Terms

Write a paraphrased definition for the key term.

Cultural Competence:

Answer Key

Chapter 1

1.1 What Is Psychology?

TEST YOURSELF

1. B
2. A
3. F
4. T
5. T

1.2 Contemporary Psychology

TEST YOURSELF

1. B
2. A
3. T
4. F
5. F

1.3 Why Is Research Important?

TEST YOURSELF

1. T
2. F
3. F
4. T

1.4 Approaches to Research

TEST YOURSELF

1. T
2. T
3. F
4. F

1.5 Analyzing Findings

TEST YOURSELF

1. The two variables of interest are not related to each other.
2. Negative correlation
3. The inability to make causal statements

1.6 Ethics

TEST YOURSELF

1. F
2. F
3. F
4. F

Chapter 2

2.1 Human Genetics

TEST YOURSELF

1. T
2. T
3. F
4. T

2.2 Cells of the Nervous System

TEST YOURSELF

1. F
2. F
3. F

2.3 Using Context for Unfamiliar Words and Phrases

TEST YOURSELF

1. C
2. B
3. A

2.4 The Brain and the Spinal Cord

TEST YOURSELF

1. T
2. F
3. F
4. T
5. C
6. B
7. A

2.5 The Endocrine System

TEST YOURSELF

1. C
2. A
3. A
4. T
5. F
6. T
7. T

Chapter 3

3.1 What Is Consciousness?

TEST YOURSELF

1. B
2. C
3. A
4. F
5. F
6. T
7. T

3.2 Sleep and Why We Sleep

TEST YOURSELF

1. D
2. A
3. T
4. F
5. F
6. T

3.3 Stages of Sleep

TEST YOURSELF

1. B
2. C
3. B
4. B
5. T
6. F
7. T
8. F

3.4 Sleep Problems and Disorders

TEST YOURSELF

1. T
2. T
3. F
4. T
5. T
6. F
7. T

3.5 Substance Use and Abuse

TEST YOURSELF

1. C
2. C
3. B
4. F
5. T
6. T
7. T
8. F

3.6 Other States of Consciousness

TEST YOURSELF

1. F
2. T
3. T
4. F
5. T
6. B
7. A
8. C

Chapter 4

4.1 Sensation versus Perception

TEST YOURSELF

1. C
2. A
3. C
4. F
5. T
6. T

4.2 Waves and Wavelengths

TEST YOURSELF

1. F
2. T
3. T
4. A
5. D
6. D

4.3 Vision

TEST YOURSELF

1. D
2. B
3. A
4. C

4.4 Hearing

TEST YOURSELF

1. B
2. B
3. A
4. F
5. F
6. F
7. T

4.5 The Other Senses

TEST YOURSELF

1. C
2. A
3. Medulla, thalamus, limbic system, gustatory cortex
4. Limbic system, olfactory cortex

4.6 Gestalt Principles of Perception

TEST YOURSELF

1. B
2. C
3. Good continuation
4. Similarity

Chapter 5

5.1 What Is Learning?

TEST YOURSELF

1. B
2. A
3. C

5.2 Classical Conditioning

TEST YOURSELF

1. B
2. A
3. A
4. D
5. B
6. "This won't hurt a bit."
7. The needle jab
8. Cringing in fear
9. Pain from the needle

5.3 Operant Conditioning

TEST YOURSELF

1. A
2. D
3. B
4. A
5. B
6. Variable ratio
7. Fixed interval
8. Variable ratio
9. Fixed interval

5.4 Observational Learning (Modeling)

TEST YOURSELF

1. B
2. B
3. A
4. F
5. F
6. T

Chapter 6

6.1 What Is Cognition?

1. F
2. T
3. F
4. D
5. B
6. C
7. A

6.2 Language

1. B
2. A
3. D
4. A
5. B

6.3 Problem Solving

1. A
2. D
3. C
4. C
5. B
6. Representative bias; you think of what is "typical" for a "type of person."

6.4 What Are Intelligence and Creativity?

1. Creative intelligence
2. Practical intelligence

6.5 Measures of Intelligence

1. D
2. D
3. C
4. F
5. T
6. F

6.6 The Source of Intelligence

1. B
2. B
3. A
4. T
5. T
6. F

Chapter 7

7.1 How Memory Functions

TEST YOURSELF

1. T
2. F
3. F
4. T
5. C
6. A
7. B

7.2 Parts of the Brain Involved with Memory

TEST YOURSELF

1. A
2. C
3. F
4. T
5. F

7.3 Problems with Memory

TEST YOURSELF

1. A
2. B
3. A

7.4 Ways to Enhance Memory

TEST YOURSELF

1. B
2. B
3. C
4. F
5. T
6. F

Chapter 8

8.1 What Is Lifespan Development?

TEST YOURSELF

1. C
2. A
3. A
4. The statement is not true. Research shows that language development in children follows a similar sequence. All children coo, babble, and then use single-

word statements. Being in a different culture does not influence this sequencing.
5. The statement is not true. Given that child care practices differ by culture, some children are not given the same opportunities as others. For example, some children are kept largely immobile during infancy, which may result in them walking later than children who are provided more freedom to move early on.

8.2 Lifespan Theories

TEST YOURSELF

1. B
2. C
3. A
4. Freud focused on psychosexual development, but Erikson felt that social aspects were more important than sexual aspects. In addition, Erikson felt that development occurred through the lifespan, whereas Freud focused largely on childhood development.
5. The baby is developing cognitive skills that are largely developed by experimentation. Whenever the baby throws something off the high chair, he learns aspects about the object and the rules of the world. Although annoying, the friend should allow the baby to continue this behavior.
6. 1. Sensorimotor 2. Preoperational 3. Concrete operational 4. Formal operational

8.3 Stages of Development

TEST YOURSELF

1. B
2. C
3. C
4. C
5. C
6. T
7. T
8. F
9. F
10. T

8.4 Death and Dying

TEST YOURSELF

1. B
2. B
3. T
4. F

Chapter 9

9.1 Motivation

TEST YOURSELF

1. C
2. D
3. B
4. F
5. T

9.2 Hunger and Eating

TEST YOURSELF

1. A
2. C
3. A
4. T
5. F

9.3 Sexual Behavior

TEST YOURSELF

1. D
2. B
3. B
4. T
5. F
6. F

9.4 Emotion

TEST YOURSELF

1. C
2. A
3. A
4. B
5. T
6. F

Chapter 10

10.1 What Is Personality?

TEST YOURSELF

1. B
2. C
3. A
4. Freud placed great emphasis on psychosexual behavior and the idea that personality was developed by the time individuals were approximately 6 years of age. The Neo-Freudians agreed that childhood experiences mattered, but they focused on the social environment of the child instead of the sexual aspects.

10.2 Freud and the Psychodynamic Perspective

TEST YOURSELF

1. B
2. D
3. B
4. Displacement
5. Regression
6. Reaction formation
7. Projection

10.3 Neo-Freudians: Adler, Erikson, Jung, and Horney

TEST YOURSELF

1. B
2. D
3. F
4. F

10.4 Learning Approaches

TEST YOURSELF

1. B
2. C
3. A
4. T
5. T
6. T

10.5 Humanistic Approaches

TEST YOURSELF

1. A
2. B
3. The ideal self represents who we want to be, whereas the real self is who we actually are.
4. Congruence

10.6 Biological Approaches

TEST YOURSELF

1. C
2. A
3. B
4. Endomorphs
5. Mesomorphs

10.7 Trait Theorists

TEST YOURSELF

1. A
2. B, C
3. Conscientiousness, agreeableness
4. Neuroticism, extroversion

10.8 Cultural Understandings of Personality

TEST YOURSELF

1. indigenous approach
2. comparative approach
3. combined approach
4. collectivist
5. Selective migration

10.9 Personality Assessment

TEST YOURSELF

1. F
2. T
3. T

Chapter 11

11.1 What Is Social Psychology?

TEST YOURSELF

1. D
2. B
3. C
4. A
5. F
6. T
7. F

11.2 Self-Presentation

TEST YOURSELF

1. B
2. A
3. C
4. T
5. F
6. F

11.3 Attitudes and Persuasion

TEST YOURSELF

1. D
2. C
3. A
4. D

11.4 Conformity, Compliance, and Obedience

TEST YOURSELF

1. C
2. A
3. B
4. Normative social influence
5. Informational social influence
6. obedience
7. Social loafing
8. Social facilitation

11.5 Prejudice and Discrimination

TEST YOURSELF

1. Ageism
2. Sexism
3. C
4. A
5. B

11.6 Aggression

TEST YOURSELF

1. The bully, the victim, and bystanders
2. Hostile
3. Instrumental
4. B
5. A
6. B

11.7 Prosocial Behavior

TEST YOURSELF

1. Intimacy, commitment, passion
2. Commitment
3. Passion, intimacy
4. A
5. C
6. B

Chapter 12

12.1 What Is Industrial and Organizational Psychology?

TEST YOURSELF

1. Organizational psychology
2. Industrial psychology
3. Human factors psychology
4. C
5. C
6. B

12.2 Industrial Psychology: Selecting and Evaluating Employees

TEST YOURSELF

1. Structured
2. Unstructured
3. B
4. B
5. B

12.3 Organizational Psychology: The Social Dimension of Work

TEST YOURSELF

1. Transactional
2. Transformational
3. C
4. B
5. D
6. B

12.4 Human Factors Psychology and Workplace Design

TEST YOURSELF

1. T
2. F
3. T
4. D
5. B

Chapter 13

13.1 What Is Stress?

TEST YOURSELF

1. Secondary
2. Eustress
3. A
4. D

13.2 Stressors

TEST YOURSELF

1. Daily hassle
2. Life change
3. D
4. B
5. C

13.3 Stress and Illness

TEST YOURSELF

1. F
2. F
3. T
4. C
5. D
6. B

13.4 Regulation of Stress

TEST YOURSELF

1. B
2. B
3. Stable
4. External
5. Global

13.5 The Pursuit of Happiness

TEST YOURSELF

1. C
2. C
3. C
4. F
5. F
6. T
7. T

Chapter 14

14.1 What Are Psychological Disorders?

TEST YOURSELF

1. F
2. T
3. T

14.2 Diagnosing and Classifying Psychological Disorders

TEST YOURSELF

1. American Psychological Association
2. American Psychiatric Association
3. *Diagnostic and Statistical Manual of Mental Disorders*
4. *International Classification of Diseases*
5. World Health Organization

14.3 Perspectives on Psychological Disorders

TEST YOURSELF

1. B
2. S
3. DS
4. B
5. DS
6. S

14.4 Anxiety Disorders

TEST YOURSELF

1. A, B, D, E
2. A, C, E, G, H, J

14.5 Obsessive-Compulsive and Related Disorders

TEST YOURSELF

1. A
2. C
3. B

14.6 Posttraumatic Stress Disorder

TEST YOURSELF

1. D
2. A

14.7 Mood Disorders

TEST YOURSELF

1. D
2. C
3. D
4. T
5. F
6. T
7. T

14.8 Schizophrenia

TEST YOURSELF

1. A
2. D
3. D
4. Paranoid
5. Grandiose
6. Somatic

14.9 Dissociative Disorders

TEST YOURSELF

1. A
2. B
3. D
4. The individual experienced severe trauma early in life and handled the situation by disassociating.
5. Multiple personality disorder
6. Depersonalization revolves around disassociation from the self, whereas derealization is disassociation from the world.

14.10 Personality Disorders

TEST YOURSELF

1. A
2. C
3. C
4. Cluster C
5. Cluster B
6. Avoidant and schizoid
7. Fearlessness, impulsive antisociality, and callousness

14.11 Disorders in Childhood

TEST YOURSELF

1. C
2. C
3. T
4. T
5. F
6. F

Chapter 15

15.1 Mental Health Treatment: Past and Present

TEST YOURSELF

1. C
2. C
3. C
4. T
5. T
6. T
7. F

15.2 Types of Treatment

TEST YOURSELF

1. D
2. B
3. A
4. C
5. Classical conditioning; counterconditioning; aversive conditioning
6. Aversive conditioning and exposure therapy
7. Rational emotive therapy
8. The ABC model refers to Action, Belief, and Consequences. CBT will focus on changing the beliefs in the situation so that the consequences are altered.

15.3 Treatment Modalities

TEST YOURSELF

1. A
2. B
3. F
4. T
5. F
6. T

15.4 Substance-Related and Addictive Disorders: A Special Case

TEST YOURSELF

1. D
2. A
3. C
4. Prefrontal cortex
5. Family therapy
6. Two times as likely

15.5 The Sociocultural Model and Therapy Utilization

TEST YOURSELF

1. B
2. C
3. F
4. T
5. T

Notes

Notes

Notes

Notes